PUBLISHED ON THE LOUIS STERN MEMORIAL FUND

Thomas Otway

Printed for Tho. Bowles ... & ... & ... Newman's Pools Church Yard, & Io. Bowles ... at ... Black Horse ... Cornhill London.

From an engraving attributed to W. Faithorne, Jr., after the
painting by Soest.

Otway and Lee

Biography from a Baroque Age

Roswell Gray Ham

Assistant Professor of English in Yale University

New Haven

YALE UNIVERSITY PRESS

London · Humphrey Milford · Oxford University Press

1931

Preface

NOWHERE in the history of English literature may one instance a more curious reversal of taste than that Otway and Lee—now hardly more than names—for over a century and a half packed the theaters with their plays, and that a race of critics from Dennis and Steele down to Hazlitt did not hesitate to couple their names with the greatest. Thus, in the *Memoirs of the Life of Robert Wilks* (1732), it was remarked that "as *Shakespear* exceeded in Nobleness of Thought, so *Otway,* of all our Tragic Writers moved the Passions with greatest Violence." This was nearly the unanimous judgment of an age pluming itself upon a fine discrimination of taste. The question arises whether perhaps we have not lost something of value by our rejection of heroic and sentimental tragedy. In this work I have attempted no more than to touch upon reputations, nor have I been concerned overmuch with the extensive stage history of the plays, since both subjects have been treated elsewhere. It has seemed rather that the answer lay in the men themselves and in the conditions that gave rise to their style.

Otway and Lee have been selected as type-figures, who between them explain the salient characteristics of Restoration tragedy. In writing thus a dual biography, I have attempted the difficult task of managing two personages as though they were one. It has been assumed that between them they tell almost the whole story—the more truly so, since neither was of that stature to rise entirely superior to his time. Happily, Otway and Lee insist upon such treatment, for they present a striking parallel of the old struggle between personality and its age, and in the end they merge their lives and work to a single *dénouement*. Two figures of this sort, like the two plots of *King Lear*, have a clear advantage over one. If children be cruel to their parents once, it is a singular occurrence; twice, it argues a world gone awry. How much more so if the two cases tend to coalesce and form what seems to be a pattern.

The biographies were not originally composed in their present form. A large part of the material upon Otway was embodied in a thesis submitted in 1925 as partial fulfilment for a degree of Doctor of Philosophy at Yale. During the academic year of 1926–27 I was greatly assisted by the grant of a Sterling Fellowship for the study abroad of Restoration tragedy. It was at that time and by the gradual discard of other material that the present work shaped itself. Meanwhile, I published, in various periodicals, certain notes upon Otway from my original thesis. These I am obliged to mention because of the inevitable comparison which will arise between this study and that of the Rev. Mr. Montague Summers, printed at the end of 1926 in his edition of *The Complete Works of Thomas Otway*. It would doubtless be assumed, otherwise, that I am heavily in his debt. On the contrary I owe him scarcely anything, save the discovery of Otway's translations from Tibullus; while anyone caring to pursue this matter may discover in his life of the poet a great number of new biographical details and judgments taken from my work without acknowledgment, sometimes verbatim and always with a close similarity of phrase and arrangement. In my notes I have indicated only a few of these instances. As to my own quotation, I have endeavored to be fair to my authorities by proper acknowledgment, accuracy, and that minimum of editorship which would make a clear text. This book in no way pretends, however, to be an edition of certain disused poems, but rather an excursion into the byways of dramatic personality.

Whoever undertakes a study of this sort cannot but be impressed with the results already accomplished in the general field of Restoration drama. I am particularly indebted to Professor George H. Nettleton, who introduced me to the study of the period, and who subsequently by his friendly criticism and encouragement aided me beyond what I am able to express. Were not dedications sometimes a doubtful return of kindness, this book should go to him. Instead I absolve him from any responsibility for its matter or style. To Mr. Allardyce Nicoll I am indebted for a fund of information contained in his *Restoration Drama,* and for a delightful afternoon of general discussion. To various other authorities who have supplied me with general background, my appreciation can only partially be expressed by due acknowledgment in the notes. Unhappily, the brilliant studies in Restoration tragedy by Mr. Bonamy Dobrée appeared too recently to be laid under contribution; otherwise I should doubtless have been under obligation to him.

The biography of Nathaniel Lee has hitherto not been attempted on such a scale, though the outlines were sketched by various writers of the eighteenth and nineteenth centuries, culminating in the article for *The Dictionary of National Biography* by Sir Sidney

Preface

Lee. The thesis of Professor Douglas S. Beers, largely a study of sources, I did not utilize in the composition of this work. It is to be hoped that he will at some time publish his results. Lee has been an important figure in the history of English drama, but his comparative neglect may be indicated by the fact that even his most popular plays have remained unedited for over two centuries. This task I myself hope to undertake in due time. Otway has been more liberally handled, but only with a comparative fulness of detail. The work of a Swiss scholar, Dr. Edgar Schumacher, is easily the best. It appeared after my thesis was written and had discovered independently some of the facts I had already unearthed. A very substantial piece of research, its design is entirely different from this. My chief debt for material upon the lives is to the first-hand sources discoverable only through liberal aid of the Sterling Fellowship and the courtesy of the officials of the Yale Library, the British Museum, the Victoria and Albert, Bodleian, Cambridge, Huntington, and Harvard libraries, to all of whom go my sincere thanks. I am happy, also, to express my appreciation to Mr. George Parmly Day and the Yale University Press for their unfailing consideration. To Mr. J. A. Venn, for verification of the Cambridge records, and to Professors Arthur E. Case and Charles B. Welles, for a variety of favors, I hereby express gratitude. Finally, there remain certain of my colleagues at whose kindness in reading and criticizing this work I may only marvel. To Professors Robert Dudley French and William Clyde DeVane and that excellent colleague, my wife, for their help in infinite ways I can only set down my heartfelt gratitude.

R. G. H.

New Haven, Connecticut,
  October, 1930.

Contents

Illustrations

Chronology

of the Drama of Otway and Lee

Lee, *The Tragedy of Nero, Emperour of Rome* (D.L. May, 1674), 1675.

Lee, *Sophonisba: or, Hannibal's Overthrow* (D.L. April, 1675), 1676.

Otway, *Alcibiades* (D.G. September, 1675), 1675.

Lee, *Gloriana, or the Court of Augustus Caesar* (D.L. January, 1675/6), 1676.

Otway, *Don Carlos, Prince of Spain* (D.G. ca. June, 1676), 1676.

Otway, *Titus and Berenice. . . . With a Farce call'd The Cheats of Scapin* (D.G. ca. December, 1676), 1677.

Lee, *The Rival Queens, or The Death of Alexander the Great* (D.L. March, 1676/7), 1677.

Lee, *Mithridates, King of Pontus* (D.L. ca. March, 1677/8), 1678.

Otway, *Friendship in Fashion* (D.G. April, 1678), 1678.

Dryden and Lee, *Oedipus* (D.G. ca. August, 1678), 1679.

Otway, *The History and Fall of Caius Marius* (D.G. ca. September, 1679), 1680.

Lee, *Caesar Borgia; Son of Pope Alexander the Sixth* (D.G. ca. September, 1679), 1680.

Lee, *The Massacre of Paris* (written ca. 1679, produced D.L. November, 1689), 1690.

Otway, *The Orphan: or, the Unhappy Marriage* (D.G. ca. February, 1679/80), 1680.

Otway, *The Souldiers Fortune* (D.G. March, 1679/80), 1681.

Lee, *Theodosius: or, The Force of Love* (D.G. ca. September, 1680), 1680.

Lee, *Lucius Junius Brutus; Father of his Country* (D.G. December, 1680), 1681.

Lee, *The Princess of Cleve* (D.G. 1681, or end of 1680), 1689.

Otway, *Venice Preserv'd or, A Plot Discover'd* (D.G. February, 1681/2), 1682.

Dryden and Lee, *The Duke of Guise* (D.L. November, 1682),
  1683.

Otway, *The Atheist: or, The Second Part of the Souldiers Fortune*
  (D.G. *ca.* September, 1683), 1684.

Lee, *Constantine the Great* (D.L. November, 1683), 1684.

Chapter I

AN ODE TO PITY

There first the Wren thy Myrtles shed
On gentlest *Otway's* infant Head,
  To Him thy Cell was shown:
And while He sung the Female Heart,
With Youth's soft Notes unspoiled by Art,
  Thy Turtles Mix'd their own.
                COLLINS, "An Ode to Pity"

SEVEN years after the return of Charles II to his ancestral estates
and pleasures, the antiquarian Anthony Wood took survey of England and found it wanting. The passage of time and a complete
reversal of government had wrought the most profound changes,
and now in Wood's judgment both the state and her microcosm at
Oxford were given over to every kind of abomination: "whores
and harlotts, pimps and pandars, bauds and buffoones, lechery and
treachery, atheists and papists, rogues and rascalls, reason and
treason, playmakers and stageplayers, officers debauched and cor-
rupters."[1] And presumably affairs had not greatly mended by May
27, 1669,[2] when Thomas Otway—playwright in embryo—matriculated at Christ Church, a matter of but four months after his fellow
tragedian, Nathaniel Lee, had entered Trinity, Cambridge.

Otway came immediately under the tutelage of the famous
scholar upon whom Tom Brown meditated:

I do not love thee, Dr. Fell.
The reason why I cannot tell. . . .

But, for various reasons, it might have been forecast that something of the furious doctor would have counteracted the malignant
influence of the age upon the young poet, had not a single tragic
flaw unhappily conspired against all that good work to which he
seemed predestined. It appears, incredibly enough, that the great
Dr. Fell was devoted to the theater, and that as early as 1664 he
had permitted his students to stage the comedy of *Flora's Vagaries*[3]
in the great hall.

The undergraduates, actors thereof [complained Wood], arrived to
[a] strang degree and streyn of impudence, especially from the encour-

agement of the deane and cannons. The deane gave them a supper; Dr. Allestree gave each of them a booke of 7s price. They gave themselves upon this to drunkenness and wantonness, especially among themselves. Dr. Mayne spoke before them a speech commending them for their ingenuity and told them he liked well an acting student.[4]

And thus the little mirror at Oxford reflected the outward order of things. As Trevelyan remarks of the landing of Charles at Dover Beach, 1660, "The wittiest company of comedians that history records had come to tread the stage for a while."[5]

The business had just begun at the university. On July 9 to 12 of the year of Otway's matriculation, Oxford turned out *en masse* to welcome the stage players. The Duke of York's company from London had unpacked their scepters, unrolled their green cloths, and set up their temples of Aphrodite in the Guildhall yard. Their discovery of theatrical Oxford, with its two crowded performances a day in place of the lean holiday season of London, was manna alike to the players and playmakers.[6] Their gratitude was expressed in a prologue to the act of 1671:

> Gentlemen
>   Your civil kindness last year shown,
> A second time hath brought your Creatures down,
> From the unlearned and Tumultuous Town;
> Where Pride and Ignorance in a full cry
> Dare all the power of art and witt defy:
> To the calm dwelling of the Muses here,
> Where all things soft and gentle do appeare,
> Whose sacred Learning flouresheth in peace,
> And without noise each moment doth encrease.
> Hither we come, and with such pleasure too,
> As we are in despair of giving you. . . .
> What pleasure is it to give you delight
> When each of you is fit to judge and write![7]

It was devastating flattery.

To a young scholar with an inclination more to the composition of heroic tragedy than to the study of Greek verbs the descent of the stage players was of tremendous consequence. At this unnoticed crisis in his life, Otway probably had his first introduction to Betterton, who thenceforward was to take possession of his destiny; to Nokes, of the vast empty visage; to Harris, the friend of Pepys, an actor cursed with a beautiful voice; and to Smith, a notable follower in the Bettertonian tradition. Whether Shadwell with his "mighty mug of potent ale" was there in the flesh to complete the poor scholar's deliquium does not appear. Elkanah Settle, late a commoner of Trinity College, was much more certainly in evidence. His play *Cambyses, King of Persia*, lately staged with some little applause at Lincoln's Inn Fields, was to be acted the next visit but one to Oxford.[8] This much we do know, however, upon the unquestioned authority of Wood, that the players "carried away *de claro* 1500 *li*. Scholars pawn'd books, bedding, blankets—laughed at in London—but afterwards they grew wiser."[9] Not so our poet. It may be conjectured that sans books, bedding, and blankets, Otway turned from the huffing company with his wits left behind him. The closing of the curtains, on the afternoon of July 12, 1669, appears to have been the one stroke that was required to cut short any latent aspirations that he may have had to the clergy. It needed but one other event to set him finally adrift into infinitely more treacherous waters.[10]

The horoscope of Thomas Otway was cast many centuries before his birth. Could he as a child have entered the church at Trotton, near which he was born, and scraped away the successive layers of whitewash and plaster, he might have discovered there a wall painting for the sinners of an earlier generation, but one not a little apropos to his own. The process of repair has since revealed our Lord, together with his servant Moses, judging the good and evil of this world. Figuring prominently in the design is wicked mankind, surrounded by his Seven Deadly Sins. His feet significantly point in opposite directions, and his figure is crudely daubed—all save the head. That seems either to have been retouched by some finer artist or else to have been added later than the rest as something of an afterthought, since the grotesques upon the side walls are singularly enough composed only of a body. It is somewhat dubious whether young Otway, playing about the church of which his father was curate, would have let this homily sink into his soul. But at the other end of the nave, beneath the altar, rested a tomb that the fitness of things demanded he should have observed. Within were gathered all the mortal remains of Elizabeth Camoys, to us more truly memorable as Hotspur's Kate. Elizabeth Percy was scarcely a Belvidera, much less a Mistress Barry; she was nevertheless a lady of ladies, and as such might well have tutored the boy in many things useful to the future panegyrist of her sex.

Humphrey Otway, the father of Thomas, never during his entire pastoral career strode into aggressive prominence.[11] In his modest demeanor and loyalty to the crown, he anticipated similar characteristics in his son, and formed with him a notable contrast to the more variable Lees. For the biographer the result is not happy, since there remains of the elder Otway only the most slender store of biographical material upon which to form an estimate. It may all be reviewed very briefly. First, there is a slight but attractive character sketch written some thirteen years prior to the birth of the poet. Shifting then peacefully from Christ's to St. John's Cambridge, he was officially commended in the great admissions book over the signature of one Tho. Bainbrigg, tutor:

I am very well content that the bearer hereof Mr Otway bee admitted of any other Colledge besides Christs. . . . For his carriage whilst he resided in the Colledge, I know no exception against him, nor since his goeing away did I heare but that he was faire and approoved, so as he was well liked and loved where soever he lived. Octob.3.1638.[12]

Other entries, in the records of the two colleges, discover him at Christ's contemporaneously with the sojourn at Caius of the more vigorous Richard Lee.[13] The history of the elder Otway until May 25, 1627, when he came up to Cambridge at the age of sixteen, was one of painstaking education.[14] He had left his father's rectory, at Braughing, Herts, to attend schools successively at Battle, Sussex, at Edinburgh, and at Sedbergh, Yorkshire, the latter being the seat of the Otways of Ingmer Hall. The territory of his wanderings was of sufficiently broad extent to indicate one of two things: either considerable wealth in his sire, or strong family support. Probably it was the former, since young Thomas in his turn was to receive as careful an education.

Neither father nor son seems to have been unduly proud of his connections, who supported "arms argent, a chevron sable, over all a pile azure counterchanged, and a crest out of a ducal coronet or two wings displayed sable."[15] Thomas Otway never alluded to his ancestry, nor did he indulge in the occasional harmless vanity of Nat. Lee, and other plebeian dramatists, of appending *Gent.* to his printed name. The days of his extremest penury could never bring him to call for succor upon his more prosperous cousins, the loyal Bishop of Ossory and the equally loyal Vice-Chancellor of the County Palatine of Lancaster. Indeed, so far as any evidence in his writings is concerned, these worthies need never have existed.[16]

According to Anthony Wood, our sole informant in the absence of early parish records,[17] Otway was born at Trotton, Sussex, the third of March, 1651/2,[18] and by the poet's statement, in his *Satyr Against Libells,* he was an only child:

> My Father was (a thing now rare)
> Loyall and brave, my Mother chaste and fair.
> Their pledge of Marriage-vows was onely I:—[19]

This was accepted without question until the recent discovery of his mother's will.[20] There, after the bequest of a flagon[21] to the church at Woolbeding—where she was to be buried beside her husband—and numerous small legacies to kinsfolk of the name Emes, Elizabeth Otway left her residuary estate to a daughter, Susanna. It appears, then, that the poet's sister was at least nine years of age when he passed thus lightly over her existence, that being the space that had intervened between the death of his father and the composition of the poem. The failure to mention her may have arisen from his desire for literary effect, or perhaps from the fact that she was greatly his junior. Yet all of Otway's relations with his family are shrouded as much in mystery as those of young Lee with his. Despite the fact that both of their mothers seem to have inherited comfortable estates, the two prodigals chose rather to starve than to call upon them for aid. Was it from pride, or was it perhaps the custom of the age, after the somewhat dubious examples of Cowley, Butler, and Spenser? In his time of final penury, Otway was to cite these poets as precedent, in a prologue written advisedly for a play by his starving colleague.

But now in his youth, untroubled by such specters, Otway lived a retired and tranquil existence at Trotton and Woolbeding:

> Alone I liv'd their much-lov'd fondled Boy:
> They gave me generous Education, high
> They strove to raise my Mind, and with it grew their Joy.
> > The Sages that instructed me in Arts
> > And Knowledge, oft would praise my Parts,
> > And chear my parents longing hearts.[22]

The Woolmer forest, in which he played, is as unspoiled now as it was during his childhood. A luxuriant growth of fir, yew, beech, and chestnut shadows its deeply cut lanes. And past the tiny church at Trotton, the Rother hurries down to join the river Arun. We may picture the boy loitering by the great tithe barn, and over the bridge—flung centuries ago across the river by the family of Camoys—and up to the parish church of St. George. There his father retained a curacy sometime after he had come into the larger living of All Hallows at Woolbeding. Once the church had a monastery hard by, but now few relics of that remained. A commonplace of criticism should hasten to add that bridge, church, tithe barn, and the somnolent whisper of the river would have had little concern to a poet of the urbane court of Charles II. Yet an amazing number of vestiges of them remain in the writings of Otway, touches of nature that stand almost unique in the drama of his period. Thus that which follows may be duplicated time and again from his works:

> All the wild Herds are in their Coverts Coucht;
> The Fishes to their Banks or Ouze repair'd,
> And to the murmurs of the Waters sleep.[23]

He was a poet endowed with an eye for the more helpless aspects of nature. It is therefore not strange that in his later reveries from the "iron city" he should recall his father kneeling close to the gray walls of the rectory:

> You took her up a little tender Flower,
> Just sprouting on a Bank, which the next Frost
> Had nipt; and with a careful loving hand
> Transplanted her into your own fair Garden.[24]

But the landscape of the "tender Otway" was not forever soft and lovely. Beside the many scattered images of storms, hawks, and ravenous wolves—in which, however, he is invariably sympathetic toward the victim—there is his opening to *The Poet's Complaint*, suggestive in diminished scale of the macabre landscape of Spenser, and foreshadowing some of the characteristics commonly associated with the romantic generation. Perhaps it was reminiscent of more extensive rambles across the only barren region of all the neighboring downs:

> To a high Hill where never yet stood Tree,
> Where onely Heath, course Fern and Furzes grow,
> Where (nipt by piercing Air)
> The Flocks in tatter'd Fleeces hardly graze.[25]

There are also unremarked flashes out of homely country existence, all too rare in their generation. Such are the shepherds in *Caius Marius,* whose startling appearance in the midst of the Roman campagna cannot disguise their true English habitat: their talk all of the untoward weather, omens of a bald-faced heifer that stuck up her tail eastward and ran into the new quickset, just made to keep the swine from the beans, and of a family of swallows that had fallen, nest and all, into the porridge pot and spoiled the broth.[26] It is the same friendly humor—so unlike the ordinary run of city wit— that hovers over his portrait in *Friendship in Fashion* of the impoverished village curate welcoming the landlord's coming down.[27]

Once Otway seems even to have sketched a portrait of his father, or at least what has been accepted as such for over a hundred years. In *The Orphan* the elder Otway appears perhaps as the chaplain, otherwise a purely gratuitous character. He here develops a philosophy of accommodation—a matter ever to be an issue with his proud spirited son—and in praising his lord draws almost unconsciously the curtain from his own placid existence:

> he has good nature,
> And I have manners;
> His Sons too are civil to me, because
> I do not pretend to be wiser than they are;
> I meddle with no mans business but my own;
> I rise in the morning early, study moderately,
> Eat and drink cheerfully, live soberly,
> Take my innocent pleasures freely:
> So I meet with respect, and am not the jest of the Family.[28]

This paternal philosophy of the golden mean, Otway was to reemphasize in a fine rendition of *The Sixteenth Ode of the Second Book of Horace,*[29] significantly the only translation from the poet that he left behind. Later he was to remark the impassable gulfs which separated that course of life from his own distempered career:

> 'Twas far from any Path, but where the Earth
> Was bare, and naked all as at her Birth,
>   When by the Word it first was made,
>   E're God had said,
>   Let Grass and Herbs and every green thing grow,
> With fruitfull Trees after their kind; and it was so,
>   The whistling Winds blew fiercely round his Head,
>   Cold was his Lodging, hard his Bed;

Aloft his Eyes on the wide Heav'ns he cast,
Where we are told Peace onely's found at last:
And as he did its hopeless distance see,
Sigh'd deep, and cri'd, How far is Peace from me![30]

That, however, anticipates much of the story. Otway's life at first ran placidly enough, protected as it was by the love and good will of his early tutors.

Despite the indefatigable correspondence of Anthony Wood,[31] we have from him only the most meager outline of the poet's career. Thus though it is said that he was educated at the famous school of William of Wykeham at Winchester, he was in attendance there for a period hardly exceeding that passed at Oxford. It is remarked in a note written from the school in 1670 that "12 years is a good age to come thither,"[32] but unless all the evidence is awry Otway was nearer sixteen when he quitted his early tutors and journeyed down to Winchester. We first discover his name upon the *Winchester Long Rolls*[33] as admitted *ad Winton* in the year 1668, and as a commoner of September, the same year. He had been preceded thither by his father's cousin, the first Thomas Otway, and by a kinsman of his mother, William Emes, one time scholar and in 1672 fellow of the college.[34] Doubtless through their influence it was that the boy was sent to Winchester, though not necessarily at their expense. At the time, the future bishop was merely the rector of Etchingham, near by in Sussex, before being translated to Ireland, and was very likely no more prosperous than the poet's father, while William Emes was not yet designated a prebendary of Chichester Cathedral. There seems, in short, no good reason why Otway should be saddled with patrons at this early date, when he was to be sufficiently cursed with them throughout his brief London career.

The rolls of Winchester reveal, beside the poor scholars, an aristocratic and wealthy young race, with whom thus early Otway undertook those disproportionate friendships so unhappily pursued in his later years. Of all their names, the most interesting is that of the young "Ld. of Falkland, *commensalis ex collegio*,"[35] the offspring of a great line, here taking his tentative steps in foppery. It was only a few years later that a scurrilous lampoon sketched in his portrait, and showed to what a strain of proficiency he finally arrived:

His Grandfather, honour'd by all is confest,
Was with Wisdom and Riches like *Solomon* blest,
But he left him nothing, and 'twas his hard Fate
To inherit no more of his Parts than Estate.
    A Mimick he is, tho a bad one at best,
Still plagu'd with an impotent Itch to a Jest;
In appurtenant Action he spares no Expence,
He has all the Ingredients of Wit but the Sense.
    His Face oft of Laugh and Humour is full,
When his Talk is impertinent, empty and dull:
But if so low buffooning can merit our Praise,
Frank Newport, and *Jevon*, and *Haines* must have Bayes.
    Or if *French* Memoirs read from *Broad-street* to *Bow*
Can make a Man wise, then *Falkland* is so.
And for full confirmation of all she did say
She produc'd his damn'd Prologue to *Otway*'s last Play.[36]

Poor Otway—later entangled in the patronage system—penned a
dedication to this boyhood friend, wherein he alluded to their
common bond:

For heretofore having had the honour to be near You, and bred under
the same Discipline with You, I cannot but own, that in a great measure
I owe the small share of Letters I have to your Lordship. For your Lordship's Example taught me to be asham'd of Idleness; and I first grew in
love with Books, and learnt to value them by the wonderfull Progress
which even in Your tender years You made in them: so that Learning
and Improvement grew daily more and more lovely in my Eyes, as they
shone in You.[37]

There was appended much more, of which in summary it is possible
to say that under pressure of dedication Otway overstated his
debt. Falkland, at the time, was some five years the junior of the
Rector's son.

    Otway was one of the few commoners who lived *in collegio*.
Many of the others were *filii nobilium et valencium*, and like the
Lord of Falkland sought more comfortable quarters outside. It
may have been their board, as well as their "enlightened discourse,"
that charmed the young poet, accustomed as he was perforce to
the fare of the scholars and commoners of the college:

    Sunday. *Morning*. Beef broth
             Noon. Roast mutton and beef
             Night. Boiled mutton and broth

Monday. *Morning*. Beef broth made of the dinner beef
     Noon. Boiled beef cold or sodden in water
     Night. Boiled mutton and broth
Tuesday, Wednesday, and Thursday.
     A similar diet of mutton, broth, and beef.
Friday. *Morning*. Nothing
     Noon. Cheese and butter
     Night. Nothing

The spirit of its founder still hovered over the school.

Upon Vigils, Rogation Days, Ember Days, and the Eves of Gaudies nothing was allowed for supper. The diet was meagre in Lent at this period. The quantity of near half a pound of good wheaten bread was allowed to each scholar at every meal, and something more than a pint of beer to each scholar at dinner and at supper, and something less than a pint to him at breakfast, besides beavor beer after dinner and supper in summer time.[38]

Under such a *régime* it is not surprising to discover that the death rate in the Winchester of 1668 was extraordinarily high. Despite the bread and "beavor" beer, it seems a diet excellently calculated for the novitiate of a young poet foredoomed to starvation.

His day began with the cry of the Prefect at five o'clock, a scurry into gown, breeches, and shoes, and the chant of a Latin psalm. After a splash of water, a lick and promise of a comb, and the tidying of his room, the shining pupil made his way to chapel at half-past five, to pray God for guidance, protection, and blessing upon his studies. At six, empty of stomach, he put in his appearance at school.[39]

His drilling in the classics proceeded apace. Perhaps not so thorough as at Westminster, where the scholars of Busby in 1661 wonderfully astonished Evelyn—"such youths, some of them not above twelve or thirteen years of age, composing extemporaneously in Greek, Latin, Hebrew, and Arabic"[40]—the discipline, nevertheless, at Winchester seems sufficiently strict. At least it answers the oft-repeated dictum of Goldsmith that Otway "appears to have had no learning, no critical knowledge."[41] It would be ungracious to reply to the age following *Irene* that classical decoration and parade has little or nothing to do with the soul of tragedy. Otway knew his Latin and some Greek, if a few excellent translations from his hand and this routine of Winchester in the year 1670 have any value as evidence:

They read Virgil by themselves.
At Christmas and such times they learne for tasks abundance of Homer
exactly.
They turne Virgil into English verses & Hesiod into Latine. . . .
They speake Latine everywhere.
Erasmus, Ovid de Tristibus, was the lowest book they learnt in the low-
est form in the School.
They made verses every night except Friday in their chamber at night
on a theme given by the Prepositor and not shewed to their Master.
The Prepositors take the exercise and examine it ere the Master hath
it. . . .
Once in a quarter they had a . . . triall, viz. how they profit. . . . 'Tis
their emulacion that makes them schollars.[42]

Of which the latter remark is borne out by his own modestly
boastful words:

> When I was call'd to a Dispute,
> My fellow-Pupills oft stood mute:
> Yet never Envy did disjoin
> Their hearts from me, nor Pride distemper mine.[43]

But in addition to these disciplinary measures in the handling of
Latin verse—thus bending him in the direction he was to grow—
Otway read from Hesiod and Museus, with much more of the
Latin writers than here set down. Most interesting of all, as show-
ing what was deemed proper nurture for the callow youth of the
Restoration, he was given unlimited Catullus, Propertius, and
Ovid. Thus the *De Arte Amandi* is said to have been a schoolbook
of Winchester at the period of his sojourn there.[44] Needless to say,
he gazed back upon these years with all the fondness of reminiscence.
   But we must leave unstudied the more kindly aspect of Otway's
life at Winchester. That it had its charms we may know. From
Collins to Lionel Johnson, the race of its poets have lavished many
of their happiest lines upon this place, of whom one writing anony-
mously at the beginning of the next century must be our valedic-
torian to the spired city:

> Say, father *Itchen,* genial river, say
> What stripling bards on Catherine's summit stray;
> Where the deep Danish foss, and shatter'd heap
> Of turf-rais'd ramparts, crown'd th' encircled steep

> For many an infant muse in years unripe,
> Of thy rude reeds first fram'd his artless pipe.
> Thou in the vale hast spied thine Otway roam,
> To yon old mansion's hospitable dome;   (St. Cross)
> Where kind Religion lavish'd heretofore
> On the poor pilgrim all her social store;
> Where still Religion's charity bestows
> Help to the wayworn traveller as he goes.[45]

"In the beginning of 1669," we are told by Wood, "he became a Commoner of Christ Church, and left the university without the honour of a degree."[46] Elsewhere the date of his matriculation is set down definitely as May 27.[47] All beyond that is merest conjecture, since Oxford may as well never have existed for Otway. Its traces upon him were negligible, save only those wrought presumably by the strolling players. In all the pages of his works there is neither reference to his stay at Christ Church nor to his friends there. Even those illuminated parables—so grateful to the early nineteenth century—of the gentleman commoner dissipating away his days and nights with Falkland and Plymouth must now be abandoned, with much else that depends upon them. Falkland matriculated at Christ Church on May 21, 1672,[48] when almost certainly Otway had departed, and Plymouth seems never to have attended the university. The history of the playwright at Oxford then resolves itself to certain conviviality, but with whom we know not, a brief continuance of his classical studies, and the flare upon the horizon of the Duke's Company of stage players.

What was it, beside this latter, that put so sudden a period to his youth? The answer is set down in *The Poet's Complaint*. It recounts the first of those many tragic turns in his brief downward course:

> Thus my first years in Happiness I past,
>   Nor any bitter cup did tast;
> But, oh! a deadly Potion came at last.
>   As I lay loosely on my bed,
> A thousand pleasant Thoughts triumphing in my Head,
>   And as my Sense on the rich Banquet fed,
>   A Voice (it seem'd no more, so busy I
>   Was with myself, I saw not who was nigh)
> Pierc'd through my Ears; Arise, thy good *Senander's* dead.
> It shook my Brain, and from their Feast my frighted Senses fled.[49]

There have been various conjectures passed upon the identity of the friend whose death caused the final break from youth and plunged Otway into unready manhood. It has been argued that this *Senander* must have been an unknown patron who had assisted the promising youngster in his education. But, as we have seen, there is hardly a vestige of evidence for this assumption. The more plausible answer is that *Senander,* despite its hybrid coinage, was from the Latin *senex,* old, and the Greek ἀνήρ, man.[50] By the coincidence that Otway appears to have left Oxford around 1670, the old man of these lines seems possible of but one identification. Upon turning over the parish register, we find under date of 1670 that, "Mr. Humphrey Otway, Rector of Woolbeding, was buried Feb. 9."[51]

His son doubtless returned from the university to give what aid he might to his mother and sister, who were now left truly impoverished. As for himself, he said that "a steady Faith and Loyalty to my Prince was all the Inheritance my Father left me."[52] Was it at this period, while revisiting, perhaps for the last time, the pleasant haunts about Woolbeding, that he scribbled in the parish register those formless Latin mottoes that discover him vaguely attempting to unravel his own destiny? Out of those jottings only one stands with any distinctness. It is no very profound answer to his quest, but perhaps as good as he was ever to discover. Thus he wrote in a great scrawl, *"Mors omnibus communis,"* seems to have considered it awhile, and then appended his name, "Tho. Otway."[53]

Chapter II

THE VICAR OF BRAY

In good King Charles's golden days,
    When loyalty no harm meant,
A zealous High Churchman was I,
    And so I got preferment;
To teach my flock I never missed,
    Kings were by God appointed,
And damn'd are those who do resist,
    Or touch the Lord's anointed.
                                    ANON.

THE life of Nathaniel Lee had been affected by drama some six years prior to that of Otway. On November 29, 1663, the Lord Mayor of London, the Aldermen, and a great assembly of loyal citizens gathered in old St. Paul's to give thanks for deliverance and restoration. And though the clangor of its bells may have caused certain of the less penitential brethren of Newgate and the Fleet to reflect moodily upon the turn of events, one at least of their number prepared now to mount the pulpit for perhaps the climactic pronouncement of his career.[1] It is altogether suitable that Richard Lee, Doctor of Divinity and the father of mad Nat. Lee, should have anticipated drama not far from the scene of his son's future greatness; and perhaps it is not too much to assume that the boy was released for the moment from the rigors of Charterhouse to attend upon his father's triumph. As the elder Lee afterward remarked, it was altogether "an Auditory, (though greater then had been known in the memory of man) yet composed into a spirit and posture suitable to the Majesty, Holiness, and Presence of that God in whose House we were."[2] One may conjecture whether the size of the auditory was determined entirely by the desire for thanksgiving, or whether it was not augmented by a just curiosity concerning the Rev. Richard Lee of Hatfield. He had been a considerable figure under the Commonwealth, the chaplain of General Monk, a stern administrator of the Puritan code, and in short "a Godly, learned, and orthodox divine."

Judging by the comment of an irreverent brother, this was not Lee's first appearance at Paul's, nor the first time that he had delivered his celebrated recantation. He had held a dress rehearsal at St. Mary's, Cambridge, where he had been received *ambabus ulnis*,[3] and upon November 5 previous he had been honored with the duty of preaching at Paul's in commemoration of Guy Fawkes's Day. It was apropos of the latter sermon that the irreverent Dr. Wild composed a ditty, called: *The Poring Doctor, or the Gross Mistakes of a Reverend Son of the Church, in Bowing at the Name of Judas, at St. Pauls, Novemb. 5th, 1663*.[4] Upon the greater occasion of the twenty-ninth, Wild again was ready with a squib, representing "Penitent Proteus, alone in the Tyring-house before his entrance to the Pulpit." "Oh I am almost mad," he cried,

> 'twould make one so,
> To see which way *Preferments* game doth go.
> I ever thought I had her in the *Wind*,
> And yet I'm cast above *three years* behind.

> *Three times* already I have turn'd my Coat;
> *Three times* already I have chang'd my Note:
> I'le make it *four*, and *four and twenty more*,
> And turn the Compass round ere I'le give ore.

Perhaps it was because Lee was fearful of just this sort of thing that he was particularly attentive to recall to Gilbert Burnett the observations of his late sacred majesty, "of glorious and eternal memory." In his Εἰκὼν Βασιλική Charles I advised his son, "That none will be more loyal and faithful to You and to Me, than those Subjects, who being sensible of their own Errors and Our Injuries, will feel in their souls vehement motives to Repentance, and earnest desires to make some reparations for their former defects."[5] Thus Richard Lee had journeyed down from his rectory at Kings Hatfield, with consecration of spirit, "to address himself to this service, (finding so much reason to distrust his own abilities)."

It is to be feared that young Nathaniel, if he were present, nodded under the booming pulpit, as period after period unrolled from the text of *Cor Humiliatum & Contritum*. But for those curious concerning the involved terminology and the appeal to church fathers, which passed in the mid-seventeenth century for the perfection of homiletics, the sermon is available, as printed and bound in several splendid editions at the express command of the Bishop of London. As we read, it is not surprising that the son of Richard Lee should later have forsworn the pulpit for the more tangible flying devils and visions of the cross which were purveyed in the theater at Dorset Garden.

The irreverent Dr. Wild, however, shortly rushed from the press an account of the whole procedure, under the title of *The Recantation of a Penitent Proteus; or, The Changeling: As it was Acted with good Applause at St Maries in Cambridge and St Pauls in London, 1663. To the Tune of Doctor Faustus.*[6] A scurrilous thing, it tells, nevertheless, something of our poet's father and of what stuff the youngster was composed. In part it runs as follows:

> Atend good People, lay by scoffs and scorns,
> Let *Roundheads* all this day pull in their horns,
> But let *Conformists* and brave *Caviliers*
> Unto my doleful Tone prick up their Ears. . . .
> In learning my poor Parents brought up me,
> And sent me to the Universitie,
> There I soon found *bowing* the way to *rise:*
> And th' only *Logick* was the *Falacies.*
> In stead of *Aristotles Organon,*
> Anthems and Organs I did study on;
> If I could play on them, I soon did find,
> I rightly had Preferment in the *Wind.*
> I follow'd that hot scent without controul,
> I bow'd my body, and I sung *Fa Sol;*
> I cozen'd Doctor *Couzens,* and e're long
> A Fellowship obtained *for a Song.*
> Then by degrees I clim'd until I *got,*
> Good Friends, good Cloaths, good Commons, and what not?
> I *got* so long, until at length I *got*
> A *Wench with Child,* and then I got a Blot. . . .
> But as I scorn'd to *Father* mine own Brat,
> 'Twas done to me as I had done with That.
> The Doctors all, when Doctor I would be,
> As a *base son,* refus'd to *Father* me.

At this point we may pause a moment to summarize the less sensational facts of the career of Richard Lee, as they are set down in the records of his college. The son of William, a merchant of Nantwich in Cheshire, Lee was admitted a sizar of Caius at the age of seventeen, November 2, 1629, and proceeded to his B.A. in 1633/4. In 1636 he was a fellow of Peterhouse, whence he received his master's degree in 1637. He was ordained deacon at Peterborough the same year, and was made rector of St. Martin Orgar in London, and of St. Leonard, Shoreditch, in 1643 and 1644, respectively.[7] But we run ahead of the sermon—

> *Cambridge* I left with grief and great disgrace,
> To seek my fortune in some other place. . . .
> But though I bow'd and cring'd, and crost and all,
> I only got a Vicaridge very small.
> E're I was warm (and warm I ne're had been
> In such a starved hole as I was in)
> A fire upon the Church and Kingdome came;
> Which *I* strait help't to blow into a *flame.*

The second part of this doggerel shows Richard Lee's rapid advancement to the post of chaplain to Monk's army, and certain of his quixotic adventures at the time of the Covenant.[8] It all furnishes a prevision of the days of the Popish Plot, when his son was to ride forth on headlong adventure, spouting the language of new committees and new associations. But young Nathaniel at least was to be a bit more consistent than his father, whom we may allow to continue:

> My Conscience first, like *Balaams Ass,* was shy,
> Bogled, and winc't; which when *I* did espy,
> I cudgel'd her, and spurr'd her on each side,
> Until the Jade her paces all could ride.
>   When first I mounted on her tender back,
> She would not leave the *Protestant dull Pack,*
> Till in her mouth the *Cov'nant Bit* I got,
> And made her learn the *Presbyterian Trot;* . . .
>
> From *Hatfield* to *St. Albans* I did ride,
> The Army call'd for me to be their *Guide;*
> There I so spur'd her, that I made her fling
> Not only *dirt,* but *Blood* upon my *King.*
> When *Cromwel* turn'd his Masters out by force,
> I made the Beast draw like a *Brewers* horse;
> Under the *Rump* I made her wear a *Crooper,*
> And under *Lambert* she became a *Trooper.*
> When Noble *Monk* the KING did home conveigh,
> She (like *Darius Steed*) began to *neigh.* . . .
> If the *Great Turk* to *England* come, I can
> Make *Gospel* truckle to the *Alchoran;*
> And if their *Turkish Sabbaths* should take place,
> I have in readiness my *Friday face.* . . .

There follows a not inconsiderable confession of sin, to which he adds:

> My *Leicester* sins, my *Hatfield* sins are many,
> But my *St. Albans* sins more red than any.
> To *CHARLES the First* I was a bloody Foe,
> I wish I do not serve the *Second* so:
> The only way to make me leave that trick,
> Is to bestow on me a *Bishoprick.*
> This is St. *Andrews* Eve, and for his sake
> A Bishoprick in *Scotland* I could take. . . .
>   Now may this *Sermon* never be forgot,
> Let others call't a *Sermon,* I a *Plot,*
> A Plot that takes, if it believed be;
> If not, I shall repent *Unfeigned-Lee.*

The preacher descended from the pulpit, was "received by the Lord Bishop, embraced and blessed."[9] So much for the libelous report of Dr. Wild, by whom Lee is painted as forbear to the Vicar of Bray. On the contrary, he appears frequently in the Journals of the Commonwealth House of Commons as a "Godly, learned, and orthodox divine," moving quietly to the appropriation of various sequestered livings, ordaining presbyterian ministers, and controlling hospitals—variously in the company of Whalley, Okey, Nye, Greenhall, and "such of their gentry."[10]

One would like to discover at just what point he first collided with Dr. Wild. The latter shortly thereafter died and left Lee in peace; but the barb remained with him. There is still extant a catalogue of the sale of his library, "at the parsonage-house, Hatfield, Tuesday the 28th Day of April, 1685,"[11] containing one particularly interesting item, a copy of Wild's *Iter Boreale, with other select Poems.* The presence of this volume may paint for us a picture: under the candlelight the Rev. Richard Lee, in the quiet of his soul fingering the pages of *A Penitent Proteus,* his ten-odd children and chaste wife having some time since retired for the night.

From the aspect of his father's library, we may conclude that young Nathaniel passed an edifying childhood in the parsonage at Hatfield. In the catalogue, just alluded to, were listed 79 *Libri Theologici* in folio, 63 in quarto, 169 in octavo and duodecimo, besides immeasurable Divinity, volumes of sermons and tracts bound and unbound, with more entertaining consideration of alchemy and witchcraft—both of which were to play some part in the future drama—the works of Prideaux and Jeremy Taylor, Lessius' *Right Course of preserving Health to extreme Age,* with at least seventeen other treatises upon health, etc., all of which were doubt-less indispensable to the composition of those sermons which the merry court of Charles so approved toward the latter end of Richard Lee's life. In passing, however, we must note under date of September 29, 1671, that Lieut. Gen. Lyttelton Annesley com-ments in his diary as follows: "Heard Mr Lee of Hatfield the morning at Court; no such great preacher as famed."[12] Annesley's was but one idle voice; the elder Lee continued regularly to appear at court until the end of his life in 1684, when mad Nat. had burned out his flame for the time being, and was safely snuffed away in Bedlam. Can it be that his renegade son helped to keep alive the glory of Richard Lee in a court more interested in an Alexander and a Statira than in a *Cor Humiliatum & Contritum?*

Nevertheless, there were links between these distant worlds of the library at Hatfield and the rattling stage of Dorset Garden. The tastes of a young playwright were here in embryo, though needless to say the shelves contained no copies of *Cassandre* or of *Cléopâtre,* works to be read to better purpose than the ten treatises of William Prynne, which were here. There was *The Great Evil of Health-Drinking, with the original of that Sin,* in which the boy might in time instruct his thundering sire. We may note a *Description of the Grand Turk's Seraglio,* and a volume of the *Acts of the English Votaries and their unchaste practices.* Of greater import was *The History of Justin, with the Epitome of the Lives of the Roman Emperors,* out of which were to come hints, prodigiously magnified, for several of our poet's plays, including his *Sophonisba.* Then there was *Modern Policies out of Machiavel, Cesar Borgia, etc.* The names were to be familiar enough among his plays. Other strange lumber in this library was *The Muster Roll of the Evil Angels; Mystagogus Poeticus; Politeuphieia, or Wits Common-wealth;* an *Epitome of the Lives of the French Kings;* Henry Foulis' *History of Romish Treasons;* and a *History of the Inquisi-tion.* We may only trust that the latter was illustrated with curious woodcuts of writhing martyrs, for a youth with a Renaissance fancy for such horrors. The truth is, that as we consider the titles of his plays—*Nero, Hannibal's Overthrow, The Court of Augustus Caesar, Constantine the Great, Caesar Borgia,* and *The Massacre of Paris*—we may easily be led to remark that the bent of his genius was perhaps traceable to the influence of Richard Lee and this puritan library. Certainly no other dramatist of his time shows quite the same dour *dramatis personae*. Thus, however much we may talk of other influences, it should not be forgotten that Nat. Lee was the son of his father.

Finally, like an apparition in all this hodgepodge of divinity and history, appeared the one work that perhaps may date the boy's final severance from the parental yoke. We find, after the death of his father, that Elizabeth Lee authorized the sale of the sole relic of her son's composition. At the end of the *Miscellanies in Quarto,* and the only play in all this terrifying catalogue, appeared *Sophonisba, or Hannibal's Overthrow, a Tragedy, by Nat. Lee, 1676. Nero,* his first, was hardly a play presentable to the rector of Hatfield, but this second was more becoming. Afterward there followed a decline into the depths of obliquity.

Before we may continue with Lee's further adventures, it is fitting that we should pay our respects to the Earl of Rochester, whose name is to figure largely in these pages. It was Rochester who misled several generations of scholars upon the early schooling of Nathaniel Lee. Through him the tradition held well into the twentieth century, that Lee was lashed almost to insensibility by the great Dr. Busby:

> When *Lee* makes temp'rate *Scipio* fret and rave,
> And *Hannibal* a whining, Amorous Slave,
> I laugh, and wish the hot-brain'd Fustian Fool
> In *Busby*'s Hands, to be well lasht in School.[13]

Recently there was a rereading of Rochester's jest, and the matter became obvious. It was not a historical anecdote, as it had been taken by Oldys and Malone, but merely a genial wish. Busby thus stood exonerated and it was conjectured that Lee's existence at Westminster might have been relatively untroubled.[14] If, however, the lines be probed further, it will be found that Busby's correction of Lee is little more than the conclusion of a temporal subjunctive. Rochester was never too scrupulous in what he wrote. He once remarked to his father confessor, Burnet, that "The lyes in these Libels came often in as Ornaments that could not be spared without spoiling the beauty of the *Poem*."[15] Busby's flogging of young Lee, then, may be considered merely as such an ornament. The name of the poet nowhere occurs in the records of Westmin-

ster, nor is there other evidence to assign him to that school. Indeed
he was in attendance all the while at Charterhouse.

His father seems to have led the small boy up to the Earl of
Salisbury, near by at Hatfield, who, "finding him endowed with
extraordinary promise," nominated him for a vacancy in the
school, May 20, 1658.[16] But the date produces further difficulties.
Lee has been accepted as altogether precocious. Bowman, the actor,
told Oldys that Lee was nineteen when he produced *Sophonisba,*
and Oldys, forgetful of the great age and mellowed memory of the
actor, figured it out upon the margins of his *Langbaine,* coming to
the conclusion that Lee was born in 1657.[17] Apparently he boggled
at this and refigured it to 1654, whence it was duly set down as
1653 in the *Dictionary of National Biography.* But the date unhappily would bring the poet into Charterhouse at five or six,
granted that he entered immediately upon his election. The rub
comes in the rules of the establishment. They were undeviating in
their observance of ten as the earliest age of admission.[18] This
would fix his birth around 1648/9, and would send him up to Cambridge as an exhibitioner, in July of 1665, at about the age of
seventeen, an age more in accord with the rest of the conservative
world, including that of his brothers.[19]

Thomas Sutton, in founding Charterhouse, had intended it for
the sons of the poor: "No Children shall be placed there whose
Parents have an Estate in Lands to leave unto them but only the
Children of poor Men that want Means to bring them up."[20] In
applying to the governors, of whom Salisbury was one, Richard
Lee was obliged to urge the claims of poverty. Places were frequently filled by children of high connections, but by far the
greater number of them were sons of the country clergy. Thus the
comrades of Nat. Lee were more nearly of his own social order
than those of Otway. Otherwise Charterhouse appears to have
offered a discipline resembling that of Winchester.

If we know nothing about the boy's experiences at Charterhouse, we know as little of those at Cambridge. In 1665 Trinity
College had a tradition of scholarship and poetry which was outstanding. John Dryden was one of its recent graduates. Its sons
were thoroughly schooled in the classics, but that was nothing unusual. Lee had more of its discipline perhaps than was summed up
by his degree of 1668/9.[21] From his earliest bit of published verse,
we may infer that he lingered on at Trinity for several years after

his graduation. The poem appeared in a volume of Cambridge elegies, brought forth in 1670 upon the death of the great Duke of Albemarle.[22] It was an unskilled and turgid product of immaturity, yet somehow it gave an inkling of his later dramatic style. There was present a marked fondness for theatrical pageantry, permeating even the dim regions of his underworld:

> Arise ye Ghosts of ancient Heroes fled
>   To shades below,
> Where all things hush'd in silence gently flow,
> Forsake awhile the mansions of the dead:
>   In all your honours mantled,
>   With all your glories garnished,
>   With lawrels crown'd, draw near,
>   Approach with Panick fear;
>   Come all, with jealous wonder come,
> And kneeling bow your heads before our *Gen'rals* tomb.

The lines may serve as a link between the past and future of the young poet. Richard Lee had followed Albemarle faithfully for many years, while the latter was still General Monk, and now doubtless was well pleased at the threnody composed by his son. And that son, with this final backward glance, plunged forthwith into the world of panegyrics and spoken drama. It is, therefore, to Dorset Garden, wherein the dual career of Lee and Otway was chiefly to be enacted, that we may now direct our attention.

Chapter III

STAGE AND ACTORS

The purple Emp'rors who in Buskins tread
And rule imaginary Worlds for Bread.
ANON.

THE interval immediately following the death of his father was by Otway's own confession one full of perplexity:

> From thence sad Discontent, uneasy Fears,
> And anxious Doubts of what I had to do,
>   Grew with succeeding Years.
> The World was wide, but whither should I go?
> I, whose blooming Hopes all wither'd were,
> Who'd little Fortune, and a deal of Care?
> To *Britain*'s great Metropolis I stray'd,
>   Where Fortune's generall Game is play'd;
> Where Honesty and Wit are often prais'd,
> But Fools and Knaves are fortunate and rais'd.[1]

Young Otway's descent upon theatrical London was truly the uncharted voyage of an unskilled pilot. The honesty of youth, his inexperience, and his "praised parts" made him dream sudden glory in the fabulous world about the playhouses. The pull thither had been irresistible. It is noteworthy that he is first heard of in connection with the Duke's company of stage players, the same that had in all likelihood destroyed his peace of mind at Oxford. At nearly the same time, young Lee somehow had managed to attract the attention of the Chancellor of Cambridge, the witty Duke of Buckingham, and quitting the university had been led to the metropolis in the train of that great man. Whereupon, in the manner of the times, he too had been unceremoniously spilled into the whip tides of Dorset Garden, and left there to sink or swim.[2]

The two adventurers shortly found themselves cast upon the shores of a *terra ignota*, such another as theatrical history has never seen before nor since. A brief description by a member of the Florentine embassy of 1669 may serve to orient us. In London he found that,

There are two theatres for comedy, and three companies, all English. The first is called His Majesty's, the second that of the Duke, and the third is no more than a school for young comedians, who sometimes recite in the theatres, habituate themselves to the stage, and at times enter the other companies aforesaid. They rehearse every day during the whole year, except Sundays; these days are here universally sanctified with superstitious devotion.[3]

Sanctity otherwise was rarely permitted to resolve the discord of atheism and bad manners that ruled the playhouses. Writing in 1697, when conditions had improved only slightly, a certain M. Misson viewed the playhouses with Latin eyes. One of them he found "large and handsome, where they sometimes act Operas, and sometimes Plays:"—this was the Duke's Theatre of earlier days, planned sumptuously by Wren for the spectacles devised by Betterton—"the other something smaller, which is only for Plays"—this latter was the Theatre Royal, at our period merely projected in Wren's mind for a company specializing upon comedy and heroic drama, without the appurtenances of song and flying devils.

The Pit [continued Misson], is an Amphitheater, fill'd with Benches without Back-boards, and adorn'd and cover'd with green Cloth. Men of Quality, particularly the younger Sort, some ladies of Reputation and Vertue, and abundance of Damsels that hunt for Prey, sit all together in this Place, Higgledy-Piggledy, chatter, toy, play, hear, hear not. Farther up, against the Wall, under the first Gallery, and just opposite to the Stage, rises another Amphitheater, which is taken up by Persons of the best Quality, among whom are generally very few Men. The Galleries, whereof there are only two Rows, are fill'd with none but ordinary People, particularly the Upper one.[4]

Though this theater was certainly dominated by the modish pit and boxes, rather too little attention has been directed toward the upper galleries. Aloft were a fair number of the city class, that in spite of the discredit to which the theaters had fallen worked as a slow leaven toward greater stability. But they were few in number and scorned by the wits. It was in the vacations particularly that the solid citizens turned to the theaters for the relief that the courtiers sought at Newmarket and at Tunbridge Wells.[5] New plays by new playwrights and with new actors were then given trial. But during the remainder of the year the house was well stabilized. The town gallant's daily ritual included at least one visit to the playhouse—

STAGE OF THE DUKE'S THEATRE, DORSET GARDEN, 1673.

*From an engraving in the first edition of Settle's "Empress
of Morocco."*

. . . the young brisk men who think it fit,
To spend no afternoon but in the Pit—[6]

and the feminine devotee was timed to as irrevocable an attendance
—"till Five in Visits, till Seven at the Play."[7]

The more assertive fops made a show of guiding theatrical taste,
particularly in comedy, but it was the ladies, with their moistened
handkerchiefs, who were the true rulers of tragedy. Here they admitted man's sway only upon sufferance. They were a curious
mélange; the punks of the middle gallery were able to dab their
handkerchiefs as furiously as their more respectable sisters of the
boxes, while both discovered in the high heroism and eternal constancy of tragedy an agreeable relief from the transient affections
of the universal fop. The feminine influence, however, was not
always a sedative:

About one *Jilt* a hundred *Fops* shall crowd,
So talkative, impertinent and loud,
That who e're hither comes to see the *Play,*
For what they hear, might as well stay away.[8]

As to the rest of the pit and gallery, Dryden has characterized
the tribe in a half-dozen brilliant prologues and epilogues, of which
this for the opening of the King's new playhouse, March 26, 1674,
may serve as well as any:

But you, loud Sirs, who thro' your Curls look big,
Criticks in plume and white vallancy Wig,
Who lolling on your foremost Benches sit,
And still charge first, (the true forlorn of Wit)
Whose favours like the Sun, warm where you roul,
Yet you like him, have neither heat nor Soul;
So may your Hats your Foretops never press,
Untouch'd your Ribbons, sacred be your Dress;
So may you slowly to old Age advance,
And have th' Excuse of Youth for Ignorance;
So may Fop corner full of Noise remain,
And drive far off the dull, attentive Train;
So may your Midnight Scowrings happy prove,
And Morning Batt'ries force your way to love;
So may not *France* your Warlike Hands recal,
But leave you by each other's Swords to fall,
As you come here to ruffle Vizard Punk,
When sober rail, and roar when you are drunk.[9]

When you come to a new Play [remarked the wise Tutor of Pacheco], and know the Author is no fighter, and you may venture to abuse him; first sit grave and unconcern'd, and be sure to cast an eye upon some fam'd wit of the town, and take him for your pattern.

Pac. But how if there be none there *Tutor?*

Tut. Why then if any thing takes in general you may venture to smile a little; if only amongst some few, and you imagine it not good, cast a scornful look about you, as if you pittied their ignorance. Above all things commend nothing without some exception. . . .

Pac. Nay, they almost take me for a wit already, I know all the *Poets* Christen names; and call *Tom* and *Jack* with as much confidence, as if I had been their God-father.

Tut. That's well: There's very much in that. You may take occasion to give them the familiar shrug, talk aloud and swear, *Tom* the humour in thy last Prologue was high and new. Pox on thee for a rogue, thou'lt grow famous. A whisper now and then, with a great laugh after it does well.[10]

Youth, with ambitions to enter this rarefied society, needed most of all some sort of introduction by nobility or recognized wit. Buckingham supplied it for Lee; but we have no information who performed a like service for Otway. Possibly it was Rochester. We read, in a letter of 1675 from Falkland, an expression of profound gratitude to that dictator of wit for his many favors.[11] Was perhaps our poet one of the recipients? Already a patron of Lee, Rochester was shortly to become interested in Otway. He was a powerful friend or enemy, a petty despot in this little kingdom.

We may picture Otway upon the outer edge of fops' corner, with his ear attuned to the loud wisdom of the great men. They discourse upon the relative value of rhyme and blank verse—a question which at the moment is rending the theatrical world. Thence they move to stage lighting, scandal, opera, the unities, decorum, and all the multifarious critical dicta now pursued in full cry by a court only recently returned from its foreign travel. In the intervals, Aphra Behn conducts a vizarded campaign at shorter and shorter distance against a Captain of Horse. Ravenscroft and his friends from the Inns of Court haggle with Orange Moll over the price of fruit. Brawny Settle presses boldly among the great with authoritative criticism upon the management of scene and machine. Crowne has philosophical glimmerings, in an age not much given to them. "The first Harvard playwright," in starched cravat, collects such crumbs of Hobbism as fall from the lips of Rochester and Sedley, and lays them by for a *Siege* he is projecting. Another "brother of the orange and cravat-string," Beau Hewitt perhaps,

values not the Play, his Province lyes in the Boxes, ogling away his Half Crown admission fee, or running from *side Box* to *side Box* to the inviting Incognitoes in black Faces, or else wittily to cry aloud in the Pit *Bough* or *Boyto,* and then be prettily answer'd by the rest of the *Witts* in the same *Note,* like Musical Instruments tun'd to the same pitch.[12]

Meanwhile the play continues: "a damned dull opera" of *Macbeth,* by Shakespeare, of which altogether the pleasantest parts are a dance by the witches to flutes and kettledrums, and the heroics of Betterton. When Betterton speaks, fops' corner for the moment is silent.[13] The other actors are not so favored. A newcomer is cast for the part of Duncan, King of Scotland, one Nat. Lee, son of the court preacher. The chorus of "Boytos" rises triumphant, and the little tragedian, from his advanced post, turns a distorted countenance upon his tormentors.

But attention shortly is distracted to Ravenscroft and his crowd, who have discovered Hewitt in a side box. The rest of this business —reënacted time and again in the Restoration playhouse, where it was of tragic implication to the development of serious drama— may be set down at some length in the words of a spectator. Henry Ball, writing July 4, 1673, notes that

The quarrell on Monday att the King's Theatre was occasioned thus: one Mr. Ravenscroft having half a yeare since received an affront from Sir George Hewitt in the play-house, and having ever since studied retalliation, came that day to the play, where finding him there, beate him with his cane and so went away; presently after which my Lord Buckhurst and Capt. Bulkley going out with intentions to the other playhouse, were followed by chance by Coll. Strode, so that all three being at the doore and Mr. Ravenscroft and company going by, and my Lord by chance blaming the action, Mr. Ravenscroft presently fell to words, and then they all drew. My Lord was hurt in the body, Capt. Bulkley in the necke, and the Collonel in the hand, and eare, but all their hurts are now cured.

The fracas was not yet ended. It all came to the ear of Charles, to whom the theater was like a rich crown province, rendering periodical tribute of wit, mode, and beauty.

His Ma[ty] sent an order to the Earle Marshall to seize Sir George

Hewitt for sending a challenge to Ravenscroft, and to take the three
brothers of them into custody for falling upon my Lord Buckhurst and
his company, resolving if possible to prevent those ill consequences which
such disorders will produce.

Four days later this tumult among the wits received its final notice:

> This quarrell between Sir George Hewitt and Mr. Ravenscroft is not
> yet composed, nor the latter rendered themselves, his Majesty having
> commanded the Marshall to make them peremptorily quitt his kingdomes
> if they come not in and be punished, which makes the Inns of Court men
> rayle horridly at the actions of the Court, and draw themselves into
> parties to affront the courtiers anywhere, so that it's feared that foolish
> quarrel may have too ill consequences.[14]

> A harmless *jest*, an accidental *blow*,
> Touching their *Cuffs*, or treading on their *Toe*,
> With many other things too small to name,
> Does blow the *Sparks of Honour* to a *flame;*
> For such vile trifles, or some viler *Drab*,
> They roar, they swear, look big, lug out and stab.[15]

A few years later, at another performance of *Macbeth*, Sir Thomas
Armstrong killed Mr. Scroop, the two fighting across the benches
of the pit;[16] and in time we shall see young Otway performing with
like heroism to the mingled delight and discomfort of the spectators, though he at least did not climb upon the stage and frighten
the squeaking actresses to the tiring-room.

Ravenscroft's career of turmoil was typical of the bolder of his
contemporaries in stagecraft. Settle seems to have led a harried
existence. Crowne said that he had reason to fear his enemies, but
that he did not expect them to drop from the clouds.[17] Dryden's
unhappy adventure of the Rose Alley ambuscade, in which he was
the victim of Rochester's venom, is too well known to demand
repetition. Even the fair Aphra found herself lingering in prison
from the overvigorous use of her talents. It was part of the playwright's heritage that perhaps made violence of plot and portrai-
ture a necessity.

Otway was receiving his final lessons in foppery. After telling
of his melancholy journey to London, he added:

> My forward Spirit prompted me to find
>   A Converse equall to my Mind:
> But by raw Judgment easily miss-led,

> (As giddy callow Boys
>   Are very fond of Toys)
> I mist the brave and wise, and in their stead
> On every sort of Vanity I fed.
> Gay Coxcombs, Cowards, Knaves, and prating Fools,
> Bullies of o're-grown Bulks, and little Souls,
> Gamesters, Half-wits, and Spendthrifts, (such as think
> Mischievous midnight Frollicks bred by Drink
>   Are Gallantry and Wit,
> Because to their lewd Understandings fit)
> Were those wherewith two years at least I spent,
> To all their fulsome Follies most incorrigibly bent.[18]

Here Otway listed both the audience and the *dramatis personae* of the Restoration stage: in comedy to provide originals for the actors and the species of wit; in tragedy to exert as marked an influence by reason of a complete and unalterable perversion of taste. By the writers of both it was recognized as an audience volatile and malicious, and as such was condemned almost universally throughout the range of prologue, epilogue, and epistle dedicatory.

And before these worldlings Otway first ventured his fortunes. He had discovered in the amiable Mrs. Behn a friend complacent enough to hazard upon him a small part in her first play. *The Forc'd Marriage, or the Jealous Bridegroom* was produced at Lincoln's Inn Fields, December, 1670, a matter of eleven months after the death of his father, though there is no certainty that Otway's appearance came at that specific time, his rôle being assigned by the printed cast to one Westwood. But this much information we have from old Downes, that:

> *In this play Mr.* Otway *the Poet having the inclination to turn Actor;* *Mrs.* Bhen[19] *gave him the King in the Play, for a Probation Part, but he being not us'd to the Stage, the full house put him into such a Sweat and Tremendous Agony, being dash't, spoilt him for an Actor. Mr.* Nat. Lee *had the same Fate in Acting* Duncan *in* Macbeth, *ruin'd him for an Actor too. . . . from that time, their Genius set them upon Poetry.*[20]

The tinsel world of the stage itself was as important to the formation of the finished playwright as that of the adjoining pit and gallery. At the Duke's it was ruled by the friendly nod of Betterton, and at the King's, by Hart and Mohun. While these three divided empire, there was spared neither care nor expense in the mounting of plays. And a school of actors arose that time has judged unexcelled in their particular provinces, limited though they were by the tawdriness of their environment. The most perfect description of their mimic world came toward the end of the century from an anonymous hand.[21] It was written when Hart and Mohun had disappeared from the scene, but while Betterton still kept alive the old traditions, and hence parts of it may be admitted in this place. The satirist describes the theater known in our earlier time as the Duke's in Dorset Garden:

> Where gently Thames in stately Channels glides,
> All England's proud Metropolis divides,
> A Lofty Fabrick does the Sight invade,
> And stretches o're the Waves a Pompous Shade,
> Whence sudden *Shouts* the Neighbourhood surprise,
> And *Thund'ring Claps* and dreadfull *Hissings* rise.
> Here Thrifty Rich hires Heroes by the Day
> And keeps his *Mercenary Kings* in Pay,
> With deep-mouth'd Actors fills the *Vacant Scenes,*
> And rakes the Stews for *Goddesses* and *Queens;*
> Here the leud Punk with Crowns and Scepters grac't,
> Teaches her Eyes a more *Majestick Cast,*
> And hungry Monarchs with a numerous Train
> Of suppliant Slaves, like *Sancho,* Starve and Reign.
>   But enter in, my *Muse,* the Stage survey,
> And all this Pomp and Pageantry display;
> Trap-doors and Pit-falls from th' unfaithfull Ground
> And Magick Walls encompass it around:
> On either Side Maim'd Temples fill our Eyes,
> And intermixt with Brothel-Houses rise;
> Disjointed Palaces in Order stand, ⎫
> And Groves obedient to the Mover's Hand, ⎬
> O'er shade the Stage and flourish at Command. ⎭
> A Stamp makes broken Towns and Trees entire:
> So when *Amphion* struck the Vocal Lyre,
> He saw the Spacious Circuit all around
> With crowding Woods, and rising Cities crown'd.

We turn thence to the tiring-rooms, where some few hints are given that illuminate the fantastic careers of Goodman, Nell Gwyn, Joe Haynes, and a score of others:

> But next the Tiring-Room survey and see
> False Titles, and promiscuous Quality,
> Confus'dly swarm from Heroes and from Queens,

To those that swing in Clouds, and fill Machines;
Their various Characters they choose with Art,
The frowning Bully fills the Tyrant's Part:
Swoln Cheeks and swagging Belly make a Host,
Pale Meagre Looks, and Hollow Voice, a Ghost;
From careful Brows, and heavy down-cast Eyes,
Dull Cits, and thick-scull'd Aldermen arise. . . .
The Mincing Dame continues as before,
Her Character unchang'd, and Acts the Whore.
   Above the rest the Prince with haughty stalks,
Magnificent in Purple Buskins walks:
The Royal Robes his awfull Shoulders grace
Profuse of *Spangles* and of *Copper-Lace:*
Officious Vassals to his mighty Thigh,
Guiltless of Blood th'unpointed Weapon tye;
Then the Gay Glittring Diadem put on,
Pondrous with Brass, and starr'd with Bristol-Stone.
His Royal Consort next consults her Glass,
And out of Twenty Boxes culls a Face;
The Whit'ning first her Ghastly Looks besmears,
All Pale and Wan th'unfurnisht Form appears;
Till on her Cheeks the blushing Purple glows,
And a false *Virgin Modesty* bestows;
Her ruddy Lips, the deep Vermilion dyes;
Length to her Brows the Pencil Touch supplies,
And with black bending Arches shades her Eyes.
Well pleas'd, at last the Picture she beholds,
And spots it o'er with Artificial molds;
Her Countenance compleat, the Beau she warms
With Looks not hers, in spight of Nature's Charms.
   Thus artfully their persons they disguise,
Till the last Flourish bids the Curtain rise.
The Prince then enters on the Stage in State,
Behind a Guard of Candle-Snuffers wait:
There swoln with Empire, terrible and fierce,
He shakes the Dome, and tears his Lungs with Verse:
His Subjects tremble, and submissive Pit
Wrapt up with silence and Attention sit;
Till freed at length, he lays aside the Weight
Of Publick Business and Affairs of State,
Forgets his Pomp, dead to Ambitious Fires,
And to some peacefull *Brandy-Shop* retires,
Here in full Gills his anxious Thoughts he drowns,
And quaffs away the Care that waits on Crowns. . . .

Otway perforce abdicated after his first appearance; and seems never to have essayed another flight at kingship. Lee was of better acting stuff. In addition to his Duncan, he appeared as Captain of the Guard in the cast of Nevil Payne's *Fatal Jealousie*, August, 1672, and perhaps in another small walking part, that of Marcellus in *Hamlet*.[22] That he had some ability is witnessed by a story told of the great Mohun. This actor, who had come to England with the reputation of being the finest in the world, is said to have heard Lee declaiming one of his own plays and at the end to have thrown down his scrip with the magnificent remark: "Unless I were able to *play* it as well as you *read* it, to what purpose should I undertake it?"[23] The compliment was amply repaid in kind by the heroic Lee, who once is purported to have exclaimed after a performance: *"Oh Mohun, Mohun! Thou little Man of Mettle, if I should Write a hundred Plays I'd Write a Part for thy Mouth!"*[24] Lee seems to have been less precipitously driven from the stage than Downes would imply. Indeed, it may have been that he withdrew voluntarily in order to devote himself entirely to composition; for it was but a short while afterward that he produced his first tragedy.

Both Lee and Otway turned this slight ability to some account, and therein lies its present relevance. We need only picture the playwrights in the full frenzy of composition. The details are supplied by Gildon, with certain sage admonitions to beginners, that he incidentally followed with such rare success as to land among the demi-heroes of the *Dunciad*.

When the general Plan is form'd [said he], the Poet should endeavor, before he sets to write, at any time during his penning of the whole Piece, to imitate with his own Body the Gestures and Actions of those Dramatic Persons, to whom he is about to give Words and Sentiments proper to the Passions they are possess'd with; to which I must add, that he should likewise imitate the Voice and the Utterance; all which join'd together will fix in his Soul the Passion and Characters he is writing, and by that means he can never miss drawing them according to Nature. This was the Method that *Otway* follow'd, as I have been assur'd by an intimate Acquaintance of his; and to this Method I must in great measure attribute his admirable touching of the Passions.[25]

Otway composed his plays with an eye ever upon the actor, and we know that Mrs. Barry, for one, was accustomed to consult the poet for his individual interpretation.[26] The feeling which he obviously threw into composition partly explains why Otway, by Dryden's own admission, had a moving power beyond that of the laureate. The latter, apparently, was devoid of any acting ability.[27]

But meanwhile Otway's one misadventure upon the boards kept rising unhappily to plague him. According to the habit of the age, it was never quite forgotten nor forgiven. Three years later came forth a pasquinade, reflecting upon it cruelly:

> But *Apollo* had seen his Face on the Stage,
> And prudently did not think fit to engage,
> The scum of a *Play-house* for the Prop of an Age.[28]

It was a sneer so unseasonable as to draw down a duel upon the head of its author.

The trials of Otway and Lee seem to have been occasioned by the shortage of actors at both playhouses during the early seventies. Cademan, stabbed in the eye during a stage duel, was retired to his pension and to bookselling, whence his name was to appear upon our poets' title-pages. Others had either withdrawn or had died in various degrees of violence. Certain actresses, in the words of Downes, had been "erept the stage by force of Love." Of the newcomers, many were of the greatest significance in the creation of the tragedy of ensuing years. Betty Currer had a genius for acting "the trim built carack of the town"; and her success in comedy inevitably was to cause parts to be written for her in tragedy. Thus, there was something more than the prevalent English taste for tragi-comedy behind the creation of her great rôle of Aquilina in Otway's most famous play. The mountebank Tony Leigh, also, was to insinuate his buffoonery into the pity and terror of *Venice Preserved*. Another comedian, though one less a newcomer to the stage, James Nokes, may be mentioned for the part he was to take in the evolution of tragedy. By reason of his demonstrated capacity as Mrs. Beardly, in Durfey's *Virtuous Wife*, he was to shamble into Otway's perversion of *Romeo and Juliet* and sink the nurse to incalculable depths:

> Pleasant Buffoon! to what an artfull Screw
> His wither'd Chops the merry Whoreson drew,
> What Pencil can describe his grotesque Mein,
> The Cuckolds sneaking Leer, the Noncon Grin,
> The wire-hung Limbs, sunk Eyes, and pecked Chin.

Thus furnish'd, thus deform'd, thus bent with Age,
With feeble Steps he limp'd across the Stage,
There drawling Nonsense from his haggard Jaws,
Dispell'd the Spleen which Betterton had caused.[29]

Among others who appeared in the early seventies was Bowman. He was to last through whole packs and sets of great ones and recount to Oldys indistinct reminiscences of Lee and Otway. Bowman had joined the Duke's Company as a boy gifted with a lovely singing voice. That voice, and others like it, should also help to shape tragedy, though at last into the byway of trills and quavers. Gillo, Williams, Percival, Mrs. Butler, and "the Great Mrs. Barry," according to Downes, were some of the others who entered at about this time. There can be no suggestion that any of the newcomers introduced revolutionary changes into the technique of acting. Mrs. Barry did not spring full panoplied from the brain of Rochester, but had to undergo years of probation, and ultimately owed her mastery over tears to the endless care of Betterton and a play or two wrought by the devotion of Otway. The tyros merely fell in step with the conventions of the stage. They had their initiation from Betterton and his talented wife, or from Hart and Mohun, into a technique direct by descent from Shakespeare, Burbage, and the great actors of the Jacobean era, with a most liberal admixture of current French practice.

After the Restoration, the conventions of acting seem to have commenced to harden into elaborate formulas, with the development of heroic tragedy tending to accelerate the process. The heroic lovers of Beaumont and Fletcher still preserved some of the gentle accent of Shakespeare's creatures; those of Dryden had cast away discretion, and, in their striving to achieve in tragedy the effects of Rinaldo in epic poetry, had merely risen to the realm of the baroque. A single couplet by Lee may serve to demonstrate the extreme limits of the new fashion:

We'l drown the talking Gods with our last cry,
And Earth shall thunder back upon the Sky.[30]

The audience demanded this sort of line, the line tolerated but one sort of actor, and the actor of necessity aimed at one sort of audience. In the vicious circle, the use of voice and gesture grew more rhetorical. Surrounded upon three sides by unruly spectators, the actor began to partake of the qualities of the platform demagogue.

He was the moving statue, not yet the moving picture, depending for his effects upon the force of broad movement, of posture, and of compelling accent to ravish away his audience. To what extent mere rhetoric and formal elocution ruled the stage may be deduced from any description of the great artists of the period. Cibber makes the following observations upon the more general principles:

In the just Delivery of Poetical Numbers, particularly where the Sentiments are pathetick, it is scarce credible upon how minute an Article of Sound depends their greatest Beauty or Inaffection. The Voice of a Singer is not more strictly ty'd to Time and Tune than that of an Actor in Theatrical Elocution: The least Syllable too long or too slightly dwelt upon in a Period depreciates it to nothing; which very syllable if rightly touch'd shall, like the heightening Stroke of Light from a Master's Pencil, give Life and Spirit to the whole. I never heard a Line in Tragedy come from *Betterton* wherein my Judgment, my Ear, and my Imagination were not fully satisfy'd.[31]

A few years after Betterton's death, the unscrupulous Gildon brought forth a *Life of Mr. Thomas Betterton*[32] purported to have been gathered from the conversation and the notes of the actor. How far we can trust it as derivative of him is very much of a question. It does show, however, to what degree of petrifaction the free but careful art of genius could harden when observed by weak imitators. In the pages of this book is to be found half the reason for the decline of English tragedy toward the end of the seventeenth century. We have page after page of carefully catalogued look, attitude, and gesture. Hanging down of the head was the consequence of grief and sorrow; tossing the head, pride and arrogance; carrying it aloft, joy and triumph; a hard and bold forehead was the mark of obstinacy, perfidiousness, and impudence. Denial, aversion, dissimulation, and neglect were shown by turning away the eyes. The hand put on the mouth was the token of silence, lifting one hand upright or extending it was expressive of force, vigor, and power.[33] The constrained theatrical engravings of Wilks as Jaffeir or of Barry as Zara were probably not so far afield from the actor's actual representations of love, hate, and despair.

The comedian was freer in his technique. Nokes, Jevon, and Haines were *improvisatori* on or off the stage. Of the first of these, Cibber wrote what may stand for his fellows.

His excellence may be comprehended in one article, viz, a plain and palpable Simplicity of Nature, which was so utterly his own that he was often as unaccountably diverting in his common Speech, as on the Stage. I saw him once, giving an account of some Table talk, to another Actor behind the Scenes, which a Man of Quality accidentally listening to, was so deceived by his Manner, that he ask'd him if that was a new Play, he was rehearsing?[34]

The unconstrained art of the comedian, so long as it was not shackled by sentimentality, permitted the free development of comedy; and that is some part of the reason why the next age is better known to us for its Congreves and Farquhars than for its Southernes and its Rowes.

It is worth observation that the gradual accretion of rules and formulas of tragic acting, under which Hart, Betterton, and Mohun labored in varying degree, had its exact facsimile upon the French stage.[35] In 1663 Molière caricatured the exaggerated declamation of the rival company at the Hôtel de Bourgogne,—a company more famous for its tragedy than his own of the Palais-Royal. His rapier spared Floridor, the Hart of the rival company, but the smaller fry received just chastisement. These were the actors and actresses applauded by Charles during his exile, and by the company of English actors which he patronized at Paris. Betterton had observed them hardly less attentively than Mohun. It is not improbable that the two rival companies of the French stage, with their fine balance of power, were the models upon which were formed the twin companies of the English stage. With the ascendancy of Racine, a great actress of the natural school arose in France to interpret his rôles. He saw in Mlle de Champmeslé the same possibilities that Otway discovered in "the great Mrs. Barry."[36] But if La Champmeslé was of the natural school, the term is used in the comparative sense. Her declamation, we read, was not so exaggerated as that of her predecessors, yet she retained a marked tragic cadence. After the union of the two French companies in 1680, which significantly anticipated the English union by two years, Baron took his place as the chief tragedian of France. He too was of the so-called natural school of acting, and may serve as a parallel to Betterton. "Il ne déclamoit jamais, pas même dans le plus grand tragique, et il rompoit la mesure des vers de telle sort que l'on ne sentoit point l'insupportable monotonie du vers alexandrin."[37] Following Baron and La Champmeslé came actors who succumbed entirely to the spell of the Alexandrine. So the battle ebbed and flowed for a century across the channel, as in England. The passing of the individual genius of Racine and Otway does not altogether explain the decline of tragedy in both countries that followed their deaths.

We may seriously question whether the English tragedy of the later seventeenth century was ever able to free itself from a somewhat artificial chant. Tony Aston said of Mrs. Barry's acting that "neither she, nor any of the Actors of those Times, had any Tone in their Speaking, (too much, lately, in Use)."[38] But the reliability of Aston's statement is weakened by his qualification, that she "had a Manner of drawing out her Words, which became her, (but not Mrs. *Braidshaw* and Mrs. *Porter*)." It would be but natural for one first bred in the heroic drama, and in the strange refinements of spectacle, chant, and frequent song that passed for Opera, to carry "tone" over into straight tragedy. Lowe questions the statement of Aston, with a sound summary of the evidence.[39] "Tone" had become predominant when Victor wrote in the early eighteenth century. He speaks of the "good old Manner of singing and quavering out their tragic Notes."[40] And that this was the predominant style appears conclusive from the preface to *The Fairy Queen*, 1692, where Settle remarked that: "He must be a very ignorant Player, who knows not there is a Musical Cadence in speaking; and that a Man may as well speak out of Tune, as sing out of Tune."[41] Later, as this chanting style took complete possession, the acting of Mrs. Cibber was thus described: "In a key, high-pitched but sweet withal, she sung, or rather recitatived Rowe's harmonious strain . . . it was so extremely wanting in contrast, that though it did not wound the ear, it wearied it,"[42]—a reflection as entirely applicable to her contemporaries of the French tragic stage.

Restoration tragedy will probably never be revived, except at sporadic intervals and under the impulse of antiquarian enthusiasm. *The Orphan* and *Venice Preserved*, because of their importance in the history of the English stage, will suffer resurrection about once in every fifteen years, as the memory of the last failure disappears; and because of their quick extinction, we shall be prone to draw hasty generalizations concerning the intelligence of our ancestors. How much more would this be true, were we to select for such revival plays even closer to the main current of Restoration drama, as, for example, *The Rival Queens* or *Sopho-*

nisba. The cause of their failure would lie with us. We have lost an
art as distinct from that of the modern stage as sculpture is from
painting. By banishing "tone," by reducing the play into a two-
dimensional stage, by improving acoustics so that elaborate and
formal declamation is no longer a necessity, by flooding the stage
with light so that the slightest movement may pass across the foot-
lights, and finally by overrationalizing the audience, we have
erected a barrier that forbids retrogression. It is not all pure profit:
our actors in their pursuit of subtlety within the picture have lost
the magnificent sweep of gesture and the operatic use of the vocal
cords. An Alexander or a Hannibal played by any of the thousand
nameless but careful artists of today is unthinkable. The last actors trained to such rôles were of the generation of Kean, O'Neill,
and Macready, when the dramatic conditions that created Betterton and Barry still lingered on. Nor is the recent revival of interest
in Restoration comedy more than a futile gesture of understanding.
The Way of the World may be performed upon the modern stage
with no great depreciation of its brilliance or its wit. But, contrary to the general opinion, wit tells only one-half the story of the
Restoration. To understand the age one should turn, first of all, to
the great baroque tragedies, such as *Theodosius, Don Carlos, The
Rival Queens,* and *Mithridates.* It is to these works of Lee and
Otway, therefore, that we shall first direct our attention.

Chapter IV

YOUTH COMPOSES A TRAGEDY, 1674/5

I Cannot choose but laugh, when I look back and see
The strange Vicissitudes of Poetrie.
Your Aged Fathers came to Plays for Wit,
And sat Knee-deep in Nut-shells in the Pit.
Course Hangings then in stead of Scenes were worn,
And Kidderminster did the Stage adorn.
But you, their wiser Off-spring, do advance
To Plot of Gigg; and to Dramatique Dance;
But when the Reign of Gigg and Dance is past,
Whither the Devil will you go at last
What yet unheard-of Way can Poets try,
To please these Modern Criticks of the eye.
Prologue to CORYE's *Generous Enemies*, 1671

I MUST confess [wrote Otway in the somewhat forward manner of his time], I had a Tittillation to Poetry, but never durst venture on my Muse, till I got her into a Corner in the Country, and then like a bashful young Lover, when I had her in private, I had Courage to fumble, but never thought she would have produc'd anything, till at last, I know not how, e're I was aware I found myself Father of a Dramatique birth, which I call'd *Alcibiades*.[1]

Nathaniel Lee, having already suffered the pangs of fatherhood—at least of an Ode—appears not to have been so completely rebuffed by his ill success as an actor, but to have remained hard by Lincoln's Inn Fields for the composition of a robust tragedy, to which he gave the name of *Nero*.[2]

It is hardly correct to call either play a heroic tragedy, without making at the same time some sort of qualification. Both have been so catalogued. Of the two, that by Otway—who was to depart farthest from the style set by Orrery and Dryden—was the closer to the norm. But each had traces, even in this *juvenilia*, of the newer style that was to transform English tragedy.

The heroic in our drama is traceable to various antecedents, and is in itself a study of such complexity as to pass the bounds of this place. However, we may safely conclude that the Rinaldo of Tasso was more surely the prototype of Almanzor than the Achilles of Homer, or, less certainly, the Artéban of La Calprenède. Though

Dryden professed to admire the Grecian demigod beyond the ruffled French hero,[3] it was nevertheless the chop-logic of the latter and the unparalleled magnanimity of the noble Rinaldo that together composed the *mélange* which was Almanzor. The Restoration audience, which in turn partook of the greater European culture, demanded of its heroes an epic egotism transcending any example, either from the Elizabethan stage or from Homer or Virgil. The epic was understood mainly as the boundless assertion of individuality; its complete embodiment was discovered in the heroism of the artificial epic of Italy and the "epic" romance of France. Almanzor and his fellows huff their way through all the countries of the Grand Khan, Pizarro, and Cortez without for a moment losing their superiority to time or space. The courts they serve are veritable tinder boxes of conspiracy and ungoverned lust, and yet all alike are foredoomed to extinction before heroic love and heroic friendship. These heroes are all of a piece in their rapturous rhetoric of egotism, never descending—at least consciously—from their high pedestals. And as an *obbligato* to all their turgid magnificence was added infinite song, rhyme, and dance.

The surface formula of heroic drama was neatly characterized by Shadwell. He, who "never deviated into sense," was one of the few to maintain his balance during the heroic seventies, and now it was with satisfaction that he observed that

> He has no cautionary Song, nor Dance,
> That might the Treaty of his Peace advance,
> No kind Romantick Lovers in his Play,
> To sigh and whine out passion, such as may
> Charm Waiting-women with Heroick Chime,
> And still resolve to live and dye in Rhime;
> Such as your Ears with Love and Honour feast,
> And play at *Crambo* for three hours at least:
> That Fight, and Woo, in Verse in the same breath
> And make Similitudes, and Love in Death.[4]

Lee and Otway were not conscious revolutionaries. Youth is generally derivative. It thumbs old folios in the quiet rectories of Woolbeding and Hatfield, and designs for itself a play. One half the scheme reëchoes the familiarized drama of early reading, the other the standardized formulas of the contemporary stage. The wise Tutor of Pacheco again has much apposite instruction:

I take a subject [he said], as suppose the Siege of *Candy,* or the Conquest of *Flanders,* and by the way Sir, let it alwayes be some war-like action; you can't imagine what a grace a Drum and Trumpet give a Play. Then Sir I take you some three or four or half a dozen Kings, but most commonly two or three serve my turn, not a farthing matter whether they lived within a hundred years of one another, not a farthing, Gentlemen, I have tryed it and let the Play be what it will, the Characters are still the same.

PIS. Trust me Sir, this is a secret of your art.

TUT. As Sir you must alwayes have two Ladies in Love with one man, or two men in love with one woman; if you make them the Father and the Son, or two Brothers, or two Friends, 'twill do the better. There you know is opportunity for love and honour and Fighting, and all that.

PED. Very well Sir.

TUT. Then Sir you must have a Hero that shall fight with all the world; yes i'gad and beat them too, and half the gods into the bargain if occasion serves.

ANT. This method must needs take.

TUT. And does Sir. But give me leave and mark it as infallible, in all you write reflect upon religion and the Clergy; you can't imagine how it tickles, you shall have the Gallants get those verses all by heart, and fill their letters with them to their Country friends; believe me this one piece of art will set off many an indifferent Play, and, but you are my friends—

ANT. You honour us.

TUT. Last of all be sure to raise a dancing singing ghost or two, court the Players for half a dozen new scenes and fine cloaths (for take me if there ben't much in that too) put your story into rime, and kill enough at the end of the Play, and *Probatum est* your business is done for Tragedy.[5]

Many years after this was written, Richard Steele seems to have come upon a tradition concerning Lee's technique of composition that lays bare the complete rigmarole as our poet found it in possession of the stage. But what Steele set down in this prologue of 1717, as descriptive of Lee, was perhaps even more applicable to Otway at the beginning of his career,—inasmuch as Lee did not arrive at his formula until his second or third play. The recipe may be used to supplement that just given:

> *Nat Lee,* for Buskins fam'd would often say,
> To Stage-success He had a certain Way;

Something for all the People must be done,
And with some Circumstance each Order won;
This He thought easy, as to make a Treat,
And, for a Tragedy, gave this Receipt.
    Take me, said He, a Princess Young and Fair.
Then take a Blooming Victor flush'd with War;
Let Him not owe to vain Report, Renown,
But in the Ladies Sight cut squadrons down;
Let Him, whom they themselves saw win the Field,
Him to whose Sword, they saw whole Armies yield,
Approach the Heroine with dread Surprise,
And own no Valour Proof against bright eyes:
The Boxes are your own—The thing is hit, ⎫
And Ladies, as they near each other sit, ⎬
Cry, oh! *How movingly that Scene is writ?* ⎭
For all the Rest, with Ease, Delights you'll shape,
Write for the Heroes of the Pit, a *Rape:*
Give the first Gallery a *Ghost;* on th' Upper,
Bestow, tho' at that distance, a good *Supper,*
Thus all their Fancies, working their own Way,
They're Pleas'd, and think they owe it to the Play.[6]

It was with remarkable fidelity that Otway followed the precepts of young Nathaniel, in this first play of *Alcibiades;* and however distasteful to us, the dish was pleasing to the *bons vivants* of his own generation. After the production, the Duke of York graciously permitted Otway to kiss his hand, and straightway took upon himself the protection of the poet's next play,—an unexampled display of favor.[7] But why not? The heroine was young and fair; a whole series of rapes was projected, albeit the untimely arrival of the hero frustrated the consummation of any; while the hero himself narrowly escaped ravishment by a lustful queen. For this escape Otway, the country youth, felt constrained subsequently to apologize to the city wits.[8] The last act was perfect of its kind, furnishing, besides a ghost and a banquet, a welter of destruction beyond all specification. Throughout, the decorums were nicely observed. The king was stabbed by the queen, when the villain unexpectedly developed scruples. Decency it seemed demanded that royalty alone should dispose of royalty; and, besides, faint echoes of *Hamlet* were running through the young playwright's mind when he wrote the climactic speech:

There is in Majesty a secret charm
That puts a fetter on a Traytor's arm.[9]

This was all bait to the groundlings and the royal box.

But everywhere Otway worked according to the public mind. Unlike Lee in his *Nero*, the younger poet adhered strictly to the fashionable rhyme, even though there were serious mutterings against it in powerful quarters. Otway was conventional, likewise, in his adherence to the conventional claptrap of pulleys and windlasses. In more respects than this one, *Alcibiades* came perilously close to opera, as it was then understood. Thus in the fifth act, while Timandra sleeps, *A Spirit comes and sings*. After which *The Scene changes to Elizium. Several Spirits of the ayr descend, and Dance. . . . A glorious Temple appears in the Ayr, where the Spirits of the Happy are seated. A song. The whole Body of the Temple moves downward. They all vanish, and the Scene changes again to the Tent*.[10] It is entirely a product of the time, in its new emphasis of back drops and complicated machinery.

The architecture of these tragedies was of a characteristic bastard origin. Side by side with French and Italianate galleries in the full efflorescence of rococo adornment, are to be found ponderous outworks, or even whole stories, in the Tudor and Jacobean manner. The Poppea of Lee's *Nero* awhile strides unabashed as the familiar lustful queen of heroic tragedy, and then is metamorphosed into a pale Cressida with momentary pangs of conscience, only to die at length, a woman killed by kindness. Tissaphernes, of Otway's first play, plots death and destruction with all the tortuous convolutions of a villain out of Settle or Dryden, and then shades off into an irrational Iago. His character develops by endless soliloquy, much of it copied from Shakespeare's villain, but subtly shifts from the Elizabethan themes of "will" and "reputation" to those upon the scale of the Restoration mind, "the futility of conscience" and "ambition."

It was, however, in the character of the heroine, Timandra, that Otway was most certainly feeling his way toward the new tragedy. A rather colorless courtesan, as she appeared in Plutarch,[11] she first led Otway to observe her closely perhaps by her tender collection of the ashes of Alcibiades, after his death at the hands of her outraged brothers. We may ponder at length upon the flood of tears that might have been unloosed, had the poet written of her some few years later. But her earliest mutation, at his hands, was into the type-heroine, for whom the hero "cuts whole squadrons down," and who, like her kind,

> With all the hast Joy could, or love afford
> Flies to congratulate her Conqu'ring Lord.[12]

As we regard Timandra, however, she undergoes almost insensible transformation to a creature more gentle and better resigned to the strokes of her unkind fortune. She is the curious mixture of Elizabethan softness and the high-flown emotionalism of the Restoration stage. In her are to be observed the first premonitions of the typical Otwavian heroine, later to play so important a rôle in the development of English tragedy; and though the resemblances here are too vague for ultimate certainty, her antecedents ought to be more easily traced at this early date than later, when other forces should have exerted their influence. Much of her character may be attributed easily enough to the nature and family background of Otway himself. For that, comment in this place would be useless. Otherwise, the one certainty is that Otway was reproducing in Timandra's the general situation of Desdemona, and that her personality faintly reflected that of Shakespeare's gentlest heroine. We have already observed that the play has its Iago, and now we discover the docile object of his machinations. But the sorrows of this new Desdemona as yet fail to move us. It was to take some further study, on the poet's part, before they should become contagion; and then ultimately should be created two heroines over whom, in the estimation of Scott, were to be shed more tears than ever for Juliet or Desdemona.[13]

Alcibiades, himself, likewise forecast a race typically Otwavian. By contemporary usage these heroes of ranting tragedy were as variable as the moon, their changes dictated only by their boundless egoism. Otway discovered in Plutarch the outlines of a character gifted with a genius for sudden change; and this he necessarily retained, as well as his extraordinary prowess. The material was present in Plutarch for another Almanzor, to whom the side should matter little, so long as it could afford him the opportunity to shine in use.[14] But Otway added certain incongruous qualities of loyalty and goodness. His hero was a traitor to his country, following Plutarch, and yet, after the heroic scheme, he risked his life to keep fair the name of an alien state; he was a drunken reveler, and yet a model of masculine continence. A year or so later, when twitted upon the subject, Otway had no defense ready: "For my Hero to do him right, was none of that squeamish Gentleman I make him, but would as little have boggl'd at the obliging the passion of a young and beautiful Lady, as I should my self, had I the same opportunities, which I have given him."[15] But at no time was Otway able to laugh off the purblind half-morality of his characters. Of the other traits of heroism, as they were commonly practiced on the contemporary stage, there was lacking from Otway's Alcibiades some of the sublime egoism but none of the chronic waywardness. This utterly unhistorical Athenian, with his loyalty and nobility in conflict with his heroic duplicity, was, therefore, a link between the paladin of Restoration tragedy, and the oncoming race of Polydores and Castalios. These latter indecisive persons were in reversion, not only to the wayward channels of Otway's personality, but to the wholly irresponsible and tempestuous heroes of early Restoration tragedy.

What was true of the juvenile work of one playwright, was hardly less true of that of the other. Lee appears to have possessed the more vigorous nature. In him the heroic instinct was more deeply bred, so that the insufficient hero of Otway was never quite permitted to emerge. Lee's heroines, on the other hand, were perhaps more Elizabethan; and from the outset he strove to wring the hearts of his fair auditors as no dramatist hitherto.

> I'm told that some are present here to day,
> Who e're they see, resolve to Dam this Play,
> So much wou'd interest with ill nature Sway;
> But Ladies, you we hope, will prove more civil,
> And charm these witts that Dam beyond the Devil.[16]

Immature as was the motivation of his subplot of Cyara and Britannicus, Lee's basic design for his *Nero* was quite obvious. Britannicus runs mad after the fashion of Hamlet, and on occasion ponders reminiscently upon death:

> It is a truth? or does Fame tell us lyes,
> When it reports that the Soul never dyes,
> But mantled sits, and acts in gloomy shrouds,
> Like *Cynthia*, when she's hemm'd with circling clouds?[17]

The lines illustrate the general debilitation of Shakespearean vigor that was a part of the age. They do not show so well the heavy drafts of sentimentality which were taking its place. This is more typical:

> When the soft partner of our griefs and joyes,
> With trembling hands shall close our dying eyes,
> When in sad sort our friends shall stand and mourn,
> To see the Fatal torch those relicts burn,
> Is there an end of thought? no farther care?
> No throne of bliss, nor caverns of despair?[18]

Finally, to the infinite wellspring for tears of a gentler Hamlet gone mad, but not yet dreaming of revenge, add a heroine disguised as a page to minister to her lord, as in *Philaster, or Love lies a Bleeding,* and behold we have the old tragedy transmogrified into the new![19]

Lee consolidated his position by other and more commonplace devices. It is notable that Nero poisons his mother in the first act, after various other crimes, and that he pursues his villainy to the end, urged on by the gusto of the pit and the ghost of Caligula. But Nero is no mere demigod of ordinary Restoration villainy. He stands before us one-half Elizabethan or Jacobean, one-half what the uneducated rakehells of the pit took to be a Hobbist.

It is worth while, at this point, to observe the philosophical background of the Restoration courtier. He is supposed to have been without such background, and yet the devotee of hard living was sometimes actuated by more than his unrestrained animal passion. He was no worse, probably, than his predecessors in vice, only a bit more systematic in the pursuit of it. He first developed his philosophy as a protest against the restrictive morality of the roundheads; and thence he passed to a code of negative ethics, as elaborately conceived, so he judged, as the positive code of any doctrinaire religion. Vice became religiously conventionalized under hard rules, ultimately as devoid of pleasure as the system it strove to supplant; it was followed for many years. Rochester, to whom Lee's *Nero* was dedicated, was high priest, "whose sayings astonish the Censorious, and whose Writings are so exactly ingenious, Princes treasure them in their Memory as things divine";[20] the prophet was Hobbes; the patron, Charles himself. The prophet doubtless never contemplated the far-fetched conclusions of his avowed disciples, and yet, by his mechanistic philosophy, his agnosticism, his violent distrust of civil religion, his devout adherence to royalty, with various other shreds and patches of belief, it finally resulted that he was canonized by the court party. This was an action the more orthodox, since Charles himself had at one time been pupil to Hobbes, and Rochester and Buckingham had never lost an occasion to glorify his name.[21]

So much did Hobbes dominate worldly fancy that even the *laissez-faire* church ultimately had to take notice of his doctrines and to answer them in several semi-official manifestoes, the most elaborate being that of Thomas Tennison: *The Creed of Mr. Hobbes Examined, In a feigned Conference Between Him and A Student of Divinity*, 1670. As the Creed itself, let alone the examination, is too protracted for adequate treatment in this place, a part of it only will be set down, for the important bearing it has upon any study of Restoration tragedy. Significant of its popularity with the wits is the fact that it was incorporated into various commonplace books of the late seventeenth century,—those same books being otherwise given over to the scandalous epistles to Julian, profane satires, and the tag ends of plays.[22] Hobbes's important *Credo,* then, in part runs as follows:

I believe that God is Almighty matter; that in him are three Persons, he having been thrice represented on earth; that it is to be decided by the Civil Power, whether he created all things else; that Angels are not Incorporeal substances, (those words implying a contradiction) but preternatural impression on the brain of man; that the Soul of man is the temperament of his Body; that the Liberty of Will, in that Soul, is physically necessary; that the prime Law of nature in the soul of man is that of self-Love; that the Law of the Civil Sovereign is the obliging Rule of good and evil, just and unjust. . . .[23]

The creed might have furnished a complete philosophical armament for all the followers of Almanzor, had they paused long enough to consider it.

By Rochester and the other libertines of the age, these doctrines were diluted and applied. Thus, in his final conversations with Dr. Burnett, the Earl set down two principal maxims of morality: "that he should do nothing to the hurt of any other, or that might prejudice his own health,"—rules grievously transgressed in his own career as voluptuary. "And he thought that all pleasure, when it did not interfere with these, was to be indulged as the gratification of our natural Appetites."[24] Tissaphernes gave utterance to similar doctrines, and they were worked into countless contemporary plays, nowhere more incisively than in Otway's *Don Carlos*:

> Why should dull Law rule Nature, who first made
> That Law, by which her self is now betray'd:
> E're man's Corruptions made him wretched, he
> Was born most noble that was born most free:
> Each of himself was Lord; and unconfin'd
> Obey'd the dictates of his Godlike mind.
> Law was the Innovation brought in since,
> When Fools began to love Obedience,
> And call'd their slavery Safety and defence.[25]

That was written when Otway sat at the feet of Rochester. But one might term it all a redevelopment of Renaissance egotism.

Unadulterated villainy appertained no more to Otway's final design than to that of the great men at court. The speaker of the lines just quoted, one Don John, cultivated certain very engaging human traits along with his enthusiasm for man in the original state of nature. If, then, we should demand at this point another influence to account for him, aside from current Hobbism, we might discover it in the person of Edmund, the superman of Shakespeare's *King Lear,* to whom Don John had not a few resemblances besides his bastardy. Edmund was the model for his reliance upon nature as his goddess, for his rejection of love and hate, and for his abandonment of all gentler human emotions,—until he likewise should discover that human sympathy was as necessary to him as to the weaklings he betrayed. In Don John, however, the scale was lowered infinitely. The superman became the Restoration rake. His argument was for no ruthlessness beyond that of free love:

> How vainly would dull Moralists Impose
> Limits on Love, whose Nature brooks no Laws:
> Love is a God, and like a God should be
> Inconstant, with unbounded liberty,
> Rove as he list—[26]

To carry out the analogy, it was as though Edmund had set his goal at the seduction of Goneril and Regan. Thenceforward Don John was merely the glorified beau.

When Rochester passed from ethical doctrine and came to explain his notion of the Deity, he seemed most closely to approximate the views of Hobbes.

He said, He looked on it as a vast Power that Wrought everything by the necessity of its Nature: and thought that God had none of those Affections of Love or Hatred, which breed perturbation in us, and by consequence he could not see that there was to be either reward or punishment. He thought our Conceptions of God were so low, that we had better not think much of him: And to love God seemed to him a presumptuous thing, and the heat of fanciful men. Therefore he believed there should be no other Religious Worship, but a general Celebration of that Being, in some short Hymn: All the parts of Worship he esteemed the Inventions of Priests, to make the World believe they had a Secret of Incensing and Appeasing God as they pleased.[27]

This was the confessional of a votary whose step had lost its quickness at thirty-two. Shortly thereafter it was to be written of him in elegy that

> The mighty ROCHESTER, a *Convert* Dies,
> He fell a Poet, but a Saint shall Rise,
>
> .   .   .   .
>
> Himself his *looser Lines* to Flames bequeaths
> And *Hobs's creed* with Detestation leaves.[28]

The speculations of Hobbes and his followers rarely became explicit in the drama of the Restoration, though now and again they were to be found in the works of Crowne, and once, notably, in the mouth of Pierre in Otway's *Venice Preserved*.[29] Nevertheless they were behind much of the tragedy of the time, and their reverberations were to be noted for some decades yet. The age was duly grateful to Rochester. After his death there was to be celebrated, at the presentation of his *Valentinian,* perhaps the first public commemoration of an author in the history of English literature.

It was small wonder that to Lee the name of Rochester was almost beyond praise. Despite some barbs directed against him by that nobleman, it was Lee who was one of the first to elegize him. In *The Princess of Cleve,* he wrote of Rochester, that

He was the Spirit of Wit—and had such an Art of guilding his Failures, that it was hard not to love his Faults: He never spoke a Witty thing twice, tho to different Persons; his Imperfections were catching, and his Genius was so Luxuriant, that he was forc'd to tame it with a Hesitation in his Speech to keep it in view—But, Oh! how awkward, how insipid,

how poor and wretchedly dull is the imitation of those that have all the
affectation of his Verse, and none of his Wit![30]

In 1674, when Lee produced his *Nero,* and in the two succeeding
years, when Otway brought forth his *Alcibiades* and his *Don
Carlos,* the cult of libertinism was flourishing. *Nero* seems to have
been its completest dramatic expression, even more than Shadwell's
Libertine of 1675. For a time Lee's play created a kind of Nero
cult. At about the same period, Oldham wrote a satire upon morality—presumed incidentally upon its anonymous publication to
have come from Rochester himself[31]—and in its summary of the
demigods of libertinism, the Emperor Nero was held to the climax:

> Yet greater was that mighty Emperor;
> (As greater crime befitted his high Pow'r)
> Who sacrific'd a City to a Jest.[32]

Oldham may have proposed this as a satire upon the court hector,
who was its speaker, but at the time his intention was none too
clear. Newcomers to this world of wit and elegance were of necessity completely dazzled. It is amazing to discover the complete-
ness with which the rector's son of Hatfield gave expression to his
recently discovered philosophy. Ostensibly upon the side of good
morals, he nevertheless presented the other doctrine with great
clarity and greater sympathy. Thus the tragedy opens with an unspeakable crime by Nero against his mother, his excuse being
that—

> Virtue's a Name; Religion is a thing
> Fitter to scare poor *Priests,* than daunt a KING.[33]

And from that point forward, the emperor mounts from crime to
crime, until at last, urged on by the ghost of Caligula, he plunges
to ruin.

The young novice apparently practiced what his elders preached.
Oldys mentions sundry escapades of this "handsome and ingenious" youth, which ultimately "restricted him to a milk diet." When
later "some of Lee's university friends visited him, he fell to drink-
ing with them beyond all reason, which flying up into his face
broke into those carbuncles, which were afterward observed
therein."[34] Or, as Settle impudently remarked,

> By the Rubyes in's Face, he could not deny
> But he had as much Wit as Wine could supply.[35]

In those early years Lee was advancing with youthful ardor toward a complete and consistent philosophical system, and managed to surcharge his material with great vigor. It was only after time and an injured physique had discovered to him the emptiness of Rochester's professions that his enthusiasm broke. The preface to *Gloriana,* his play of 1676, spoke of dashed hopes, and the next year he followed with a dedication of his *Rival Queens* to Rochester's inveterate enemy, Mulgrave. The latter he praised for his admirable continence:

How commendable therefore is such Reservation; how admirable such a Solitude! If you are singular in this, we ought to blame the wild, unthinking, dissolute Age; an Age whose Business is senseless Riot, Neronian Gambols, and ridiculous Debauchery; an Age that can produce few Persons besides your Lordship, who dare be alone.[36]

In the beginning, however, it was probably the libertinage of his first play which gained Lee his hearing, and that not alone from the great high priest, but, with a certain amused toleration, from the patron himself. The production of *Nero,* May 16, 1674, holds interesting implications. We know that upon that date Charles almost certainly honored it with his attendance.[37] The King by that time had been well accustomed, through Hobbes, Orrery, and Dryden, to the similarly zealous absolutism of young Lee. It could cause no amazement. But the remainder of the youth's philosophy may have proved startling. Sin varied inversely to Lee as the elevation of its protagonist. So, upon the verge of death, Poppea—the mistress of Nero—found excuse for her misdeeds:

> In pity say this of me, when I'm dead,
> She was not easily to ruin led;
> 'Twas not a common Crown her virtue bought;
> But mighty Glory with great Courtship wrought.

To which she added, for comfort to the errant ladies of the seventeenth century, a Restoration paraphrase of Othello:

> Then she was young:
> This, *Sir,* perhaps, may mitigate my fault.[38]

Such speeches could disturb no one. But what were the thoughts of Charles, surrounded as he was by his harem, when Hart at the end of a singularly passionate act turned to the royal box with the opening words of his soliloquy?

Let phlegmatic dull KINGS call Crowns their care:
Mine is my wanton; and does Beauties share
Above my Mistress' Eyes. On, *Nero*, on;
Spend thy vast stock, and riot in thy Throne.
If there be pleasure yet I have not found,
Name it, some GOD: 'Tis mine, though under ground:
No nook of Hell shall hide it from thy sight,
But I will conjure't into open light.
My Scepter, like a charming rod, shall raise
Such sports as would old *Epicures* amaze:
Pleasures so rich, so various, and so new,
As never yet the *Gods*, my great Fore-fathers, knew.[39]

The first scene closes. Had not the King been so royally endowed with a sense of humor toward his beloved stage, the scene might easily have closed forthwith upon our hopeful playwright. Instead Lee appears to have been encouraged with some royal favor and to have set about to compose another play, of more sentimental design, for his majesty's fair consort in libertinage, the Duchess of Portsmouth.

Chapter V

PATRONS AND PROFITS

Wit which was formerly but Recreation,
Is now become the Business of the Nation;
Prentices write Lampoons, your Justices ⎫
Have quirks for Courtiers late debaucheries, ⎬
And Constables with quibbles break the peace. ⎭
Your formal Citizen turns man of sense,
And has to Ingenuity pretence:
Treats Miss in Box, which was but Punk with you, ⎫
Gripes her craz'd knee, and treads upon her toe, ⎬
And cries, I' fack my dear this Play will do. ⎭
LEE, Prologue to Gloriana, 1676

NAT. LEE betook himself to the dedication of his *Nero.* One half
the business of a young playwright, in the year 1674, was to provide himself with a patron,—at once wealthy and powerful enough
to protect him from the plague of damning critics. On his first appearance he seems to have been so unfortunate as to have had none
such at hand. Buckingham had abandoned him, and he was otherwise so far unprovided as to lack even a "prologue-writing gifted
friend":

> It is the Fate of Strangers to the Town,
> To have the Play and Prologue too their own:
> Whilst Writers here for one another sweat,
> Clubbing like Carr-men when a Brother's set.
> Nay, dull insipid Farce you will commend
> For sake of Prologue-writing gifted Friends;
> Some gentle follower of the Wits, who thinks
> He sucks in Poetry when-e're he drinks.[1]

Neither of our poets at the outset appears to have been favored by
those cabals of critics that sometimes gathered to boost the stock
of an incipient muse; and indeed with Lee it was quite the contrary, for the gay parasites had assembled early to the snuffing of
his flame. For succor, the poet turned quite properly to the all-
powerful Rochester, stating in his dedication:

Your protection & favour is implor'd by this Humble Supplicant in the
behalf of a Civil Tyrant [Nero], at least one whom I have so represented,

and for which I have been sufficiently censur'd, perhaps unjustly enough; since 'tis not impossible for a man to love and hate, to be brave and bad. From the Criticks, whose Fury I dread, those Killmen, and more than *Jews*, I appeal to your Lordship, as the Saint did to *Caesar*.[2]

We cannot judge at this distance how far that protection extended. The play is to be found in the Bodleian bound in the original vellum and gold stamp of Rochester's library, apparently Lee's gift, with the printer's errors corrected in his own hand. Doubtless the poet was rewarded by a donation commensurate with the favor.

Otway, in his quest for a patron, chanced as happily upon the famous Earl of Middlesex, Buckhurst, afterward Earl of Dorset. He was a powerful friend at court, and like Rochester had poetical pretensions of his own. To the world he was famous as "the best good Man with the worst natur'd Muse"—an arbiter of taste rivaling Rochester, though one somewhat less capricious in his judgments. In his dedication, the author of *Alcibiades* confessed: "I am sufficiently sensible of my own Arrogance, in that I durst obtrude so abject a Trifle as this, under the Patronage of so eminent a Person; but that generous Candour, wherewith you oblige all the World, gave me Courage to hope you might at least pardon this first offence in me." It was a fairly safe hazard. The play had been attended, on September 22, 1675, by the King and Queen, with "a box for the Mayds of Honor,"[3] and praised by the Duke of York. Otway had been given the encouragement of the latter and his "command to go forward."[4] The Duke, it may be added, was freer of such commands than of his guineas. As to Otway's more hopeful dedication to Buckhurst, we may surmise that his lordship was altogether responsive. We have evidence of the many budding poets that he favored, and the poet's own words written in a subsequent dedication: "Your Lordship has so often and so highly obliged me, that I cannot but condemn myself for giving you a trouble so Impertinent as this is."[5]

Then or slightly later, according to the appearance of the features and the date of the painter, Buckhurst commissioned Soest to paint a portrait of Otway. It now hangs in the great dining hall at Knole, amid the brilliant company of Dryden, Wycherley, Betterton, Leigh, and many another whom the great man befriended: "On canvas very brown and ruddy. . . . Eyeballs blue black. Eyebrows broad and brown, cheeks red, lips full and strong red colour, youthful face. Hair sepia, full and flowing. The handling of this flatter and softer than the Betterton next it."[6] Weariness and scorn were already settling about the poet's mouth and eyes as he gazed down upon the cruel brilliance of the patronage system. Buckhurst was the best of its exemplars; he at least provided more than lip protection. Yet the unintentional satire of some portion of Otway's *Friendship in Fashion* was to prove the whimsicality of even this paragon, and to leave the poet at the mercy of his enemies. The entire episode reveals so much of the system that we may glance ahead for a moment at Otway's hopeless protestations.

As for the unluckey censures [he said], some have passed upon me for this Play, I hope your Lordship will believe I hardly deserve 'em. For to my best remembrance, when first I was accused of the thing by some people of the World who had perhaps as little reason to think I could be guilty of it, as to believe themselves deserved it, I made it my business to clear myself to your Lordship, whose good opinion is dearer to me than any thing which my worst Enemies can wrong me of else; I hope I convinc't your Lordship of my Innocence in the matter, which I would not have endeavoured, had it not been Just. For I thank my Stars I know myself better then (for all the Threats some have been pleased to bestow upon me) to tell a lie to save my Throat.[7]

The playwright alluded to the same subject in his prologue, in lines that must have been added after the report of libel had got abroad:

> Then, Gentlemen, no Libel he intends,
> Tho some have strove to wrong him with his Friends:
> And Poets have so very few of those,
> They'd need take care whose favour 'tis they lose.

The need of consulting the personalities of constantly changing patrons, their whims and fancies, of watching whatever alterations might come over their philosophies, politics, or friendships could not but involve the poet to damage of his art, particularly when those patrons were not of the fine broad design of a Buckhurst.

When Lee and Otway came down to London fired with ambition, they indentured themselves to a comparatively limited group that used the stage as its plaything. Rochester was entirely typical.

Ever since he had been at the Court, he had seldom failed to be banished from it, at least once in the year; for, as soon as ever a word came to the tip of his tongue or his pen, he immediately committed it to paper, or produced it in conversation, without any regard for the consequences. The ministers, the royal mistresses, and indeed frequently the king himself, were the subjects of his sarcasms; and if he had not to deal with the kindest hearted prince that ever was, his first disgrace would certainly have been his last.[8]

It is not surprising to discover him shuffling about his patronage with the same captious humor. A true Hobbist, continually in the state of flux, he had befriended Dryden, who had told him in one of his letters that he could write better on the meanest subject than he, the laureate, could upon the best. Wearied of this favorite, either because Dryden tended to overshadow him or else because the latter was too friendly toward his enemy Mulgrave, Rochester let his affection next shine upon Elkanah Settle. With his own hands, he wrote a prologue to the latter's *Empress of Morocco*, and otherwise so set up the brawny one that, single handed, Settle very nearly discomfited the powerful cabal of Dryden, Crowne, and Shadwell in a paper war. It was not long, however, before Elkanah was arbitrarily deposed and for a moment Lee was the favored one. Then Johnny Crowne and his masque of *Calista* was advanced. And it came to pass finally that Otway was favorite.

The friendship of the great was generally counterbalanced by the loss of other friends. Poor Settle had gathered such a host of enemies, while under the protection of Rochester, that he was never quite able to face the world once he was out of favor. It seemed to be the necessary concomitant of patronage, that one assumed most of the enemies of the patron, without gaining all the friends. When Otway was young and the blood of conflict quickened in his veins, he advanced courageously to the cause of his first patron. Buckhurst, in common with the whole camp, detested the Duke of Buckingham, and Otway tempered his speech accordingly. Thornton is probably correct in his assumption that the reference in the prologue to *Alcibiades* to

> Some false flatt'ring Minion of the Court,

was intended as a blow at the powerful statesman. Later Otway was to employ the same characterization in *The Orphan*. It was the way that one survived.

Parnassus thus began to be cut up into armed camps, with marauding expeditions and desertions to enliven the time between the great engagements. After Lee's discovery of the evanescence of Rochester's protection, he joined Dryden's forces, where the Earl of Mulgrave was acting as generalissimo. *The Rival Queens,* as we have observed, was dedicated to the latter nobleman. "Lord All-Pride," as he was known, had but few friends: Rochester had rapiered him exquisitely in a *Farewell to the Court,* and other wits were hardly less spiteful. Perhaps a part of the general dislike was from the fact that Mulgrave was playing for the high stakes of a royal marriage to the princess Ann. It was doubtless to checkmate such an ambition that the jealous monarch packed him off to the relief of Tangiers. This powerful but isolated nobleman retained the devout homage of Lee and Dryden for many years. Dryden was said to have helped in the composition of Mulgrave's somewhat lame *Essay on Satire.* If so, it is to be hoped that the rewards were commensurate with the cudgeling he received in Rose Alley on account of it from the hired ruffians of Rochester and the Duchess of Portsmouth. As to Lee's relations with Mulgrave, we know little beyond the fact that the age attributed to his hand some parts of this same satire:

> Witness the late unparalleled Essay,
> A Work which all admire, and well they may.
> For what insipid Sot can e'er write ill,
> When *Waller, Lee,* and *Dryden* guide the quill?[9]

Certainly the nobleman was shameless beyond example in the appropriation of the wit of other men, and Lee was ever ungrudging of his stock.

The poet's remarks to Mulgrave, in the dedication of *The Rival Queens,* are pertinent to an understanding of the operation of the system. We discover that not only might one contribute heavily of his own wit to the scanty measure of his betters', but also suffer the criticism and occasionally the contribution to his works of their pseudo-wit. Lee said of his play:

Alexander was more to seek for a Patron in my troubl'd Thoughts, than for the Temple of *Jupiter Ammon* in the spreading Wilds and rowling Sands. 'Tis certain too, he must have been lost, had not Fortune, whom I must once, at least, acknowledge kind in my Life, presented me to your Lordship: You were pleas'd, my Lord, to read it over, Act by Act, and by particular praises, proceeding from the sweetness, rather than the justice of your temper, lifted me up from my natural Melancholy and Diffidence to a bold belief, that what so great an Understanding warranted, could not fail of Success. . . . Praise is the greatest encouragement we Camelions can pretend to, or rather the Manna that keeps Soul and Body together; we devour it as if it were Angels Food, and vainly think we grow immortal.[10]

The manna, alas, had little of the fabled sustenance of that of the wilderness. It dissolved away as completely as once had the interest of his early protector, the great Duke of Buckingham. Only a few years later, when Lee was languishing in confinement, it was discovered that all patronage was of a piece:

> None of our new Nobility will send
> To the *King's Bench,* or to his *Bedlam* friend.
> Chymists and Whores by *Buckingham* were fed,
> Those by their honest Labours gain'd their Bread;
> But he was never so expensive yet,
> To keep a Creature meerly for his Wit.[11]

However, in justification of him, we may assume that a legitimate fear possessed Buckingham. Elsewhere are four lines that concern the indomitable appetite of the poet himself. It seems that, in pursuit of patronage, Lee at one time had partaken so heavily of the bounty of the Earl of Pembroke and had lingered at his house so long that "the butler feared he would empty the cellar":

> *Pembroke* lov'd Tragedy and did provide
> For Butcher's Dogs, and for the whole Bankside;
> The Bear was fed, but Dedicating *Lee,*
> Was thought to have a larger paunch than he.[12]

"Dedicating Lee" rivaled Dryden in the depths of humility to which he abased his muse. It may have been a trait inherited from a parent submissive to the ways of greatness. The poet's second dedication—to her grace, the Duchess of Portsmouth—is a masterpiece of such ephemera, deserving complete transcription rather than these excerpts:

Hannibal himself whose hardie spirit never bowd but to the fair imperious *Rosalinda:* nay, he who in spite of beauties Charms, durst gaze upon that sun with Eagle-eyes, and tax her with a blemish, now making his approaches to your Grace, seems awed with the source of so many rayes, and dazl'd with a presence so illustrious. He sees, with new bleedings, eyes more attractive than those of *Rosalinda,* something more delicate in your shape, and lofty in your meen; an Air so charming sweet, that 'tis miraculous it shou'd be Majestick too: Smiles of more delightful Shine than *April* Suns, such softnesses and languishings, as the almighty Poets hand cannot describe, nor Painters Pencil ever draw. For my own part, I am resolved to look upon you daily, and dedicate my Life and Labours to your Grace, to spend all the store of my yet unexhausted fancy in your unbounded Fame.[13]

For *Sophonisba*, Lee received perhaps something less than the munificent twenty guineas Otway is said to have had of Portsmouth for his *Venice Preserved*. The sum would hardly compensate for the wearisome attendance that was entailed. On the other hand, certain devotees of greatness made the time pass pleasantly enough. Shadwell, for instance, endowed as he was with an unconquerable paunch and an unabashed wit, drank with Buckhurst and Sedley in glorious aloofness, and thus paid his devoirs easily.[14]

Otway never was able to manage his affairs so well, apparently having inherited from his father an untruckling spirit, as admirable as it was useless. In *The Orphan,* he was to set down his pondered philosophy upon the matter:

> No flattery, Boy! an honest man can't live by't,
> It is a little sneaking Art, which Knaves
> Use to Cajole and soften Fools withall.
> If thou hast flatt'ry in thy Nature, out with't
> Or send it to a Court, for there 'twill thrive.[15]

In his dedication of *Friendship in Fashion,* he confessed to Buckhurst:

> I cannot but condemn my self for giving you a trouble so Impertinent, as this is: Considering how remiss I have been in my respects to your Lordship, in that I have not waited on you so frequently as the duty I owe your Lordship, and my own Inclinations required; But the Circumstances of my Condition, whose daily business must be daily Bread, have not, nor will allow me that happiness.

Even more clearly than in the case of the other derelicts, a great part of the tragedy of Otway's life must be attributed to his inability to fit himself into the patronage system. One after another of his patrons failed him: Buckhurst, Ossory, Plymouth. Finally, in the endless adventure of searching for new ones, his independence asserted itself in a dedication to his printer, Bentley. "For Mr. *Bentley*, you pay honestly for the Copy: and an Epistle to you is a sort of Aquittance, and may be probably welcome; when to a

Person of higher Rank and Order, it looks like an Obligation for Praises, which he knows he does not deserve and therefore is very unwilling to part with ready Money for."[16] It was a daring insolence, on the part of the poet, that performed no good service, unless to damaged pride.

Otway's outburst hints at the other side of the issue. In the general abuse, only rarely did the patrons themselves have an advocate, though theirs was a sufficient cause.

> No person of Quality [said Ravenscroft], how remote *soever*, can escape the Impertinences of *Poets;* for though they be Hundreds of miles off, they shall be pursu'd, and persecuted with Dedicatories o're and o're, even by the same Authors. . . . But this is excusable in them that Write for *Bread* and Live by *Dedications,* and *Third-Days.* If once in a Year they meet not with a good Audience, or a Bountiful *Maecenas,* we are to expect no *Play* from them the next; because they want Money to keep the great Wits company; from whose conversation, once in Twelve Months, they pick up a *Comedy.*[17]

In return, more often than not, these great men themselves derived a certain vicarious wit, and had in addition their gusto for the arts satisfied. It was an exciting game—for them. Both of our poets found themselves alternately supported and pursued by the fashionable witlings. Malone remarked that "there were cabals at great men's houses, where these poets used to read their poems and plays, and pre-engaged the vote and interest of those noble persons in their favour. Without such pre-engagement 'twas hardly possible for an author to pass in the world."[18] The game began with proselyting in the morning, followed by boisterous applause or equally vehement catcalls in the afternoon—

> 'Tis true, when any Favourites Plays appear,
> Then Kindness and Good-nature brings you here:
> And to secure the Censures of the Town,
> The Pit is fill'd with Friends in the Fore-noon;
> And those five long expecting hours you stay,
> Are spent in making Proselytes to th' Play.[19]

But that which was merely a sporting interest to the patron was deadly earnest to the poets. No wonder that there was occasionally a revolt in their ranks.

The unhappy pride of Otway left him chiefly dependent, at such a juncture, upon the unproductive tears of sensibility, the tenuous receipts of the poet's third night, and the slight profits of publishing, with one or two minor sources of income that would have been negligible under any other conditions. His revenue from the third night, if we may trust the offer of one of his epilogues, was hardly worth the pawn of fifty pounds. As Gildon remarked early in the next century, of his own decadent age:

> We have had extraordinary Encouragement for *Dramatick Poetry,* and that much greater than ever had been known before in this nation, which however has not been able to produce any valuable performance in that way; and several Authors have made from three and four hundred Pounds to fifteen hundred for one *Tragedy* or *Comedy;* which however never reach'd a second Season. Whereas *Otway, Lee,* and *Dryden* could never attain more for one piece than one hundred Pounds. I believe by a fair Computation, that *Mithridates, Theodosius, Alexander the Great,* and *Hannibal,* have gain'd the several actors that have succeeded each other not less than fifty thousand pounds, and yet the author scarce got one hundred pounds a piece for his labour, and dy'd at last in the very street; whereas if our *English* great men, who had power to have done it; had fix'd and order'd that the Poet should have receiv'd a reasonable share of the profits of his plays as long as they were acted in his time, as it is in *France,* he had had a comfortable maintenance from his labors, and escap'd that miserable fate that befel him. Thus, *Otway* had but a hundred pounds apiece for his *Orphan* and *Venice Preserv'd,* tho' the players, reckoning down to this time, have not got less than twenty thousand pounds by them.[20]

There is no way of telling what portion of the £100 was derived from the third night, but Otway's offered pawn may not have been far from the sum:

> But which amongst you is there to be found,
> Will take his third day's Pawn for Fifty pound?[21]

This pittance came, upon the average, once a year or less. Otway ranged from periods of six to seventeen months between his plays; Lee, a bit more providently, produced a play regularly each year, or improved his average by an occasional collaboration with Dryden. There was the pressure of poverty and of a public avid for novelties to urge them forward, neither of which was to the improvement of art. Shadwell boasted of turning off plays in record time, as though that was to his credit. Lee by nature was a more conscientious artist. In his dedication of *Theodosius,* he quoted Dryden to the point: "For, 'tis impossible in our limited Time (and

I bring his Opinion to back my own, who is without comparison the best Writer of the Age) to present our Judges a Poem half so perfect as we cou'd make it."[22] Even under pressure of an exacting contract, Dryden was unable to produce anything like three plays a year.

Third nights were rare and poets improvident. Their prospect of saving a great deal from the kites that descended upon them at seasons of affluence was negligible. Only a few years later, when Betterton's close discipline had relaxed somewhat, there was recounted the terrifying history of a play, from its inception through the poet's night. It is applicable enough to the earlier period to make it worth retelling:

A Day was appointed for the reading; a Dinner was bespoke at a Tavern for half a Score, at least that number came to judge his Play, tho' not three of 'em cou'd tell the difference between Comedy and Tragedy; in the reading of it (that is after Dinner) most of 'em dropt off, but two remain'd to hear it out, and then they walkt; so that there was but the Gentleman and his Friend left, and not a Penny all this while paid towards the Reckoning. The Play was ordered to be Licensed, so that forty Shillings for the Dinner, and forty more for the Licence, made just four Pounds, so much it cost him already. This happened to be in Lent, and the Players having then the first Day of a Play given 'em, this was bespoke; so the Author had the Mortification of having it acted in Lent; but the Devil on't was, he was oblig'd to treat every one of his Players all the while it was in Rehearsal, to keep 'em in study, and in that exploit it cost him in Coach hire and Wine near ten Pounds.

To shorten the matter, after a crowded third night, "They brought him Bills for Gloves, for Chocolet, for Snuff, this Singer begg'd a Guinea, that Dancer the same. . . ."[23] The story proceeds with losses so devastating to the poet that we must assume they were avoided by Lee and Otway after their first shearing.

Nevertheless, the infrequent rewards of production obliged them to turn to other sources. In the number of these Otway appears not to have been so happy as either Lee or Dryden. Thus the latter, for a while at least, was under some sort of contract with the theater.

After the Restoration, when the two Houses struggled for the Favour of the Town, the taking Poets were secur'd to either House by a Sort of retaining Fee, which seldom or never amounted to more than forty Shillings a Week: nor was that of any long Continuance; however that was *some* help to the support of the poet, during the time of his writing for the Stage.[24]

By the testimony of O'Keefe, Otway was retained by neither, selling his work to one or the other as occasion demanded. But the picture of this popular playwright hawking about his wares from house to house is altogether strange, especially in light of the fact that all of them were produced at the Duke's Theatre, or at its immediate successor, and always under the direction of Betterton. Indeed, shortly after Otway's death, it was remarked that:

> this best Poet, tho' with so much ease,
> He never drew his Pen but sure to please;
> Tho' lightning were less lively than his Wit,
> And Thunder-claps less loud than those o' th' Pit,
> He had of's many Wants much earlier dy'd,
> Had not kind Banker *Betterton* supply'd,
> And took for Pawn the Embryo of a Play,
> Till he could pay himself the next *third Day,*
> Were *Shakespear's* self to live again, he'd ne'er
> Deg'nerate to a Poet from a Player.[25]

The profits of publication were scarcely of greater moment. It could be written of Otway's principal publisher that "a bookseller of great repute in the Strand, can produce a receipt of Otway's given his father, for *fifteen* pounds paid for a copy of his *Venice Preserved!*"[26]

There remained a few byways off Grub Street where one might gain a livelihood. Occasional pieces were in demand for births, marriages, and funerals. The poet's broadside, for this latter crisis, with its accompanying decoration of coffins and skulls, was as inevitable to greatness as the undertaker's mutes. We have discovered Lee contributing a *Threnody* at the death of Albemarle, and while he was by no means so fecund of these ephemera as Aphra Behn or Elkanah Settle, his list was somewhat more imposing than that of Otway. In November, 1677, he composed a congratulatory address to the Prince and Princess of Orange upon their marriage, a monument of bad taste.[27] Later he had ready an address to the Duke of York upon his return,[28] and another to Dryden's *Absalom and Achitophel,* of which the latter was doubtless as much a deed of devotion as his *Epistle* to the same poet's *State of Innocence.* The writers frequently clubbed together with prologues and epilogues to one another's plays at five pounds a composition.[29] Finally the innumerable miscellanies were good for an occasional guinea. In 1680 Otway contributed a translation—it was chiefly translations that were required—of the Epistle of *Phaedra to Hippolytus* for the *Ovid* issued under the editorship of Dryden, and toward the end a place was found for his verse in the amorous collections of Mrs. Behn. Otway seems to have been highly regarded as a poet of love and as a translator, especially of the erotic poems of Catullus, Ovid, and Tibullus.

But it all simmers down to this, that in the servile world to which Lee and Otway were engaged, life itself hung precariously upon the favor of the great. The notice of the Duchess of York was a triumph that presaged fortune; the good will of His Highness and His Majesty, blessings beyond fable. Dedicating to her grace, the Duchess of Richmond, Lee alluded to this bounty: "You brought Her Royal Highness just at the exigent time, whose single Presence on the Poet's Day, is a Subsistence for him all the Year after."[30] And Otway tells of his "unspeakable Obligations" to the Earl of Rochester, "who far above what I am able to deserve from him, seem'd almost to make it his business to establish it in the good opinion of the *King* and his *Royal Highness*."[31] The Duke gave Otway permission to dedicate to him his *Don Carlos*, a favor tantamount to all earthly success. Thereafter, Otway was the completely loyal, and hence impoverished, adherent to the fortunes of James. But he could ill afford to dedicate a second play to him. Wealth for a time might be sacrificed to glory, but in the end the lesser lords paid more handsomely. Meanwhile, his triumph was of great weight. Though he was to compose far better plays than *Don Carlos*, it is doubtful whether his fortunes ever attained a climax beyond this earliest one of his career.

Chapter VI

"SO NOBLE A PLEASURE"

Pouring forth Tears at such a lavish rate,
That were the World on fire, they might have drown'd
The Wrath of Heav'n, and quench't the mighty Ruin.
LEE, *Mithridates*

BEFORE the curtain had finally descended upon the destruction wrought by Otway in his *Alcibiades,* Mrs. Mary Lee arose from the heroic dead to recite the epilogue. It was a masterpiece of sophistication:

Now who sayes Poets don't in blood delight?
'Tis true, the varlets care not much to fight;
But 'faith, they claw it off when e're they write;
Are bully Rocks not of the common size;
Kill ye men faster than *Domitian* flyes.
Ours made such Havock, that the silly Rogue
Was forc't to make me rise for th' Epilogue.[1]

Otway was wise in his generation. This was a world of play tragedy, and it ended with the fall of the curtain. The heroic type, despite its lustful queens and lascivious kings, was entirely fantastic in its reversal of everyday morality. The sordid realism of Dryden and Wycherley in comedy found its relief in the preposterous nobility of the contemporary tragedy of Lee and Otway; and the unheroic reverses in field and bedchamber of the beaux of Whitehall were here glozed over in the undying bravery and chastity of Alcibiades and Hannibal.

Less than a year after *Nero,* in April, 1675, Lee's *Sophonisba* was given its *première* at the Theatre Royal in Drury Lane. The King was then at the heyday of his play-going activity, and found the tragedy so much to his taste that he or his *entourage* occupied the royal box upon the thirtieth, with revisits at least four times within the year.[2] This was the play that appeared so incongruously in the library of the Rev. Richard Lee at Hatfield. The abandoned old court preacher for the moment appears to have basked in the greatness of his son's profane success. It was truly a play from which the most confirmed Puritan might have risen unpolluted. On the other hand, the repeated attendance of Charles would seem to argue in him an amazing love of heroism, a supposition that would destroy all preconceived notions of the King. The truth of the matter is not far to seek. It is recorded that his melancholy queen was more devoted to this than to any other play of the period; and, as to the other ladies of the court, we have Lee's dedication to Portsmouth and his appended commentary:

If *Sophonisba* received some applause upon the stage, I arrogate nothing from the merit of the Poem, but, as I ought, with the humblest acknowledgements and profoundest gratitude, impute it to the favourable aspects of the Court-Stars. [To which he added with the exact inflection of French romance:] But above all, I must pay my adorations to your Grace, who as you are the most Beautiful, as well in the bright appearances of body, as in the immortal splendors of an elevated Soul, did shed mightier Influence, and darted on me a largess of glory answerable to your stock of Beams.[3]

By Langbaine's statement, "His Muse indeed seem'd destin'd for the Diversion of the Fair Sex; so soft and passionately moving are his scenes of Love written."[4] So we may conjecture that Charles was amiably disposed to attend, while his fair jades throbbed to the amorous discourse of Mohun and Hart and wept satisfying tears at the cruel trials in love of the divine Sophonisba.

Accustomed as was the court of Charles to surrender, it is no marvel that it lost its heart completely to the personages of Lee's tragedy. Hannibal "for a mistress gave the world away," while Sophonisba in emulation challenged her foe to

> Come on, with thy brave sword rip up my breast,
> And fix my panting heart on thy proud Crest;
> There let it hang, thy valours Trophy grown,
> To all the wondring World let it be shown.[5]

They were heroes in arm and heart: beyond all example valiant, faithful to love in the conflict of great duties, tender, and dedicated to endless misfortune which they met with incredible heroism. In his second play Lee was less iconoclastic than in his first, since now he was in complete possession of his heroic formula. For the pit and gallery there was a royal feast, but for the fair despots of the boxes, infinite surrender of the most obdurate, oaths a thousand, and death to a holocaust of sighs.

> Oh *Sophonisba*, Oh!

The plaint of King Massinissa so ravished the heart of his own generation that Lee was captivated to repeat himself in later plays:

> Oh *Bellamira*, Oh!

and

> Oh *Athenais*, Oh!

At which the sigh breathed down the century in half a score of imitators to

> Oh *Jemmy Thomson*, Oh!

and to the prodigious lament of Tom Thumb,

> Oh *Huncamunca*, Oh!

But if Lee won the impressionable heart of the century by his rapture, he failed lamentably to capitalize upon it. The world of heroism remained in its splendid isolation, while the world of crowns and pounds continued to function as usual. The rise of Lee's popularity was marked by the revulsion of Rochester, who shortly expressed his displeasure in the couplets already quoted:

> When *Lee* makes temperate *Scipio* fret and rave
> And *Hannibal* a whining, Amorous slave
> I laugh, and wish the hot-brain'd Fustian Fool
> In *Busby*'s hands, to be well lasht at School.[6]

And the age was no less capricious than Rochester. Dedicating his third play to Portsmouth, who appears not to have been displeased with the bestowal of his second, our poet wrote as follows: "Judge, then how unfit I am, blasted in my hopes and press'd in my growth by a most severe, if not unjust fortune."[7]

We cannot guess the exact circumstances of his reversal, but if ever a man rendered himself liable by unexampled bombast, it was Lee in his tragedy of *Gloriana; or, The Court of Augustus Caesar*.[8] This was one of the plays severely taken to task by Addison. He granted that no English poet was better turned to tragedy than its author, and then tempered the praise by adding that Lee's thoughts were "frequently lost in such a cloud of words that it is hard to see the beauty in them. There is an infinite fire in his words, but so involved in smoke that it does not appear with half its lustre."[9] So far as Lee's audience was concerned, this doubtless was no great loss. The same audience would have grown restive, had the dramatist ventured to be clear or rational.

In what Raptures [said Cibber], have I seen an Audience at the furious Fustian and turgid Rants in Nat. Lee's *Alexander the Great!* . . . When those flowing Numbers came from the Mouth of a Betterton, the Multitude no more desired Sense to them than our musical *Connoisseurs* think it essential in the celebrated Airs of an *Italian* Opera.[10]

The high technique of bombast and rapture was first developed not by Betterton but by Hart working in collusion chiefly with Dryden, and afterward, to his greater glory, with Lee. Alexander was Hart's rôle, as was Caesario, the son of Julius Caesar, in this earlier tragedy of *Gloriana*. And how congenial to the actor's art was the grandiloquence of Caesario may be readily understood from a single speech:

> A Man! *Araspes,* I was always more.
> When me in Swadling-bands the Nurses rock'd,
> My soul was full with God-like courage stock'd;
> The sounds which first my wondrous voice did move,
> Were Father *Julius,* and Grandsire *Jove:*
> Ev'n in my Childhood I was more than Man,
> Bears in my Non-age flew, and Stags out-ran.
> *Leander* thou remembrest who art old,
> When yet nine Winters I had scarcely told,
> A half-starv'd Lion in our chase I brav'd
> And from his jaws my panting Mother sav'd.[11]

From the same Caesario we have a characterization of his potent sire, that might well stand as descriptive of this entire class of Restoration tragedy. It tells of Caesar's dalliance with the lovely Cleopatra,—a dalliance doubtless pleasant enough to Portsmouth, while the somber queen retreated behind her fan:

> 'Twas God-like and he imitated *Jove,*
> Who with excessive thundring tir'd above
> Comes down for ease, enjoys a Nymph, and then,
> Mounts dreadful and to thundring goes again.[12]

In his efforts to drug the omnipresent realities of the Restoration court, Lee drew upon every known device. Rant was followed by turgid magnificence. The figure of Ovid was brought into the play, partly as a vehicle for eroticism, partly as an excuse for florid word pictures, recalling the effects of Rubens or La Calprenède rather

than those of the author of the *Metamorphoses*. It is Ovid who thus
chants the praise of Augustus:

> Vast are the Glories, *Caesar,* thou hast won,
> To make whose Triumphs up, the World's undone:
> The *Indians* from the Eastern parts remote,
> To thee the Treasure of their Shrines devote:
> Whole Trees of Coral, which they div'd for low, ⎫
> That in the Walks of *Neptune's* Palace grow,   ⎬
> With Tritons trumpeting on ev'ry bough;   ⎭
> Pearls which the mourning Eyes of *Thetis* pay,
> When her cool'd Lover bolts through waves away;
> And Diamonds that the Sun each morning sheds,
> Driving his Chariot o're their sooty heads.[13]

This is by no means unique. Before Lee's fondness for exuberant
color should be restrained, there were to be descriptions of naked
loveliness vying with the effects of the Flemish weavers. Indeed
one might suspect that *The Rival Queens* received its first inspiration from Le Brun's famous tapestry at Versailles of the tent of
Alexander, wherein the daughters of Darius kneel in conquering
beauty before the hero. But, even more perfectly, a quotation
from his so-called "Lady's play"[14] of *Mithridates* shows to what
extent the relaxed sensuousness of the Renaissance had taken possession of the young poet:

> Behold her then upon a Flowry Bank,
> With her soft sorrows lull'd into a slumber,
> The Summer's heat had, to her natural blush
> Added a brighter and more tempting red;
> The Beauties of her Neck and naked Breasts,
> Lifted by inward starts, did rise and fall
> With motion that might put a Soul in Statues:
> The matchless whiteness of her foulded Arms,
> That seem'd t'embrace the Body whence they grew,
> Fix'd me to gaze o're all that Field of Love;
> While to my ravish'd eyes officious winds,
> Waving her Robes, display'd such handsome Limbs,
> As Artists wou'd in Polish'd Marble give
> The Wanton Goddess. . . .[15]

Lee was the child of the late Renaissance. In him magnificence
inclined to the garish. Art reveled in sudden and startling ornament: nymphs and "soft" angels in gold leaf, twisted columns, and

statuary by its very weight threatening the downfall of the building. The huge dome of St. Paul's, as well as the grandiloquence which reverberated beneath it, the vast embellished canvases of Rubens, the rhetoric and the creaking machinery of Lee were all parcel of the same tendency. It was a world in rivalry to build upon the scale of Versailles, but only upon rare occasions did it pass beyond mere pretentiousness. Of our own corner of this movement, the conscious insincerity was summarized by Dryden, the more notably as coming from one of the stage's greatest tricksters.

In a Play-house [he said], every thing contributes to impose upon the Judgment; the Lights, the Scenes, the Habits, and, above all, the Grace of Action, which is commonly the best where there is the most need of it, surprise the Audience, and cast the mist upon their Understandings: not unlike the cunning of a Juggler who is always staring us in the face, and overwhelming us with gibberish only that he may gain the opportunity of making the clean conveyance of his Trick.[16]

In the last phrase the artistic purpose was indicated of the greater part of baroque art. It was contingent upon a complete and conscious bewilderment of the critical faculties.

Glancing at only one development of the baroque, the ornate novels of the De Scudérys, Gomberville, and La Calprenède, we may be certain that rational criticism would have blighted their grand seigneurs beyond recognition. In course of time criticism would wipe away at a stroke the parallel growth of the pastoral as well as the court which delighted in it. Across the channel, the English found the unreality of heroic Almanzor and Alexander more to its fancy than that of sighing Strephon, and hence the pastoral was only intermittent in its appearance. But the process of criticism was amazingly slow in both countries. The age of reason was doomed to flourish for many years contemporaneously with these chief products of unreason.

In any treatment of Restoration tragedy the part played by the vast baroque novels of the French mid-seventeenth century should not be slighted. It is a caution that only a short while ago would have been needless. Under the rule of German and French scholarship the names De Scudéry and La Calprenède tended to appear upon every other page. But more recently there has been witnessed a complete reversal from this point of view, and now English and American scholars are equally vehement concerning the all-important contributions of the earlier English stage. The pendulum has perhaps swung far enough. It is fairly obvious that the vagabond court of Charles II, upon its return, came into a heritage of native plays and of actors drilled in the traditions of the older school, and that the plays of Beaumont and Fletcher, the chief products of the earlier heroism, were for many years more popular with Restoration audiences than the plays of Shakespeare. It is evident that *The Maid's Tragedy, Valentinian,* and *A King and No King* were such mixtures of false sentiment and divine right as the courtiers of Charles might have composed, that D'Avenant plainly foreshadowed Dryden's later flights into heroism, and that *Othello,* probably the most popular of Shakespearean tragedies, in very many respects seemed to have been written to the Restoration code. We even find that Lee himself, in his dedication of *Mithridates,* clearly announced that he had endeavored in this tragedy "to mix *Shakespear* with *Fletcher:* the thoughts of the former, for Majesty and true *Roman* Greatness, and the softness and passionate expressions of the latter, which make up half the Beauties."

I will love [he cried], *the Man that shall trace me!* . . . I desire to be found a Refiner on those admirable Writers; the Ground is theirs, and all that serves to make a rich Embroidery! I hope the World will do me the Justice to think, I have disguis'd it into another Fashion more suitable to the Age we live in.[17]

Yet a very considerable degree of resemblance between the earlier and later English stages may exist without canceling the debt to other sources. A simultaneous growth of the themes of love, honor, and divine right had proceeded in France, and one perhaps as familiar as the English to the dependents of Charles. The material was common property, a fact nowhere more plainly indicated than in the early tragedies of Lee and Otway. In the actual number of lines they borrowed and in pervasive spirit, the debt of the latter pair to the French romancers at least balanced that to the English playwrights, and was greater, if we set aside the wholesale plundering and romanticizing of material out of Shakespeare. There is but slight evidence that either dramatist composed tragedy with the folios of the Jacobeans open before him. There is ample evidence, on the other hand, that their use of the ponderous romances was first hand.

The theater, here as elsewhere, was but the reflection of its audience. Diaries, letters, and endless translations attest the popularity of French romance. It was *le dernier cri* of a court dedicated to all things French. The fashion chronicled by Dorothy Osborne in 1654 and Pepys in 1668[18] entered into the theater and took possession. How essential it was to the playwright's equipment may be observed in any source list of Restoration drama. The *Sophonisba* of Lee was heavy debtor to Orrery's novel of *Parthenissa*[19]—a seven-decker so completely in the Gallic tradition that it might have been laid down across the channel; *Gloriana* was equally obliged to the *Cléopâtre* of La Calprenède; and now *The Rival Queens*, the fourth play of Lee, turned to the same author's *Cassandre*.[20]

Lee nevertheless toned up his flaccid source material by liberal drafts from history—of the sort to be found in his father's library at Hatfield—and the effect was altogether bracing. Those portions of *The Rival Queens* derived from Curtius were more restrained and generally more powerful than those where La Calprenède ran undefiled. Thus the scenes between Clytus and Alexander in the fourth act, which were transferred in spirit and sometimes in word from the Latin, form a striking contrast in style to the preceding scenes between Lysimachus and Alexander, in their turn taken almost directly from the romance. The dialogue of the former anticipated by several years the Livian brevity of the poet's *Lucius Junius Brutus*. In *The Rival Queens*, however, the Roman accent was only fitful:

> *Clyt.* Your Father *Philip,*—I have seen him March,
> And fought beneath his dreadful Banner, where
> The stoutest at this Table would ha' trembl'd.
> Nay frown not, Sir, you cannot look me dead.
> When Greeks joyn'd Greeks, then was the tug of War,
> The labour'd Battle sweat, and Conquest bled.
> Why shou'd I fear to speak a truth more noble,
> Then e're your Father *Jupiter Ammon* told you;
> *Philip* fought men, but *Alexander* women.[21]

By contrast to this, we may discover how completely the garrulous accent of La Calprenède could enter into the speech of Lee from examination of the latter's account of the victory of Lysimachus over the lion. It may be said that the French writer gives the account to the hero himself, where Lee allows greater modesty by putting it in the mouth of Clytus. Otherwise this is little more

than a versified paragraph out of the *Cassandre,* a perfect example
of the heroic-romantic manner:

> Then walking forward, the large Beast discry'd
> His prey, and with a roar that made us pale,
> Flew fiercely on him; but the active Prince
> Starting aside, avoiding his first shock,
> With a slight hurt, and as the Lyon turn'd,
> Thrust Gauntlet, Arm and all, into his throat,
> And with *Herculean* Force tore forth by th' roots
> The foaming bloudy tongue; and while the Savage,
> Faint with that loss, sunk to the blushing Earth
> To plough it with his teeth, your conqu'ring Souldier
> Leap'd on his back, and dash'd his skull to pieces.[22]

Or, as La Calprenède remarked no less nobly: "The Lion lost all
his strength by the extreamity of that pain, and discharging the
rest of his rage against the Earth, which he digg'd up with his teeth,
and watred with his blood, he gave me the leisure to beat his skull
in pieces with my Gauntlets."[23] So likewise with the lover's jargon.
" 'Tis only my passion," we read in the novel, "the purest, the
most perfect that ever was that intercedes to you now in favour of
me. . . ."[24] Lee versified it thus:

> But Love and I bring such a perfect Passion,
> So nobly pure, 'tis worthy of her Eyes,
> Which without blushing she may justly prize.[25]

As we read this language we may understand perfectly whence
came the inflated dedications of the time. Dryden and Lee merely
carried over to their epistles what every lady and wit accepted as
the polite speech of literature. Had they been addressed otherwise
it would have been taken as bald and indecent.

But the ruling principles of this language could hardly remain
obscure to the more enlightened critics. It was repeatedly noted
that Alexander was the idol of the fair sex, and such he was to remain for many years to come. Thus around 1700 Powell was
sounding upon the same instrument that had served earlier for
Hart, Goodman, and Betterton:

> Big as the Voice of War he mouths his Roll,
> Each Accent twangs majestically full
> When *Alexander* dies, he gives the fair
> Tortures as great as those he seems to bear.[26]

The Elizabethans, it may be added, were rarely able to deflect Lee from his inflated sentiment and action. Though there was considerable reminiscence, especially in his *Rival Queens,* of lines from Shakespeare's Roman plays, they were rendered turgid by his alteration; and what virtue remained was more than vitiated by his further addition of all the Shakespearean claptrap of ghosts, signs and portents, and universal destruction at the end. He might take over for his Alexander hints for a struggle between the base and noble elements of man's nature, but he was unable to borrow, because he was incapable of understanding, the lyric love of Juliet or the quiet tragedy of Hermione. It all needed to be sentimental or colossal, so that even the "heroic Shakespeare" of *Othello* and *Julius Caesar* became hoarse when given utterance through the mouth of mad Nat. Lee.

Some years later two of his surviving contemporaries engaged in a discussion of the principles of Lee's success. It all turned upon the apparent necessity of violent action in any taking plot:

Let the Action be good or bad, it will keep the Attention of the Audience, and the more constant and violent the Action is, the more it will be attended by them; wherever there is Passion, there must necessarily be Action; those Tragedies therefore, that have a perpetual Succession of Passion, can never miscarry. It is this Quality that has preserv'd and still keeps up the Tragedy of *Alexander the Great,* which Mr. Crown found fault with, in a Discourse with me one Day, because, it was continually on the fret, as he call'd it, from the Beginning to the End; that is, the Passions were lively and strong through the whole Piece, which so took up the Audience, that they had no Leisure or Interval of Quiet to grow weary and be disgusted.[27]

But there were forces in Lee at this time operative toward quiet and naturalism. Chief of these was his desertion of the couplet. In itself the couplet was far from being the hall mark of heroic tragedy; nevertheless, by its heavy tread it seemed inexorably to suggest unrestrained hyperbole and colossal periods. Three years earlier Lee had turned certain scenes of his *Nero* into blank verse, some little time before Dryden penned his famous bill of divorcement from rhyme. Hence *Nero* was of a different substance from *Gloriana* and *Sophonisba,* where surrender to the couplet had been complete. Now, with its final dismissal, a closer imitation of Elizabethan drama became possible; and Lee, along with English drama, settled to the rediscovery of a certain calm, long since departed.

The break from ranting heroism was not so immediate with Lee as it was with Otway, for which various reasons may be advanced. First there was to be observed a clear divergence between the acting traditions of the two playhouses. The actors of His Majesty's Theatre in Drury Lane, who declaimed the lines of Lee, were closer to the French and English heroic manner than those of Dorset Garden, who performed Otway. Hart and Mohun, of the former, had risen to their full stature simultaneously with and by the aid of the early tragedy of Dryden. Mohun had been partly trained in France,[28] while Hart came out of the school that obtained prior to the closing of the theaters. Each was a very great artist after his kind, and fully capable of dominating the work of any but the greatest playwright. Hart by many was deemed a finer tragedian than Betterton,[29] which may merely signify that he was more florid. His successor "Scum" Goodman was later held incomparable as Alexander, but his mastery of the rôle appears to have chiefly consisted in following Hart's example.[30] Betterton himself is reported to have rewarded a player handsomely for giving him Hart's exact intonation of certain lines.[31] The latter's greatest successes were florid; and such were the rôles written for him at the time by Lee. Concerning the actresses of the Theatre Royal, there may be some legitimate doubt. It is questionable whether either Boutell or Marshall[32] gave any great encouragement to the dramatist who should attempt to write into their lines any of the subtleties of passion. They were both so secure in their province of declamatory tragedy that they seem to have lured no playwright into the creation of the less robustious parts. It is true that Dryden wrote his Cleopatra for Boutell, but there is little evidence that Boutell achieved any startling success in the character. Hers was a school entirely upon the large. It had already passed its grand climacteric, and offered slight inspiration to the growing playwright. The best proof of the potent influence of the Drury Lane school of acting rests in the marked change that came over the style of Nat. Lee, once he had shifted to the newer and more restrained artists of the theater in Dorset Garden.

The difference becomes conclusive when we look at Otway. Out of the oppressive glare of Dryden and the heroic actors, he had dared attempt in his first play an imitation of Shakespeare. In his second he ventured farther. *Don Carlos* was a better play than any hitherto composed by his young rival, albeit one somewhat less characteristic of the age. A heroic tragedy, as it was termed by its author, in reality it either subordinated or made a decisive break with all the more notable machinery of heroism, save only the tag of rhyme. Otway was encouraged in his revolution by a company which for the most part was still in its early youth and filled with the spirit of adventure. He dared turn for his source material to a new sort of novel: one purporting to be history, the hero of which lived in a land near by and at a recent time, instead of some ancient and mysterious kingdom of the distant east or west. It is immaterial whether Saint-Réal perverted history out of all recognition, in making the half-insane Carlos a figure of romance; Carlos was convincing, as the heroes of La Calprenède were not, and moved in conflict with an actual world.

The character and the plot of the novel gave Otway his perfect lead. It was history delicately shaded off from the heroic, with a hero curious in doing nothing at all and conventional in talking superbly. Nor was the omission of action perhaps evident either to Otway or the heroic talkers of the court of Charles. Furthermore, Saint-Réal's was a story of frustrate love, infinite in its capacity for tears, even if but tentatively developed to that end. In recasting it Otway was able to retain very many useful devices of heroic tragedy, and to add something of the relaxed sentimentality that was to mark the English stage for a century and a half. Where Lee, following the mode of double-decked romance, had struck heavily at the sense of wonder, Otway, after Saint-Réal, sought to conquer by playing chiefly upon the sentiments.[33]

We may wonder whether the playwright did not first discover his dramatic formula in this obscure historical novel. It would almost seem so, for Saint-Réal anticipated both Otwavian subject and construction. By contrast to the intricate narrative of La Calprenède, his was the bare account of a great central passion, with its minor plots properly linked and subordinated. His example of comparative simplicity, reinforced as we shall see by that of Racine, was to move Otway into close liaison with the form of French classical tragedy, and to make him in spirit as nearly French as it was possible for an English heroic-sentimentalist to be. He was to be called the English Racine, perhaps improperly enough.[34] But at any rate, it came about that early in the next century Otway was considered to have had at once a tenderness and structure the most satisfactory of any of his rivals and contemporaries.

While Otway today perhaps might not satisfy the demands of classical criticism, in his own time he more than supplied the witlings with matter for favorable comment. He was most attentive in his observance of the more obvious rules of pseudo-classicism. The plot of *Don Carlos,* as it existed in Saint-Réal, gave him the pattern; he went farther by trimming it to the simplest lines. Briefly, the plot was one of a royal father who wedded the betrothed bride of his son. The mingled fears, jealousies, and love of father and son were one half the story; the grief, and the divided love and duty of the queen, the other. Saint-Réal had unity, but not the unity of a play. Those complexities of the history—the inquisition, the intrigues of the palace, and its various amours—all were renounced by Otway whenever they did not contribute directly to the central interest. There was more doing and less talking than upon the French stage, more fury of incident and a greater welter of blood at the climax. Yet, to understand what a masterpiece of compression it was, one must contrast it to the prolixity of the novel. Being granted the scope of history, or pseudo-history, the novelist compassed time enough to bring to the queen a matter of three children, space to move through half the kingdoms of Europe, and action to divide interest between Don Carlos and Don John, not to mention a flock of generals, a queen or two, and a mysterious Juan Miques. Time, Otway compressed to thirty-six hours, thus eliminating those children so abhorrent to a squeamish audience; place, to the palace and its garden; action, to the triangle and its contributory friends and foes. One scene made an act, a very bold invention upon the stage of the Duke's Theatre, where lavish and variegated decoration was the rule. The interest was more exactly centered than in the book upon the three major characters; and from their passions rather than from external accident Otway sought to develop his plot. It was a direction quite different from that which would have been taken by Lee. Even though Otway's intuitive and highly emotional nature did not permit him to attain the delicate analysis of Racine; nevertheless, in his efforts to make the action flow naturally from the characters, he clearly answered the challenge of the French master. He strove to eliminate the purely fortuitous, and to achieve that simplicity of which *toute l'invention consiste à faire quelque chose de rien.*[35]

It was not solely by his just observance of the canons of taste that Otway won his spurs. Indeed at first glance he seems to have temporized with the heroic tradition, and in several other respects than that of the rhyme. Our hero, Smith, forgetful of classic simplicity, confronted our king, Betterton, with heaven-storming words. To be sure, he was unusual in that he perpetrated no heroic deeds, but in this he was precursor to a long line of romantic heroes possessing infinite capacity for greatness that unhappily was forever to be forestalled by callous fortune. Don Carlos had a soul foredoomed to misunderstanding by the world. Could he but reach Flanders, where his mighty ambition could be given freedom! But love, rage, loyalty, friendship, justice—in short all the motivation of the old-time heroic tragedy and the new-time romantic tragedy—strain him in unending conflict with himself. It is an internal battle beyond any contemplated by heroism, ending only as Carlos goes down to darkness triumphant in spirit, if completely negative in results. And Philip, the original villain of Saint-Réal's narrative, is another Carlos, filled with the same ineradicable pity for himself. Unlike Hamlet, and very much like Otway himself, the heroes of our dramatist were constitutionally incapable of facing their errors. Romantic sentimentalism had come in; and the audience was no longer to reason, but to be carried away upon floods of damp emotion.

One might be tempted to say that Otway's art was wholly intuitive, if he were to be judged by his critical utterances. His prefaces, dedications, prologues, epilogues, so far as they speak at all, are devoted to but one subject: the struggles of Otway and his joys and sorrows. His rejection of the customary critical approach, however, was a conscious choice. As early as *Don Carlos* he had manifested a marked distaste for the over-use of these by-products of playwriting. " 'Tis not that I have any great affection to scribling," he remarked, "that I pester thee with a *Preface,* for amongst friends, 'tis almost as poor a Trade with Poets as it is with those that write Hackney under Attorneys."[36] From his unwillingness to speak upon any other subject than his own emotions, it followed that his works were virtually devoid of those *pronunciamentos* so indispensable to a dilettante generation, and so much a part of Dryden, Crowne, and Shadwell. The mark of wit, in fact, was in one's ability to edge a fine critical distinction as much as to turn off a *bon mot*.[37] In both Otway was barren. He was too subjective, too much the child of emotion. The portrait of his muse, in *The Poet's Complaint,* is a perfect bit of self-revelation:

> No fair Deceiver ever us'd such Charms,
> T' ensnare a tender Youth, and win his Heart:
> Or when she had him in her Arms,
> Secur'd his love with greater Art.
> I fansy'd, or I dream'd, (as Poets always do)
> No Beauty with my Muse's might compare.
> Lofty she seem'd, and on her Front sate a majestick ayr,
> Awfull, yet kind; severe, yet fair.
> Upon her Head a Crown she bore
> Of Laurell, which she told me should be mine. . . .
> Nay, by my Muse too I was [often] blest
> With Off-springs of the choicest kinds,
> Such as have pleased the noblest minds,
> And been approved by Judgements of the best.[38]

It is all a naïve pleasure in his past triumphs—of which *Don Carlos* appears to have been the happiest memory—but of critical understanding of the mood and purpose of his muse, there is here no enlightenment.

One example will suffice to show the near futility of Otway as a critic. The nadir of repartee was reached at this time in his response to Dryden's gibes upon *Don Carlos*. Here, if ever, Otway was presented with an opportunity to point the direction in which his art was tending, with perhaps some inadvertent reference to the misdirection of earlier tragedy. Instead he set down the following:

A certain Writer that shall be nameless (but you may guess at him by what follows) being ask't his opinion of this Play, very gravely Cock't, and cry'd *I gad he knew not a line in it he would be Author of;* but he is a fine Facetious witty Person, as my Friend Sir *Formal* has it; and to be even with him I know a Comedy of his, that has not so much as a Quibble in it which I would be Author of; and so Reader I bid him and thee Farewell.[39]

It is somewhat surprising to discover that Otway was even vaguely aware of the tendencies of his art, or that he wrote other than by instinct. But as early as *Don Carlos* it may be noted that he was reading Racine, when the rest of critical England was for the most part unaware of the great sentimentalist's existence, and reading him with a fair degree of understanding. "This I may modestly boast of," he said, "which the author of the *French Bernice* has done before me in his Preface to that Play, that it never fail'd to draw Tears from the Eyes of the Auditors, I mean those whose Souls were capable of so Noble a pleasure."[40] The last four words, uttered in conjunction with his own praise, are worth volumes of preface for the true appraisal of Otway and his followers. The glorification of the tear was to transform English drama. The new tragedy was created by an age incapable of comprehending the difficult doctrine of tragic catharsis. It was an age dedicated to diversion, and tears were a delight. The poet, without any great critical verbiage, was nevertheless understood by the women of his audience; and ravished away by "so noble a pleasure," they were granted endless opportunity to weep. The men, moved somehow despite their natures, could attribute the emotion without further ado to the tragic catharsis approved by antiquity.

In the evolution of Otway's *tragédie larmoyante,* English elements reinforced French. More than a touch of Shakespeare was added to give body to the play; and as usual it was the influence of *Othello* that was most evident. In fact, as we study Restoration tragedy, it becomes increasingly obvious that the attack of Rymer upon Shakespeare's masterpiece was but a tribute to its popularity. The villain of *Don Carlos* was again patterned after Iago, and more obviously than in *Alcibiades* dealt with another Othello in Philip. There were significant deviations, it is true, between the two plots, deviations enforced by the age. Thus, the Spaniard of Otway *was* easily jealous—as all Restoration gentlemen descending to imminent cuckoldom would seem to have had good reason to be. Furthermore, he was made a weathercock to his every emotion, proving himself thereby a worthy descendant to the race of Almanzor. It is notable also that in the management of the incriminating letter, substituted here for Desdemona's handkerchief, Otway forestalled Rymer's criticism that Shakespeare leaned too heavily upon mere coincidence. We may add that the heroine of *Don Carlos* everywhere temporized with virtue, in a manner undreamed by Desdemona. Where the love of the latter involved higher laws, in Otway's generation there were allowed no higher laws than those of love. But it is to be credited to the account of Otway that the very faults of the queen made her and her successors far more dynamic to the movement of tragedy than were the faultless Ophelia and Desdemona. The wonder is that Otway did not perceive the implications and forestall future practice by naming his tragedy after the heroine.

Suffice it that the applause bestowed so liberally upon *Don Carlos* came to the ears of its author most pleasantly. In the preface he remarked: "I dare not presume to take to my self what a great many and those I am sure of good Judgement too, have been so kind to afford me, (*viz.*) That it is the best Heroick Play that has been written of late; for I thank Heaven I am not yet so vain."[41] His disclaimer was not received as current coin by Dryden, nor by Elkanah Settle, both of whom took to themselves some trifling credit in the field of heroics. After reading the modest boast of our poet, Elkanah discharged his bile in quantities of doggerel, with two couplets immediately to the point:

> *Tom Otway* came next, *Tom Shadwell*'s dear Zany
> And swears for Heroicks, he writes best of any:
> *Don Carlos* his Pockets so amply had fill'd,
> That his Mange was quite cur'd, and his Lice were all kill'd.[42]

The lines so enraged our playwright that he found relief shortly by way of the sword, where it appears he returned an overwhelming reply. But before we may consider that, we must direct our attention to another matter of greater import,—to the development of Otway the dramatist.

Chapter VII

LOVE AND WAR

I did but look and love awhile,
'Twas but for one half Hour;
Then to resist, I had no Will,
And now I have no Power.

To sigh, and wish, is all my Ease;
Sighs, which do Heat impart,
Enough to melt the coldest Ice;
Yet cannot warm your Heart.

Oh! would your Pity give my Heart
One corner of your Breast,
'Twould learn of yours the winning Art,
And quickly steal the rest.
OTWAY, *The Enchantment*[1]

IN spite of all efforts to explain Otway and his tragedies by this or
that influence, the matter remains that he was an individual,
though one in immediate contact less with the glorious past than
the blighting present. His was an individuality that sought in all
ways and against all odds to express itself. Thus, his plays are un-
usually distinct: the hero, forever the man Otway; the heroine, the
transfigured image of the woman he loved. To understand either
we must trace the misadventures of his hapless infatuation as it
arose and passed unrecognized across the panorama of Dorset
Garden.

"Since the first day I gazed upon you, now for seven years I
have loved your image with all the violence of despair." Such is the
distraught language of Otway's letters. They are of no date, place,
nor superscription of the mistress to whom they were addressed.
Were it not for an occasional signature, they might pass, with their
ebb and flow of passionate verse and fevered prose, as the cry of a
being detached to another world. Yet, unless all tradition is at
fault, they were directed to a woman of all women the most earth-
earthy and the most thoroughly the offspring of the hard reality
of theatrical London.[2]

The identity of the dark mistress of Otway's letters and poems
remained for a quarter of a century under a complete conspiracy

of silence. Or are we to suppose that in the fetid atmosphere, which invariably drew from the merest trifle matter for ridicule, the infatuation of Otway for the famous Mistress Barry could have remained unnoticed? The likelihood of such a love affair is very great, even were there no letters to demonstrate it. One heroine for his stage was given him throughout most of his theatrical career, with whom a thousand times, as his letters indicate, he was led to consult. And despite the unlovely portrait of Mrs. Barry painted during her later years, she was sufficiently devastating to more hardened sinners than Otway, and was calculated to throw him, as she had others, "into the very abyss of jealousy and outraged pride with her whims and ill-natured conjectures."

The letters first appeared in 1697 in a miscellany,[3] with the brief description: "Letters by the most Ingenious Mr. Thomas Otway." From the circumstance that the same volume included others, similarly without superscription, from Rochester and almost certainly to Mrs. Barry, we might be led to conjecture that she was the person from whom the publisher first received them. The probability is heightened by the discovery in the first collected edition of Lee's plays, 1713, of an advertisement of the love letters, this time phrased as being by "the ingenious Mr. *Otway,* to that excellent Actress Mrs. *Barry*."[4] The name of their recipient significantly was added the very year of her death, and by Richard Wellington, their original publisher. Did the latter perhaps rest under obligation to withhold her identity until after she should no longer fear the barbs of her critics?

For Mrs. Barry had detractors enough, dealers many of them in frightful obscenities, who detested this woman of genius beyond any of her time. Among the rest was Tom Brown, one of the mildest of them. "Should you lye with her all night," said he, "she would not know you next morning, unless you had another five pounds at her service."[5] And yet it was Brown who edited the letters, and without so much as a word as to their recipient. He was typical. Only one of her defamers appears to have had an inkling of Otway's passion, and he by reason of some peculiar intimacy with the poet, unnoted until now. Robert Gould perhaps had met Otway at Knole when the former was retained by Buckhurst and the latter was flourishing under the pleasanter aspect of that nobleman. Subsequently Gould found occasion to refer to his greater colleague in terms of utmost affection and familiarity:

> But Thee, my *Otway*, from the Grave, I'll raise,
> And crown thy memory with lasting Praise.[6]

The couplet was unique for its gentleness in a poem otherwise marked by unbridled violence of assault. In another portion of it, but recast several years later from its early version of 1685, there was delivered a terrific outburst against Mrs. Barry:

> Who counts her *Sins*, may as well count the *Stars:*
> So insolent! it is by all allow'd
> There never was so base a thing, so proud:
> Yet Covetous, she'l prostitute with any,
> Rather than waive the getting of a penny;
> For the whole *Harvest* of her youthful Crimes
> She hoards, to keep her self in future times,
> That by her gains *now* she may *then* be fed,
> Which in effect's to damn herself for *bread.*
> Yet in her *Morals* this is thought the best;
> Imagine then the lewdness of the rest.[7]

But Gould left little to the imagination, pursuing his quarry through page after page. When later, in 1696, he came to Betterton with an excellent tragedy, he found that usually amiable producer and his prima donna still seething after years of supposed quiescence. "I am not so good a *Christian* as to forgive,"[8] said Barry, and Gould's play finally came to the boards with a second-rate cast and a damning prologue by another aggrieved party.

All this appears to have been but the reëcho of his rage against her treatment of our dramatist. The following quotation gains significance from having been composed in the year of Otway's death:

> But talking of their *shifts,* I mourn, my Friend,
> I mourn thy sad, unjust, disastrous end;
> Here 'twas thou did'st resign thy worthy Breath,
> And fell the Victim of a sudden Death:[9]
> The shame, the guilt, the horror and disgrace,
> Light on the *Punk,* the *Murderer* and the *Place.* . . .
> How well do those deserve the general hiss,
> That will converse with such a thing as this?
> A ten times cast off *Drab,* in *Venus* Wars
> Who counts her *Sins,* may as well count the *Stars.*[10]

The lines refer quite certainly to Barry; as to the rest they are

vague at this distance. However, history provides no death even
hyperbolically laid at Barry's door save that of Otway, nor does
Gould let pass the opportunity to refer to the unhappy swain as
his friend. Whatever the answer, and with some considerable reservation, it may be added to our portrait of the actress.

Human motives at the distance of two centuries and a half are
difficult to appraise. It was not that Otway was unprepossessing—

Charming his Face, and charming were his Strains—[11]

nor that the coin that he offered was not of the realm: plays which
made her overnight the famous Mrs. Barry and began that considerable fortune of mills and lands that she left at her death. In
the largesse of her favors some portion might have descended upon
the poet without being missed. Otway, however, was too magnani-
mous to bargain, and Mrs. Barry too provident to bestow herself
upon a penniless poet, when she had the great and wealthy Rochester in attendance; later, according to doubtful tradition, gentle Geo.
Etherege; and finally, with interludes, St. John, the father of the
Tory statesman. "And yet," as Aston pondered, "this fine Creature was not handsome, her Mouth op'ning most on the Right Side,
which she strove to draw t'other Way, and, at Times composing
her Face, as if sitting to have her Picture drawn."[12]

One may be privileged to question a good part of the legends
that have clustered about this woman and her relations with Rochester. She was the daughter of a Royalist colonel, according to one
account. Aston would have her "Woman to Lady *Shelton* of
Norfolk (my Godmother)."[13] Another long story from the *Memoirs of Grammont* has been pretty generally credited to Barry because it has to do with an actress and the noble earl. Here he is
shown as training her for the stage:

Although he did not succeed so well in this respect as in his other instruction, still, the next winter, after he had entertained her with her
aunt for some months in the country, he got her entered in the king's
company; and the public was indebted to him for the prettiest, but at
the same time, the worst actress in the Kingdom.

Hamilton was too good a judge of beauty to make this mistake.
"Slattern Betty Barry" was first apprenticed to the Duke's Company, her name was not Sarah as in this story, and the time and
various other circumstances render her incapable of filling the

rôle.[14] But the account does show Rochester in a pose so characteristic that it may have been the basis of the legend that it was he
who trained Barry.

"Lord *Rochester* took her on the Stage; where for some time
they could make nothing of her.—She could neither sing nor dance,
no, not in a Country-Dance."[15] Colley Cibber tells of her being discharged once,[16] but after it had passed through the fingers of the
great Curll it had grown to three times.[17] The latter, or his hacks,
added details of how Rochester had wagered that he could over-
come her defects of false emphasis and her disagreeable tone, and
how she had won heavily for him by her great success before the
King and the Duke of York, and how the Duchess was so vastly
pleased with her acting that she made Barry a gift of her wedding
suit! Whether this success was in Orrery's *Mustapha* or in Otway's
Alcibiades is uncertain. Her appearance in the former rests only
upon hearsay, while in Otway's tragedy her part was so inconsiderable that it is amazing that she should have won any sort of recognition.

Meanwhile, if we are to rely upon his own words, Otway had begun his unhappy infatuation. It was always her practice to consult
even the most indifferent poet in any part that had been accepted,[18]
and, as Otway added, each day it was his chance to see or to be
near her. His rival, unhappily, had already taken possession, and it
was the poet's fate to stand aside and watch. By the very nature of
things, Otway shortly paid Rochester the compliment of a dedication to him of his third play, or rather plays. *Titus and Berenice*
with *The Cheats of Scapin* was staged about the end of 1676, and
marks perhaps the end of Otway's intimacy with the nobleman.
There is a forthright honesty about the dedication which makes us
think well of our poet. Afterward the two went their ways, nor
does Rochester, in spite of his reputation, seem to have sought to
injure the young pretender. It was probably even with a feeling
akin to pity that he regarded him. In all his verse there is but a
single line that notices Otway, one descriptive of the latter's abys-
mal lack of wit in comedy, which, as he says, "puzzling *Otway*
labours at in vain."[19] The line in itself is innocuous enough, though
only too well descriptive of the poet's position at the time. Later
Otway wrote to Barry:

With stubborn *Sufferance,* I resolved to bear, and brave your *Power:*

Nay, did it often too, successfully. Generally with *Wine,* or *Conversation*
I diverted or appeas'd the *Daemon* that possess'd me; but when at Night,
returning to my unhappy self, to give my *Heart* an account why I had
done it so unnatural a *Violence,* it was then I always paid a treble *Interest*
for the short Moments of *Ease,* which I had borrow'd; then every treacherous Thought rose up, and took your part, nor left me till they had
thrown me on my Bed, and open'd those *Sluces* of Tears, that were to
run till *Morning.*[20]

If one were ambitious to complicate the strands and make a complete romance from this passion, it would be simple enough to add
another to the eternal triangle. The question has been raised
whether Mrs. Barry did not have a rival to the attentions of Otway
in the person of Mrs. Aphra Behn. The gentleness of this lady had
been chiefly manifest in the provision of a part for Otway in her
first play, though afterward she was to appear several times in his
story. But her love is entirely conjectural, and was so amply satisfied elsewhere as to render unnecessary the drafting of "poor
Otway." She was to serve him better than by love. As arbiter of
morals, she defended the poet, as we shall see, from the charge of
undue license; and, on another occasion, in one of the few extant
letters referring to him, she clearly revealed her whole attitude. It
was addressed in 1676 to one Mrs. Price, a mutual friend.

My Dear [said she], In your last, you inform'd me, that the world
treated me as a *Plagiery,* and, I must confess, not with Injustice: But
that Mr. OTWAY shou'd say, my Sex wou'd not prevent my being pull'd
to Pieces by the Critics, is something odd, since whatever Mr. OTWAY
now declares, he may very well remember when last I saw him, I receiv'd
more than ordinary Encomiums on my ABDELAZER. But every one knows
Mr. OTWAY's good Nature, which will not permit him to shock any one
of our Sex to their Faces. But let that pass. . . .[21]

And we, on our part, may well follow the advice and return to more
solid ground.

Out of the materials of his life, Otway had already commenced
to weave his ultimate plot. It was the tragedy of two lovers in the
perpetual attitude of separation and despair; and, of these two,
though the woman is quite unrecognizable as Barry, that creature
nevertheless gave to his plays their first impulse. From her Otway
created the most lovely symbol of her sex that the Restoration
mind was able to conceive. Soft, gentle, caught herself in the web
of desire, loyal to agony, this transfigured heroine represented all

that the poet was unable to discover in reality. It is true that at first her character did not emerge clearly. In the *Don Carlos* of 1676 she was all obscure. "Let me be a woman still!" she had cried, in the person of the queen, and such she was of this earlier generation: a woman involved in all the conventional conflicts, who forever temporized and allowed her tenuous honor to be so stretched that it ceased almost to exist. She had been incapable of foregoing her love for Carlos at the very moment she had sworn eternal constancy to her husband—in 1676 it was for woman to be frail. If she did not succumb, at least she was hurried perilously close to disaster, and was subjected to all the agonies of unsatisfied love. But even so early as *Don Carlos,* we have the evident procedure of Otwavian tragedy: to draw out the tender frame of the heroine upon the rack of desire and separation until the nerves of the audience were at the snapping point, and to put upon her lips sentiments the more affecting as the punishment was less deserved. The latter was a development that here was only in embryo.

The passing of the tragic flaw from the heroine was one of the outstanding developments of Restoration drama. In time that flaw should cease likewise to exist even in the character of the hero. Whereupon, English tragedy should descend into an abyss of sentimentality. Happily Otway was preserved from such a dilemma: his heroes were created too much after his own image, undisciplined, strong and weak by turns, and forever upon the point of eruption. They were imperfect enough, doubtless, but they were not of that superb imperfection from which the greatest tragedy is wrought, their tragic flaw—for it is the same in all of them—operating in a fashion that is often fortuitous and rarely countered by even the faintest glimmerings of intelligence. Thus they differ widely in kind from Lear, Macbeth, and Hamlet, whose impressiveness is chiefly determined by the fierce power of their understanding in conflict with terrifying weakness.

The weaknesses of Otway's heroes are all too human. Turning over his letters to Barry we find endless revelation concerning these characters of his plays. In one place he remarks that he had consulted his very self, and "found how careless Nature was in framing" him; "seasoned" him "hastily with all the most violent Inclinations and Desires, but omitted the *Ornaments* that should have made those Qualities become" him. It was the same person who spoke later, as Jaffeir in *Venice Preserved*, from the depths of self-abasement:

> Tell me why, good Heav'n
> Thou mad'st me what I am, with all the Spirit,
> Aspiring thoughts and Elegant desires
> That fill the happiest Man? Ah! rather why,
> Did'st thou not form me sordid as my Fate,
> Base minded, dull, and fit to carry Burdens.[22]

Not only do we discover in these exclamations the echo of Otway's own cry, but in two of his plays, at least, the true copy of his situation as well. If, as conjectured, the plots of *Don Carlos* and *Titus and Berenice* were conceived shortly after the first appearance of Otway's love affair, the parallels are most striking, particularly in the sympathetic treatment accorded equally to the three characters of the triangle. In *Don Carlos* the hero struggles indecisively between the powerful rivalry of his royal sire and the fatal fascination of the queen; in *Titus and Berenice* a character similarly placed is torn between two great loyalties. In both the successful interloper is treated with amazing gentleness—and for a good reason. They were both written while Otway was under debt of gratitude to the great Rochester, and one of them was even dedicated to him. But as the obligation faded, the struggle of love and friendship likewise disappeared from the playwright's typical plot.

Let us glance for the moment at *Titus and Berenice* as it bears upon the life of the author. First of all, Otway was astute enough to recognize that the play in its original form was ill-suited to an English audience. Even its success in France had been owing partly to the extraneous circumstance that its auditors of the *Hôtel de Bourgogne* had discovered in Titus and Bérénice the portraits respectively of Louis and a composite of three ladies of his court.[23] Naturally, in such an *exposé*, the sorrows of a third party would have seemed an unnecessary distraction. The dual tragedy in France had been entirely able to sustain itself, even though basically undramatic; and the tears shed over Louis and his mistresses had more than compensated for those not shed for Antiochus. Transported across the channel, the play lost the greater part of this topical interest. Five acts of tears for the sorrows of two characters,[24] without the relief of one death might reasonably pall upon an audience accustomed to a stage crowded with despairing lovers and multiplied assassinations.[25] Otway answered the challenge by throwing into high relief the sorrows of the unrequited Antiochus. To that end he revealed him as a rival of Titus in the first instead of the fifth act and added whole scenes to his plot that were without warrant in the original French. The resultant drama was so excellent that the self-revelation of the poet passed apparently unobserved.

Throughout, it was with a sure perception of the differences between the two stages that Otway adapted and composed.[26] He compressed the plot to three acts, materially speeded the dialogue by simplifying the psychology, and introduced those catastrophes so essential to an English success. Curiously enough, Antiochus took a direction almost unexampled in Restoration tragedy, away from the heroic. His sentiments became altogether less noble than in Racine and, for that reason, perhaps more human. He it was who chiefly conspired to bring tears, as Otway had phrased it, "to all those whose Souls were capable of so Noble a Pleasure."

After *Titus and Berenice,* and its dedication to his rival, came the longest period of Otway's silence. Early in 1677 he may have become aware of the hopelessness of his infatuation by an incident, such only as in his world of loose standards would serve to awaken him. Perhaps it was at this time that he retreated to Cambridge for the space that Giles Jacob mentions in his note upon Otway. At any event, during December of 1677, Mrs. Barry presented the Earl of Rochester with an infant daughter. It was an event that hardly might pass unnoticed. Besides letters from Rochester himself to Barry, there is one from Henry Savile, wherein the father was duly congratulated and the wish expressed that he was looking to the welfare of the lady, "for a friend and protectrice of hers in the Mall was much lamenting her poverty very lately, not without some gentle reflections on your Lordship's want either of generosity or bowells towards a lady who had not refused you the full enjoyment of all her charms."[27] Had Barry actually convinced Otway of her poverty? When he returned to playwriting the next year, he gave her an opportunity to rehabilitate her fortunes by the lead in his cynical *Friendship in Fashion.* The title sounds appropriate.

His bit was chafing. Disillusioned in love, deprived at least for the time of Buckhurst's patronage, and holding that of Rochester only tenuously, Otway was reduced to a low ebb of fortune:

> How hard a Task hath that poor Drudg of Stage,
> That strives to please in this Fantastick Age?
> It is a thing so difficult to hit,
> That he's a Fool that thinks to do't by Wit.[28]

The speech shows to what extent the theater was beginning to pall upon him. Prematurely aged at twenty-six, he was in the mood to offer sage advice to ambitious parents:

> Who'd be a poet? Parents all beware,
> Cherish and educate your Sons with care;
> Broed 'em to wholesome Law, or give 'em Trades,
> Let 'em not follow th' Muses, they are Jades.[29]

And that the poet was fully resolved to quit them, once and for all, is evident from his next adventures.

The involved policies of King Charles provided Otway with the opportunity. For that monarch, after some adroit practice upon his parliament, at the moment that he was supporting his court by princely bribes from Louis, was now driven to recall his troopers from the support of the French and to shift them to the aid of the Dutch in Flanders. It was when Hounslow Heath was rattling with drums that the young poet resolved to become a soldier. The sounds were full of promise of escape from the petty struggles of the two playhouses, from tawdry jealousies, poverty, and despair. Tom Durfey, inspired by rumors from the world of playwriting, thereupon composed a prologue upon the subject, and handed it to Joe Haynes to speak—"in a Red Coat like a Common Souldier."

> Since there's a Dearth of Witt, and that to Play
> Is hardly worth one poor Brown George a Day;
> I from the Poet, and our Friends within,
> Am sent t' intreat, and your last Favours win,
> E're we go hence and shall no more be seen.
> For my part,—
> I'le to the *French* Campaigne, where one may get
> A certain Wholesome though a Homely Treat;
> Good Oyl and Cooling Sallads, though no meat,
> Good Company, good honest Lousie Currs.
> There's Honour to be got too—Honour, Sirs;
> Honour that makes the General's Voice sound loud,
> And serves instead of Brandy to the Crowd.

My spirits are reviv'd; Methinks I hear ⎫
A Crew of Fire-fac'd Rogues embattl'd there, ⎬
Whose Motly Noses carry Hope and Fear: ⎭
Cry out, Fall on, we shall be Kings, great Men,
Nay Emperours, the Devil knows how, and when.
Then shouting all, advance they to the Siege,
And to the Plunder fall with Priviledge.
Pray tell me then, is it not better farr, ⎫
To live abroad when other Nations Jarr, ⎬
Then 'mongst our selves to make a Civil Warr? ⎭
Are not these Bandaliers, this Sword, this Coat,
Better than Tipstaves, or a Baily's Note?
To day we Play Great Kings, strutt, bounce, and fly,
And e're next Morn the Shop's shut up—God buy,
This by your great Unkindness is our Lott,
We share, and share, 'tis true—but nothing's got,
Like lab'ring *Bees* we toyl for Witt, though poor, ⎫
Which you like Drones suck up, and hum for more, ⎬
But bring in nothing to the Winter-Store, ⎭
Witt is forgot; for with you Men of Miss,
Sense is unnatural as Marriage is—[30]

Otway's sudden urge to don a uniform is supposed to have been gratified through the good will of the Earl of Plymouth, who may or may not have secured him a commission. It is interesting, in passing, to verify the authenticity of the legend by its origin in the writings of Anthony Wood. It is set down by the latter that Otway

obtained to himself a reputation among the ingenious, and a comfortable subsistence to himself, besides the favour and countenance of Charles Fitz-Charles commonly called Don Carlos earl of Plymouth, one of the natural sons of King Charles II. In 1677 he went in the quality of a cornet, with the new rais'd English forces design'd for Flanders.[31]

Obviously there is no sure connection between the two facts. Yet upon such slight foundation a considerable superstructure by way of biography has been reared. Howbeit, Otway did secure his commission, duly signed at Whitehall the first day of May, 1678,[32] and Love airily waved her hand to a red coat on the heath.

"His Majesty and a world of company were in the field, and the whole armie in battalia, a very glorious sight." So wrote John Evelyn[33] of the adventure, but at the same time Edmund Verney, setting down his observations, was inclined to be a bit more skeptical: "The overflowing scum of our nation is listed. . . . Gaolbirds, thieves, & rogues."[34] The poet was assigned as Ensign in Monmouth's Regiment of Foot, and not, as frequently remarked, as a Cornet of Horse under the same command. The expenses of outfitting were heavy enough without those of cavalry equipment added thereto. He prepared to sail for Flanders with Captain William Bagott's company sometime about the middle of 1678.[35] It was almost certainly with the modulated farewell of Mrs. Barry ringing in his ears. Characteristically enough, she was the one chosen to recite the entirely sophisticated epilogue to Leanerd's *Counterfeits*, of which a part ran as follows:

> Gallants, I needs must pray for some of you,
> Who with such heat to the *Low-Countries* go,
> That when you come again, if e're you do,
> You may be welcom'd with the loss of some rich Friend,
> Who's made you Heir to all he's left behind.
> And be assur'd we'll prove exceeding kind
> To those who come with Scars of Honour home,
> If to inherit good Estates they come.

Thus Otway was allowed by Mrs. Barry to anticipate some of the more certain emoluments of soldiering.

The actual events of his short service abroad we may plausibly gather from various hints that he set down the next year in his *Souldier's Fortune*. The picture is more in the colors of Verney than those of Evelyn:

> *A Clumsie Fellow marches over the Stage, drest like an Officer. . . .*
> COURT. The Rascal was a Retailer of Ale but yesterday, and now he is an Officer and be hanged; 'tis a dainty in a morning to see him with his Toes turn'd in, drawing his Leggs after him, at the head of a hundred lusty Fellows. Some honest Gentleman or other stays now, because that Dog had money to bribe some corrupt Collonel withal.[36]

All of which must be scored to the account of Verney, as this likewise:

> What think you now of a cold wet March over the Mountains, Your men tir'd, your Baggage not come up, but at night a dirty watry Plain to Encamp upon, and nothing to shelter you, but an old Leager Cloak as tatter'd as your Colours?[37]

But Otway was not lost entirely to the more genial outlook of

Evelyn. He sketched an idyllic scene, which we may accept out of pity, even though it nowhere corresponds with any Flanders that we know:

> Must we never see our glorious days again? [he cried]. When shall we be rolling in the lands of Milk and Honey; incampt in large luxuriant Vineyards, where the loaded Vines cluster about our Tents, drink the rich Juice, just prest from the plump Grape, feeding on all the fragrant golden Fruit that grow in fertile Climes, and ripen'd by the earliest vigour of the Sun?[38]

Whatever the truth of the picture, the interlude was of short duration.

On July 31, 1678, the congregated blue devils of Otway's career sat themselves down permanently before his tent. For on that date Charles had concluded his disreputable peace of Nimeguen, and the troops were to come home. Captain Bagott's company did not arrive at Yarmouth from Malines until January 18, 1678/9, after a portion of the winter had been endured in the discomfort of Flanders. Bagott himself was ordered to stay at Yarmouth.[39] Otway made his way up to London by June, and found that Commons, terrorized by the prospect of so large a standing army, had passed a disbanding act. An elaborate and dilatory system for paying off the adventurers had been devised, interesting in that it required no money. In Otway's case it began operation June 5 with a debenture of £27.17.6, the paper of which was unnegotiable even at the end of 1679.[40] The remarks of Beaugard in *The Souldiers Fortune*, hence, may be termed the farewell of Otway to this phase of his life:

> A Curse on the Fates! Of all the Strumpets, Fortune's the basest; 'twas Fortune made me a Souldier, a Rogue in Red, the grievance of the Nation; Fortune made peace just when we were on the brink of a War; then Fortune disbanded us, and lost us two Month's pay: Fortune gave us Debentures instead of ready Money, and by very good Fortune I sold mine, and lost heartily by it, in hopes the grinding ill-natur'd dog that bought it will never get a shilling for't—[41]

Chapter VIII

POTBOILERS

Nay, in the Age, where Virtue is as Scarce
As Truth in Women, Wit in the last Farce,
Or Coin mongst the disbanded Sons of Mars. }
Epilogue, spoken by Mrs. Barry,
to DURFEY's *Virtuous Wife*, 1679

OTWAY's dual bill of *Titus and Berenice* with *The Cheats of Scapin* was ready for the stage by December, 1676. Aside from the sympathy that Otway felt for the theme of Racine's play and the impulse to visualize his personal problems, his ruling motive for the adaptation was one of bare necessity. Now that he was definitely sworn to the joys and sorrows of play writing, Otway perforce had come to the composition of potboilers. He was a talented adapter, even by comparison to Ravenscroft and Aphra Behn, who made it their profession. His feeling for the niceties of the French language was keen, his dialogue full of zest. If he was not completely master of the subtleties of French classical drama, he at least had absorbed enough to contribute materially to his English success. The foreign dish was so nicely flavored with English sauce that the audience could accept it without a grimace. Downes noted of the production that: "Titus and Berenice. . . . With the Farce of the *Cheats* of *Scapin* at the end . . . being perfectly Well *Acted;* had good Success."[1] And Gould added of the farce what was equally true a full century afterward:

> The *Cheats of Scapin, one,* a noble thing;
> What a throng'd Audience does it always bring![2]

Some fraction of this popularity was doubtless owing to an all-star cast. Betterton, Smith, Mrs. Lee, and Mrs. Barry were in the tragedy; Sandford, Nokes, Tony Leigh, Mrs. Gibbs, and Barry, in the comedy. Tony Leigh was the original Scapin. It was Leigh who later was characterized in our author's *Friendship in Fashion:*

My dear Mr. *Malagene,* won't you let us see you act a little something of *Harlequin?* I'll swear you do it so naturally, it makes me think I am at the *Louvre* or *Whitehall* all the time. (Malag. *acts.*) Oh Lord, don't, don't neither: I'll swear you'll make me burst. Was there ever anything so pleasant?[3]

Leigh's bit of harlequinade had little or nothing to do with the plot of *Friendship in Fashion;* its presence merely notes that his reputation was mounting from such rôles as that of Scapin, so that in the end the playwright would be forced, as we shall see, to fill his plays with bits to display his peculiar talents, even in the midst of the blackest of tragedies. And may not *The Cheats of Scapin* have been translated at the behest of Betterton to furnish a vehicle for this actor of *"Punchinello, Scaramuchio, Harlequin,* Prince *Pretty-man,* or anything"? Could he not "act the rumbling of a Wheelbarrow, a Sow and Piggs, Sausages a boiling, a Shoulder of Mutton a roasting"? He could act "a fly in a Honey-pot"![4] Yet, this versatile creature aside, what a cast remains! Even lacking knavish old Sandford, "Nurse" Nokes might easily have supported the farce upon his amorphous shoulders. And Barry herself seems to have had almost as great a genius for farce as for tragedy.

Another and extraneous interest was lent the bill by reason of the rivalry of the theaters. It appears that Otway engaged in a race to the boards with two other dramatists, and that he was victorious, in one case by the slight margin of a month. Leaving for the moment the trials of Johnny Crowne, we may listen to the complaints of another notable playwright. Edward Ravenscroft, whose very patent to greatness as a refurbisher of plays was thus challenged by Otway, brought forth at Drury Lane, May, 1677, his *Scaramouch, a Philosopher, Harlequin, A School Boy, Bravo, Merchant, and Magician,* the whole accompanied by a prologue filled with recrimination. It is this latter that chiefly concerns us:

> Very unfortunate this Play has bin;
> A slippery trick was play'd us by *Scapin:*
> Whilst here our Actors made a long delay,
> When some were idle, others run away,
> The city House comes out with half our Play.
> We fear, that having heard of this so long,
> Your expectation now will do it wrong.

The complaints of Crowne were more legitimate. For some time now he had been evolving a spectacle of siege, rape, and murder that should transcend all experience: a double-decker of ten colossal acts, parts one and two. Crowne's play finally was completed and then fell the catastrophe. We read, in a complaint from the King's Company, that

Mr. Crowne, being under . . . agreement with the Duke's House, writt a play called *The Destruction of Jerusalem* and being forced by their refusall of it to bring it to us, the said company compelled us after the studying of it, and vast expense of scenes and clothes, to buy off their clayme, by paying all the pension he had received from them, amounting to one hundred and twelve pounds paid by the King's Company, besides neere forty pounds he, the said Mr. Crowne, paid out of his own pocket.[5]

We may conjecture that Otway's *Titus and Berenice* supplanted the similar play by Crowne, for when parts one and two of *The Destruction* ultimately came to the stage, upon the twelfth and eighteenth of January, 1676/7, Crowne had so far swallowed the affront as to conceal its effects by a flank attack:

Something I intended to say in vindication of myself from theft; some Persons accused me of stealing the parts of *Titus* and *Berenice* from the *French* Play written by Mr. *Racine* on the same subject; but a Gentleman having lately translated that Play, and exposed it to publick view on the Stage, has saved me that labour, and vindicated me better than I can myself. I wou'd not be asham'd to borrow, if my occasions compell'd me from any rich Author: But all the Foreign Coin must be melted down, and receive a new Stamp, if not an addition of Metal, before it will pass current in *England,* and be judg'd Sterling.[6]

Ravenscroft and Crowne had their satisfaction. The charge that the plays were mere translations has since been carelessly repeated. At the time it was a charge disregarded by Otway. Apparently these plays were no great favorites of his, and his creative and combative energy were at a low ebb.

From December, 1676, to April, 1678, there was a long period of silence in his career. After his spectacular year in London, the twenty-fourth of his life, came the disillusionment already noted. Needless to say, no great tonic was found in the adaptation of French plays, nor hardly more in his *Friendship in Fashion,* where, as he remarked in one of his letters, he "profanely laughed at love." The decline had been precipitous. One needs only to contrast the complacency with which he disclaimed that his *Don Carlos* was the best of contemporary heroic tragedy to the complete discomfiture of the frame of mind in which he presently found himself. He described the change thus, in his *Poet's Complaint:*

But in this most transporting height,
Whence I lookt down, and laught at Fate,
All of a sudden I was alter'd grown;
I round me lookt, and found myself alone:
My faithless Muse, my faithless Muse was gone.
I try'd if I in Verse could frame:
Oft I in vain invok'd my *Clio*'s name.
The more I strove, the more I fail'd.
I chaf'd, I bit my Pen, curst my dull Scull, and rail'd,
Resolv'd to force m'untoward Thought, and at the last prevail'd.
A Line came forth, but such a one,
No trav'ling Matron in her Child-birth pains,
Full of the joyfull Hopes to bear a Son,
Was more astonisht at th' unlookt-for shape
Of some deform'd Baboon, or Ape,
Then I was at the hideous Issue of my Brains.
I tore my Paper, stabb'd my Pen,
And swore I'd never write agen,
Resolv'd to be a doating Fool no more.
But when my reck'ning I began to make,
I found too long I'd slept, and was too late awake;
I found m'ungrateful Muse, for whose false sake
I did myself undo,
Had robb'd me of my dearest Store,
My precious Time, my Friends and Reputation too;
And left me helpless, friendless, very proud, and poor.[7]

Whatever the spot to which Otway may have retired, whether to
Woolbeding, to Cambridge, or more likely to the taverns of London, his necessities—"the daily business of daily bread"—brought
him back to the stage in April of 1678. The success of Scapin had
led him to venture farther in comedy. He had progressed far since
the continency of his Alcibiades had made him a jest of the town;
and he had now resolved never again to show such absence of
breeding. He took cognizance of the world as he had found it to
compose a comedy as steel-hard as any produced during the Restoration. *Friendship in Fashion* bristled with coxcombs and ladies
of easy virtue. It was a testament of cynicism and poverty,
matched with a prologue in kind:

I' th' next Place, Ladies, there's no Bawdy in't,
No, not so much as one well-meaning hint;

Nay more, 'twas written every Word he says,
On strictest Vigils, and on Fasting Days,
When he his Flesh to Pennance did enjoin,
Nay took such care to work it chaste and fine,
He dissiplin'd himself at every Line.

Otway had not misjudged his audience. The play hissed from the boards in 1750 as indecent, was at least twice visited by the court in 1678,[8] and was acted, according to Langbaine, "with general applause."[9]

Friendship in Fashion is indecent even when judged by the rigorous standards of its time. The plot—if we may be permitted to outline it as a typical product of Otway's comic genius—turns upon the paradox of the title. Goodvile, married but one year, discovers that he is confronted with a problem demanding immediate solution. The only answer is to hurry his cousin and mistress, Victoria, to the altar with his friend Truman, before the latter shall find out the full significance of the move. To this project he adds that of seducing the beautiful Camilla, being undaunted by the fact that she is to wed his other good friend, Valentine. His duplicity is disclosed to Truman and Valentine by Mrs. Goodvile; and they plan a notable revenge. Truman is to cuckold Goodvile, whose wife has already shown a certain willingness in that way. The success that attends them, with various other *engagements d'amour* during a convenient masquerade and in a convenient grotto, comprises the plot.

Where are the great comic characters? They move across the background with a certain heartless gaiety that may be revealed by a more careful *résumé* of the various intrigues.

At the opening of the play Goodvile enters with Valentine, to invite Truman to the ball at his house. His departure is the signal for the entrance of Malagene, "a general disperser of nauseous Scandal, tho' it be of his own Mother or Sister." After attending awhile upon his backbiting, Valentine and Truman finally prevail upon him to leave, by the inopportune suggestion that he become the third party to a duel. Enter Saunter and Caper, two more fops of the town: the one "sings the *French* manner better than ever I heard any *English* gentleman in my Life," the other dances. Enter Lady Squeamish. The three conduct a school for scandal, and the act ends with song and much lively dialogue,—nothing accomplished.

We next discover the secret passion of Mrs. Goodvile for Truman, and her unqualified dislike for her husband, by which we may deduce that the stage is set. Dancers begin to arrive. Victoria is saluted with unseemly jests concerning her condition. Camilla runs "squeaking" from Truman and Valentine. Lady Squeamish enters with her *protégé*, Sir Noble Clumsey, whom she is determined to make a fine gentleman of the town, though at present she appears more concerned with being cast off by Valentine. There is much capering by Caper. Saunter is delivered of a song, having sung two or three already. The fiddles strike up. Sir Noble resists for a while the temptation of liquor and ultimately succumbs. Curtain. Still nothing accomplished.

At the beginning of the third act, Truman and Valentine, fully acquainted by now with Goodvile's designs, agree upon the revenge. The dancers come and go. Malagene fills in with drunken comedy, curses the music, sings a Scotch song and an Irish Cronan. Caper and Saunter flip across the stage to the unbounded admiration of Lady Squeamish. The latter overhears Goodvile as he attempts to arrange an assignation, and, thinking him Valentine, resolves to have her revenge by substituting herself for the lady. It all begins to resemble a series of *fabliaux*.

At the outset of the fourth act Truman carries off Mrs. Goodvile faintly protesting, and Lady Squeamish accomplishes her designs upon Goodvile. There is much running to and fro as the various parties are nearly discovered by respective wives and husbands. Truman fights with Goodvile, and Goodvile, now awakened to his wife's conduct, resolves to be rid of her. "A Wife for a Year," says he, "like a Garment that has been worn too long, hangs loose and awkwardly on a Man, and grows a Scandal to him that wears it." And so the comedy runs to its conclusion with a hectic bustle suggestive at times of the variety show. We may question whether there was any more serious purpose underlying all this seeming vitality.

Friendship in Fashion was doubtless written to amuse, for the prologue discovers no design beyond that of giving pleasure. It was a thankless business:

> How hard a task hath that poor Drudg of Stage,
> That strives to please in this Fantastick Age?[10]

The material that was bound to satisfy the wits was regarded by

the playwright with unqualified cynicism. It was Malagene who
was spokesman for this whole theory of comedy:

> Why walking along, a lame Fellow follow'd me, and askt my Charity,
> (which by the way was a pretty proposition to me:) being in one of
> my witty merry fits, I askt him how long he had been in that condi-
> tion? The poor Fellow shook his head, and told me he was born so.—
> But d'ye think how I serv'd him?
>
>   Nay, the Devil knows.
> I show'd my parts I think; for I tript up both his wooden Legs, and
> walkt off gravely about my business.[11]

Dependent as Otway was upon these wits for his existence—their
whims were the determining factors in the building of a comic as
of a tragic plot—now and again he rebelled against their cruelty
and superficiality. Lady Squeamish remarks:

> Yes, the Poet came and read to me at my Lodgings: He is but a
> young man, and I suppose he has not been a Writer long: besides,
> he has had little or no conversation with the Court, which has been
> the reason he has committed a great many Indecorums in the con-
> duct of it.
>
> SAUNTER. I did not like it neither for my part; there was never a Song
> in it, ha?
>
> CAP. No, nor so much as a Dance.
>
> MAL. Oh, it's impossible it should take, if there were neither Song nor
> Dance in it.
>
> L. SQ. And then their Comedies now-a-days are the filthiest things, full
> of Bawdy and nauseous doings, which they mistake for raillery and
> intrigue; besides they have no wit in 'em, neither, for all their Gen-
> tlemen and men of wit, as they style 'em, are either silly conceited
> Coxcombs, or else rude ill-mannerly drunken Fellows—fogh—I am
> asham'd any one should pretend to write a Comedy, that does not
> know the nicer rules of the Court, and all the Intrigues and Gal-
> lantries that pass, I vow.[12]

With his tongue in his cheek, Otway loaded his own comedy with
song and dance beyond any outside of opera, and as for bawdry
and court scandal, a reperusal of his plot and a recollection that the
friends of Buckhurst found in it material sufficient to destroy that
nobleman's patronage of the poet tells how faithfully Otway followed the procedure laid down by Lady Squeamish and her cabal.
The callow playwright of her account bears more than a slight resemblance to Otway himself in his formative years.

Regarding his more serious purpose in comedy, we find here and there disconnected comments which show Otway the artist standing apart from Otway the hack. The age, he had discovered, was served.

> Instead of Comedy, with nasty Farce.
> Would *Plautus, Terence* e're have been so lewd,
> T'have drest Jack pudding up to catch the Crowd?[13]

The assumption of moral intent was generally as vigorous for comedy as it was for tragedy. Wycherley, Congreve, Shadwell, Dryden, and our poet all professed themselves prophets in the land of darkness. Otway's was the conventional utterance of the time:

> How vain have prov'd the Labours of the Stage,
> In striving to reclaim a vitious Age![14]

Once in a while, however, the satire upon morals became too sharp, and then the clamps descended. Such was the misadventure of Dryden's *Limberham,* where the attack was upon "the crying sin of keeping," and though the edge was there dulled by the flippant attitude of the dramatist, it was still too obvious in its hits and shortly was withdrawn. We can only conjecture, in the case of *Friendship in Fashion,* where the trouble lay, but someone felt the barb and the playwright was thenceforward deprived of Buckhurst's protection. The ill luck of this comedy perhaps also had something to do with the loss of Shadwell's friendship. Only a short time before, Otway had been hailed as "Shadwell's dear zany"; it was the latter, of all the race of poets, who was closest to Buckhurst; and now, but a short time after this play, Shadwell and Otway were in open enmity. It was dangerous to exploit one's indignation too freely. The point lies in the zeal for correction that the comic artist felt impelled to follow, frequently to the verge of disaster.

Otway's methods were extraordinary. After the practice of the sophisticated Quixotes of his time, he stripped and descended into the depths, where in the confused light of the Restoration he lost half the sense of his original purpose. Temperamentally he was incapable of remaining aloof from his creatures. He was too much the idealist, by nature a tragic writer of the sentimental order, to whom solid critical thinking in the field of comedy was denied. He followed in the tracks of others, and not always intelligently. It was chiefly after Wycherley, whom by a certain similarity of outlook he was led to imitate. Each had a distinct flair for morality, however much the conduct of their lives would seem to deny it. But the colossal sneer upon the lips of his cultured elder ill suited the more gentle features of Otway. Thus, though he designed Goodvile after Wycherley's Horner, he failed to achieve in him the same easy power. Goodvile is too hysterical; and as for Otway, only when he should be thoroughly hardened by the repeated buffets of life, would he approach, in his characterization of Antonio and the depraved father of Beaugard, the *saeva indignatio* of his earliest comic master.

Comedy and tragedy had at times almost merged in the works of the elder playwright, particularly in such a product as *The Plain Dealer*. It is this fact that makes it worth while in a study of Otway, the writer of a style of tragedy that runs between sentiment and the bitterness of despair, to examine his specific debt to Wycherley. There are the more obvious resemblances, such as in the names of the characters themselves; though, recalling the habit of Restoration stage names to repeat themselves, these perhaps should not be pressed too far. We may note the following: in *The Country Wife* appears another Lady Squeamish, a Lettice in *The Plain Dealer*, a Valentine in *Love in a Wood*. This is little more than the beginning. The Lady Squeamish of Otway added to Wycherley's only a few critical pretensions, that he found elsewhere in the same playwright. Her school for scandal was very likely derived from the famous detraction scene in *The Plain Dealer*, in its turn borrowed from Molière and handed on in due course to Sheridan. Another character of the same genealogy was found in *Love in a Wood*, described as an affected widow "in distress for a husband." Malagene is a composite character of many antecedents: a bit from Plausible and Novel of *The Plain Dealer* with a seasoning of Mr. Paris of *The Gentleman Dancing Master*. In the latter play Hippolita is the same calculating schemer as Mrs. Goodvile, revealing her heart to her maid Prue much as Otway's lady of pleasure does to Lettice. Finally Goodvile himself is the false friend Vernish of *The Plain Dealer*, and accepts his cuckoldom almost in the same tone of voice as Pinchwife in *The Country Wife*, even though that conclusion is somewhat out of character. Separately these resemblances mean little, inasmuch as there was but slight invention in the whole of Restoration comedy; in the aggregate they are too considerable to be discounted. They show Otway early imitating the one writer closest to his own ultimate philosophy, and at the same time the one least likely to lead him into the free air of comedy. Under such guidance, he was to find himself more and more a Gulliver surrounded by an abhorrent race of Yahoos. Comedy does not easily flourish in that environment. But we may add that the sardonic comedian and the sentimentalist have ever been an impossible union, the one being all head and the other all heart.

At this point we may anticipate developments to glance ahead at Otway's subsequent comedy. Neither *The Souldiers Fortune* nor its sequel *The Atheist* add measurably to his stature, though neither is so devoid of merit as its comparative neglect would imply. Time and a certain refinement of taste, following the new century, made Sir Jolly Jumble of the earlier play impossible to stomach. After 1700 he was hissed from the boards, and with Sir Jolly eliminated *The Souldiers Fortune* possessed little interest. Even upon his first appearance, when tastes were not squeamish, there was at least one lady with the hardihood to protest. It followed inevitably that she was written down a prude:

> First, Says a Lady, that shall be nameless, because the world may think civilly of her; Fogh! Oh *Sherru!* 'tis so filthy, so bawdy, no modest Woman ought to be seen at it: Let me dye, it has made me sick: When the World lies, Mr. *Bentley,* if that very lady has not &c, &c, . . . But your true Jilt is a Creature that can extract Bawdy out of the chastest sense, as easily as a Spider can Poison out of a Rose: They know true Bawdy, let it never be so much conceal'd, as perfectly as *Falstaff* did the true Prince by instinct. . . . Though I have heard a Lady (that has more Modesty than any of those she Criticks, and I am sure more wit) say, She wonder'd at the impudence of any of her Sex, that would pretend to understand the thing call'd Bawdy.[15]

It has always been assumed, though upon no sure basis, that Aphra Behn was the witty and modest lady-errant of Otway's defense. Be that as it may, at this distance it would appear that the strictures upon his comedy were well taken. In Sir Jolly Jumble the race of panders reached its nadir. Nor is there any evidence forthcoming that his truth reclaimed the "vitious age."

Otway's play in 1680 was rather the cause of immediate and raucous laughter. It "took extraordinary well, and being perfectly

Acted got the company great Reputation and Profit."[16] Cibber said of Leigh that:

In Sir *Jolly* he was all Life and laughing Humour, and when *Nokes* acted with him in the same Play, they returned the Ball so dexterously upon one another, that every Scene between them seem'd but one continued Rest of Excellence—But alas! when those Actors were gone, that Comedy and many others, for the same Reason, were rarely known to stand upon their own Legs; by seeing no more of *Leigh* and *Nokes* in them, the Characters were quite sunk and alter'd.[17]

Not only had the great actors passed, but, what Cibber failed to note,—the conscience of 1680. Granted an audience of elegant savagery, the antics of Sir Jolly and Sir Davy must have been exceedingly diverting. Sir Davy, acquainted at the curtain with his cuckoldom, received his antlers with the "non-con grin" of Nokes, and cackled harshly at his own plight.[18] Lady Dunce, on her part, throughout displayed not a shred of conscience. The game of sex, the light give and take so entertaining in Etherege, to which a maidenhead was the trifling prize, had now become a downright serious business. And in contrast to Otway's tragedy, there was not in his comedy a single decent woman—at least for long. The world was in an endless ferment of lust unsatisfied, satisfied, nauseated, the most striking note of which was the entire consistency of its operation. It had gone awry in Wycherley's *Country Wife* and *Plain Dealer,* but at least in those two plays we were granted the anticipation of a satisfactory solution.

In order that he might point the moral and rest assured that it should not escape, Otway wrote his own sequel in *The Atheist; or, The Second Part of The Souldiers Fortune.*[19] The lovers of the former play became the cuckolds of this. Sylvia the chaste was reduced to Sylvia the untrue; Courtine, formerly the slave to her charms, now uttered sentiments concerning the race of wives which were doubtless agreeable enough to the hussies of the second balcony; and at the conclusion, Beaugard, the hunter of womankind, was himself trapped into matrimony—in lieu of winning by any other means. The thesis up to this point had been so roundly demonstrated that the audience was forced to perceive that the whole vicious circle had only recommenced. But it was not yet brought to its ultimate conclusion. In the spinning of life certain scum had been cast off, such as the father of Beaugard. By this poisonous old man the final *coup de grâce* was administered to the social world. One must suppose that Otway's satirical purpose was to demonstrate not only what happened in the first year to doting lovers, but also what overtook the generation of rakes when it hobbled into old age. The father to Beaugard is everything pernicious: a gambler, irreverent, and a parasite afflicted with a philosophy of libertinism grown rank with time. From his own son we discover that he has gone through the history of having killed his wife by grief, of being discovered by his child in the embraces of his housekeeper, and of coming finally to poverty by the prodigality of his vices. Now he wheedles Beaugard for money, and, after a few guineas have been slung at him, as promptly loses it at gaming. For the rest:

There's Cheating and Hypocracies still in the City; Riot and Murder in the Suburbs; Grinning, Lying, Fawning, Flattery, and False-promising at Court; Assignations at *Covent Garden* Church . . . we are overrun with a Race of Vermin they call Wits, a Generation of Insects that are always making a Noise, and buzzing about your Ears, concerning Poets, Plays, Lampoons, Libels, Songs, Tunes, Soft Scenes, Love, Ladies, Perukes, and Cravat-strings, *French* Conquests, Duels, Religion, Snuffboxes, Points, Garnitures, Mill'd Stockings, *Foubert*'s Academy, Politics, Parliament-Speeches. . . .[20]

We may be certain that the nausea they raise in us was not unintentional from one who, as time proceeded, spoke with an increasing bitterness of the scurvy fortune that had plunged him into a world of scribbling fops and enameled women. One recalls the tenderly nurtured child beside Rother stream, the mildly puritan cast of his earliest education, and then turns to this latter portrait wherein the disillusioned sentimentalist gazes upon his creatures with disgust. The contrast worked itself out into the two worlds of tragedy and comedy. The one, with its Jaffeirs and Belvideras, was the embodiment of all that he ever dreamed of life; the other, with its Claras, Squeamishes, and Antonios, all that he saw.

It was the outlook not only of "poor Otway" but of the age in which he lived. The audience of jades and jilts had its sudden revulsions when it demanded of drama a grandiose interpretation of life. We may instance the address of Lee's *Theodosius* to the Duchess of Richmond. This particular mistress of the King was haply among the less sordid of those precipitated to royal favor.

She was a lady who delighted to build castles out of cards, who—as it was noted in Grammont—"did not hate *Satyr* or *Scandal*," and who so bedeviled the King with her coquetry as almost to keep her virtue to the end. In spite of all, it seems that Richmond retained her unbounded love of constancy and high heroism. It was to her that Lee dedicated one of his most idealistic tragedies, thus:

Ziphares and *Semandra* were first Your Grace's Favourites. . . . Your Grace, who is the most beautiful Idea of Love and Glory; who to that Divine Composition, have the noblest and best natur'd Wit in the World. All I can promise, *Madam,* and be able to perform, is, That your Grace shall never see a Play of mine that shall give offence to Modesty and Virtue; and what I humbly offer to the World, shall be of use at least, and I hope deserve Imitation: which is, or ought to be, I am sure, the Design of all *Tragedies* and *Comedies* both Ancient and Modern.[21]

Chapter IX

DUELS AND RUMORS OF DUELS

'Tis very natural vain things shou'd be uppermost,
In such a World of Vanity as this;
Where massy substances of things sink down
And nothing stays but Colours, Sounds, and Shadows.
CROWNE, *The Ambitious Statesman,* 1679

THE lives of Otway and Lee during these distracted years had
come to resemble their own comedy. What with patrons, critics,
and endless jealousy, not to mention the undertone of rising political discord, the poets had sharply divided themselves into hungry
packs preying upon one another. The feuds were finally to reach
their full crescendo in the years of the Popish Plot. But whereas
then they had at least some basis of political interest, in the beginning they grew from mere personal rivalry and bitterness. One
such feud that touched the careers of our playwrights had its inception as early as 1673 when they both were hardly more than
novitiates to London. At that time a controversy had seethed
momentarily around Elkanah Settle's *Empress of Morocco.* So
great had been the success of that potpourri of dance and horror
that an ill-assorted junto of Dryden, Shadwell, and Crowne had
gathered to the attack, and, according to the well-defined judgment
of the town, had been clearly bested. Thus for some three years
Elkanah had rested upon his victory. Meanwhile Otway had risen
to his time of greatness, when, perhaps by reason of his short-
lived friendship with Shadwell, he had been added to the number
of Settle's adversaries. There were countless alignments and re-
alignments, and skirmishes by way of doggerel from both camps.

A light upon the entire business and upon the near chaos of
dramatic affairs is reflected by a satirical poem that passed in cir-
culation during the year 1677. It was quite celebrated in its day,
and hence attributed the more easily to the witty Earl of Rochester, to whose account was laid any anonymous squib of sufficient
point and vigor. Henry Savile wrote a letter to the Earl on November 1, 1677, alluding to the excitement that attended its appearance.
Said he: "The whole tribe [of poets] are alarumed att a libell

against them lately sent to Will's coffe house. I am not happy enough to have seen it but I heare it commended and therefore the more probably thought to be composed att Woodstock. . . ."[1] The answer of Rochester seems to dispose of this incorrect supposition, though nowhere does he specifically deny authorship. His response ran as follows: "For the *Libell* you speak of, upon that *most unworthy Generation the present* Poets, I rejoice in it with all my Heart, and shall take it for a Favour, if you will send me a *Copy.* He cannot want Wit utterly, that *has a Spleen to those Rogues,* though never so dully expres'd."[2]

The unworthy generation was not so easily satisfied. For some time now, Elkanah Settle had been languishing in an unpopularity to which libel came, as Otway put it, as naturally as "mud to an eale," and they recognized that this libel, *The Tryal of the Poets,* traced accurately in its orbit all his enmities and rivalries. Dryden, Crowne, and Shadwell were the chief legatees of a venom stored up for years, but next in line as their associates followed Mrs. Behn, Lee, and Otway. In all probability it was to this poem that Dryden alluded in his contemporary epistle to Lee's *Rival Queens.* He counseled his young satellite to

> Despise those Drones, who praise while they accuse
> The too much vigour of your youthful Muse.[3]

The criticism of the drones was here mild against Lee, and it was mingled with some slight praise, for Elkanah had no reason to regard him so hotly as some of the others. Young Nathaniel had written only three plays, of which but one was a serious challenge; nevertheless, as the convivial friend of Dryden, he received this telling thrust:

> *Nat Lee* stept in next, in hopes of a Prize
> *Apollo* remember'd he had hit Once in thrice;
> By the Rubyes in's Face, he could not deny,
> But he had as much Wit as Wine could supply;
> Confest that indeed he had a Musical Note,
> But sometimes strain'd so hard, that it rattl'd ith' Throat,
> Yet owning he had Sense, t'encourage him for't,
> He made him his *Ovid* in *Augustus*'s Court.[4]

Dryden himself and Otway did not come off so happily. We need recall only a couplet to motivate the rage of the latter:

> *Don Carlos* his Pockets so amply had fill'd,
> That his Mange was quite cur'd, and his Lice were all killed.[5]

Lee, handled less harshly, was content to remain silent. Dryden bided his time until the devastating assault upon Doeg, in *Absalom and Achitophel*. But Otway hurried to immediate reprisals. Our information upon this battle of the poets has hitherto been of the haziest, resting only upon the couplets Malone unearthed from Shadwell's *Tory Poets*. There Shadwell had scoffed at the pretensions of Dryden, with a passing allusion to Otway's anger:

> The Lawrel makes a Wit; a Brave the Sword;
> And all are wise men at a Council-board;
> S—*le*'s a Coward, 'cause fool *Ot*—*y* fought him,
> And *Mul*—*ve* is a Wit, because I taught him.[6]

The exact details of this appear to have rested in some obscurity until 1682, when there came forth a pamphlet filled with political diatribe against Elkanah and the sweeping accusation that he was the author not only of this *Tryal,* elsewhere called *The Session of the Poets,* but of various other Whiggish tracts of later composition. The story it tells is a curious one: "It happened about four years ago, there came out a Copy of Verses of the same *Libellous nature* of *Azaria and Hushai,* which by the greatest part of the town has been accounted his. . . ." The writer proceeds with some reference to the exalted station of those attacked in *Azaria and Hushai* before readverting to this earlier libel. He states that:

Our Malicious Buzzard [Settle] did not in those days [1676] soar so high, he only did abuse the *Poets* then into whose number he would fain have crept, which because they always scorn'd, and lookt with Contempt upon him, He endeavors thus to revenge himself; but it fell out most unluckily, for a discovery was soon made of our Author.

And Mr. O. a Man of the Sword, as well as the Pen, finding himself most coursly dealt withal, immediately call'd him to an account, and required the satisfaction of a Gentleman from him: This I must confess was something unreasonable, and did by no means agree with our *Scribblers* Constitution, who had much rather *Rail* than *Fight;* and being at this news as much surprised, and in little better pickle, than Alderman Atkins would have been upon the like occasion, beg'd he would spare his Life, and he would give him any other satisfaction he could desire, and presently taking *Pen, Ink,* and *Paper* out of his Pocket, he writ these following words, (viz.) *I confess I writ the* Session of the Poets, *and am very*

sorry for't, and am the Son of A Whore for doing it; Witness my hand
E.S. This he delivered to Mr. O. which it seems saved his Throat that
time; but I am afraid for a worse hand.[7]

This story does not agree in all particulars with that told by
Shadwell in his *Tory Poets*. Whereas it is said in the pamphlet that
the duel was narrowly averted, the other story of an actual passage
of arms very likely arose from Shadwell's effort to put the best
face on the matter for his political associate. That the pamphlet
has the better version is suggested by a possible reference to the
affair in Otway's own writings. Directly after these events he had
occasion to speak of playhouse hectors thus:

> For here you'll censure, who disdain to write
> As some make Quarrels here, that scorn to fight.[8]

In any event, we may disregard most of Elkanah's vehement de-
nials: "I was accused of being the author of a Scandalous Copy of
Verses call'd the *Session of the Poets,* an ill natured scurrilous
Lampoon, written some years since, and now as believed at the
Father's Door, being printed among Lord *R's—* Poems."[9] When
this rebuttal was penned, death had silenced the tongue of Rochester, and there apparently was no one ready to protect his memory.
But Otway was not in the mood to let the matter rest. In 1679,
while his reputation as a soldier was still fresh, he took up the cudg-
els a second time in his *Poet's Complaint*. It is now clear that the
following was his final assault upon the politically disembodied
shade of Elkanah, and not, as has been commonly assumed, upon
Rochester. Otway had just rounded off that rival with some skill
when he began upon brawny Settle:

> Next him appear'd that blundering Sot
> Who a late *Session of the Poets* wrote,
> Nature has markt him for a heavy Fool;
>   By's flat broad Face you'l know the Owl,[10]
> The other Birds have hooted him from light;
> Much buffeting has made him love the Night,
>   And onely in the dark he strays;
> Still Wretch enough to live, with worse Fools spends his days,
> And for old Shoes and Scraps repeats dull Plays.[11]

Whatever else, Rochester was no heavy fool, his features were
neither flat nor broad, and he was never given to the repetition of

dull plays for "old Shoes and Scraps." The latter was to be Elkanah's function throughout life, until he should utter his expiring
roar from the canvas vitals of a Smithfield dragon.

The reverberations of all mighty conflicts die away with time.
Thereafter Otway relapsed into a drab mutton and ale existence.
After unrequited love had come unheroic war and ignominious
home-coming. His biographer, Theophilus Cibber, after cogitating
upon this period, was impelled to speak of Otway's "cowardly
resignation of his commission."[12] The word might have been spared
had Cibber but taken the trouble to read a few pages of *The
Souldiers Fortune*. The very title itself was a sardonic comment
upon the injustice that had befallen him.

If the involved policies of the Gods and Stuarts seemed determined to deprive Otway of his glory, they reckoned without his
dauntless spirit. Upon his return from Flanders, early in 1679,
he was once more to be found in his old haunts at the theater. The
playwrights customarily were given free entrance as a stimulus, in
lieu of more substantial wages,[13] and now their horde was augmented by the flotsam of the returned army. To such, Otway himself had recently paid his respects:

> The rugged Souldier that from War returns,
> And still wi' th' heat of former Action burns,
> Let him but hither come to see a Play,
> Proceeds an Errant Courtier in a day.
> Shall steal from th' Pit, and fly up to the Box,
> There hold impertinent Chat with Tawdry Maux:
> Till e're aware the Blust'rer falls in love;
> And Hero grows as harmless as a Dove.[14]

On June 23, 1679, still gaudy in regimentals and deriving what
satisfaction he could from his illicit title of Captain, Otway found
himself in the pit with another soldier, whose returns in love and
war thus far had been infinitely more substantial. Jack Churchill,
the embryonic Duke of Marlborough, had thus early begun to
emerge from the pack of Restoration fops, though Fame was still
inclined to question upon what qualification:

> It wonders what did *Chur—ll* recommend
> Who never did to Deeds of arms pretend:
> Love, all his Active Youth, his Bus'ness was,
> Love that best suits his handsome Shape and Face.[15]

The answer to the question was not only in Churchill's exploits in Flanders, under the banner of the French king, but his more brilliant maneuver through the window of the Duchess of Cleveland's boudoir at the unexpected return of King Charles. His perfect readiness in the face of this most difficult of situations was an augury of a tactical genius notable in England's military history; while at the same time his business acumen was forecast by the skill with which he put out the annuities settled upon him by the same Duchess.[16] In time they were to multiply into England's most magnificent fortune.

It has been hitherto assumed that at this particular moment Churchill was in Flanders with James, Duke of York. But the passports of that year reveal that he made various passages to and from the continent.[17] The reason lay in another bit of his history that has remained unnoticed. Probably to represent the cause of the harassed James, Churchill had been returned from Newtown, Isle of Wight, as a member of the House of Commons for the short session summoned for March 6, 1678/9 and dissolved July of the same year. Elected with him from Newtown was one Sir John Holmes,[18] with whom we discover Churchill descending into the pit of the Duke's theater.

The town gallant observed a ritual upon these occasions:

He advances into the middle of the *Pit*, struts about a while to render his good parts Conspicuous, pulls out his *Comb*, *Carreens* his *Wigg*, Hums the Orange Wench to give her her own rates for her China-fruit, and immediately *Sacrifices* the fairest of them to the Shrine of the *next Vizor Mask*.[19]

Churchill proceeded to buy from Orange Betty, according to ritual, but at this juncture something untoward took place that remains involved in obscurity: either the thrifty Colonel was outraged at the price demanded for the fruit, or else his quartermaster's nose sniffed at its quality. There was the sudden crack of a cane, followed by an uproar not unusual in the pit and the mingled shrieks and complaints of Orange Betty. The tumult seems to have awakened our poet from his reveries, and such a storm ensued as the hero of Blenheim was unable to ride.

It may be assumed that it was to this rencounter in Tartarus that Mrs. Behn alluded in her obscure prologue to *The Young King*, recited almost immediately thereafter at the same playhouse.

As one of the more intimate friends of Otway, she derived considerable entertainment from his exploit. Her gibes have an unwonted tone of amusement, where ordinarily she would have passed over the disturbance without further notice. But she composed, instead, the mock heroic of a great soldier and the cost of oranges, of which the purport was evident enough to the denizens of the pit:

> They're Sparks who are of Noise and Nonsense full,
> At fifteen witty, and at twenty dull;
> That in the Pit can huff and talk hard words,
> And briskly draw Bamboo instead of Swords.
> But never yet Rencounter cou'd compare
> To our late vigorous *Tartarian War;*[20]
> Cudgel the Weapon was, the Pit the Field;
> Fierce was the Hero, and too brave to yield,
> But stoutest Hearts must bow; and being well can'd,
> He cries, Hold, hold, you have the Victory gain'd.
> All laughing call—
> Turn out the Rascal, the eternal Blockhead;
> —*Zounds,* crys *Tartarian,* I am out of Pocket:
> Half Crown my Play, Sixpence my Orange cost.
> Equip me that, do you the Conquest boast.
> For which to be at ease, a Gathering's made,
> And out they turn the Brother of the Blade.[21]

The brief narrative of these events is to be found in a contemporary news-letter, containing, it is true, certain apparent inconsistencies with the prologue version just quoted, but not of such difficulty as to remain insoluble. "Churchill," it says, "for beating an Orange Wench was challenged by Capt. Otway (the poet), and were both wounded, but Churchill most."[22] The difficulty here is twofold: in the greater seriousness of the duel and in the poet's somewhat dubious title. Neither should trouble us. By reason of much chatter among the wits, a duel of canes easily might assume more threatening proportions, particularly when the names were well known and the teller had not seen the duel. Nor should our belief in Otway's part in these events be more disturbed by his new and illicit rank of Captain. Such titles were as easily bestowed in that day as in this. In fact it was matter of but a few months when Otway bestowed upon himself the identical rank. In his epilogue to *Caius Marius* he put into the mouth of Mrs. Barry a line alluding at once to his own military experiences and to her late leading rôle in Shadwell's *Woman Captain*. She had said:

> For t'other day I was a Captain too.

Thus for all the agony it may have cost him, Otway apparently cherished a secret pride in his title; and it may be very easily assumed that had he perused the letter he would have passed the addition unchallenged. Our newsmonger, however, was not finished with the account. Gossip of the duel had traveled about the town and finally had arrived at the highest quarters. There Sir John Holmes, the colleague in parliament of Churchill, was called upon to present his version: "The relation being told the King, . . . as Churchill thought to his prejudice, he challenged him Holmes, who fighting disarmed him Churchill."[23] It was a sorry train of events for the future duke that Otway had started.

For himself it probably was the stimulant that his system required. By his duel he had found occasion to issue from eclipse, and now he stood full in the light of public admiration—as a soldier, a man of honor, and a defender of orange wenches in distress. Most noteworthy of all, he administered to Churchill the earliest and almost the unique reverse of that great soldier's career.

Chapter X

POLITICS

[*Enter a mad man.*] And I am come to the nine and fortieth point, the downfall of the Whore of *Babylon*. Mark me, the Judgments of the terrible Approach, of the falling into nothing of the polluted and sinful World, shall be turned and converted to Confusion and Distress, and then, you shall behold the Crowns of the Earth be tumbled on Heaps, and the Seas, and the Moon, shall vanish into Vapor—but then—

Mr. Turbulent (1682). (ANON.)

MEANWHILE the gaining of a livelihood by one "whose Business must be daily Bread" had perforce to go forward. After the first exhilaration of adventure, Otway found himself relapsing once more into despondency:

> It was a dark and gloomy Day,
> Sad as the Bus'ness, sullen too,
> As proud Men, when in Vain they woo,
> Or Soldiers cheated of their Pay.[1]

By September, 1679, less than three months after the duel with Churchill, he had produced another tragedy, a piece of hack work, yet not without a certain novelty of approach. A profound change had come over London in the interval of his absence, a change equally decisive upon its mirror, the stage. Titus Oates had already begun his infamous attack upon the character and the religion of those closest to Charles; and it was managed with sufficient plausibility to inflame the prejudice of one-half England. There was some half-perceived justification in his practice. Charles himself had designed by secret treaties with France to deliver England over to the Catholic Faith, but after burning his fingers in lesser related matters, he had been shrewd enough not to press the cause. The heir to the throne lacked the same even balance, and thus James became in his turn the hope of the militant Jesuits of France and Spain and the secret foreboding of the more peacefully inclined Catholics of England. The latter desired little more than that the king should guarantee them a decent quiet in which to celebrate their masses. But their wishes unhappily were foredoomed. The vague rumors which the renegade Oates had gathered while a

Jesuit at Valladolid and St. Omers, provided him with the tissue, and thence he evolved his superb fabrication of lies. It seemed by his report that there was "a hellish plot to fire the city, raise the Catholics in Ireland, conquer England by French and Irish arms, massacre every protestant who refused to recant, and murder the King." This, said Oates, had been agreed to at a Jesuit convocation of April 24, 1678, to which he had been admitted. Certainly a meeting of some sort had been held in the private apartments of James, though Oates hardly knew the place, nor much more than that the Duke's Catholic secretary, Coleman, had been present. With this as a start, it took a certain period of incubation to bring affairs to a head. Charles meanwhile was most adroit in uncovering the lies of Oates, and the whole court party strove mightily to quiet the business. But the chance discovery of documents in the chambers of Coleman, revealing long and treasonable communications with France, together with an extraordinary murder of the magistrate, Sir Edmund Godfrey, before whom the informant had laid his deposition, suddenly shot the flames sky high. Overnight London became a city of terror. It was feared that Godfrey had been only the first victim, and that a St. Bartholomew's Eve of Protestants was to come, with ultimate destruction of the city by the incendiary. The patriots undertook measures for defense, and the tramp of trained bands and the clatter of pikes seemed the only warrant for sleep through the interminable winter nights.[2]

At just what point the Earl of Shaftesbury had seen fit to use the lies of Oates, to the end of constructing for himself a powerful political machine, is not entirely clear. Out of the tumult of his intellect, with its mingled discontent and patriotism, arose the Whig party and policies that in the long run were to be justified. Once he had been the heart of the Cabal ministry; now Shaftesbury was the most detested antagonist of the court. His figure, lean, sinister, and wasted by disease, was set up by the Tories as the symbol of destruction. His personal character was vilified by indecent attacks. To the city, on the other hand, he was demigod, as he jolted through Aldersgate surrounded by his noisy green-ribboned myrmidons. The union of boundless personal ambition and far-sighted statesmanship, Shaftesbury was easily the most interesting politician of the latter end of the century, if we set aside for the moment the omnipresent and untroubled figure of the King himself.

It has been necessary to enlarge upon the actors and events of this period because they were the subject matter for much contemporary English tragedy.[3] Politics took the place upon the stage formerly occupied by French romance. Shaftesbury and James in their various disguises became as clearly recognizable as had been the outright figures of Mithridates or Alexander. But with the greater vitality of actual events, no matter how disguised by historical or romantic nomenclature, and with the stage transformed for the time into a political arena, tragedy advanced farther in four short years than it had in all the eighteen since the Restoration. That violence of action which had been merely conjectured before was now ready at hand in the subterranean intrigues of the great plot, in the assassination of Godfrey, and in the wholesale execution of the Papists.[4]

The writers naturally took direction according to their patrons' interests. Dryden at first appears to have wavered. Settle attached himself to the Whig cause as a pamphleteer and for a while rushed along triumphantly as one of the most powerful dealers in political invective. He became celebrated as the director of gorgeous Pope-burnings; while his quondam enemy, Shadwell, was to be found close to Shaftesbury, at the inner councils of the Green-Ribbon Club, as one of the chief "character men"[5] for the vast streams of libel that belched from the unauthorized press. The defenders of the succession were somewhat slower in formation. They were as yet hardly aware of a cause, and they had no such political genius as Shaftesbury to marshal them. It was at this indecisive period that Nat. Lee discovered that of all professions and cults that only of pure poetry failed to thrive:

> On Poets onely no kind Star e'er smil'd
> Curst Fate has damn'd 'em ev'ry Mothers Child:
> Therefore he warns his Brothers of the Stage,
> To write no more for an ingrateful age.
> Think what penurious Masters you have serv'd;
> *Tasso* ran mad, and noble *Spencer* starv'd:
> Turn then, who e'er thou art that canst write well,
> Thy Ink to Gaul, and in Lampoons excell.
> Forswear all honesty, traduce the Great,
> Grow impudent, and rail against the State;
> Bursting with spleen, abroad thy Pasquils send
> And chuse some Libel-spreader for thy Friend:
> The Wit and Want of *Timon* point thy mind,
> And for thy Satyr-subject chuse Mankind.[6]

Time and the valiant heeling of the Tory leaders shortly helped the more indecisive to solve their problem. It was something of a choice by necessity: as playwrights, with the productive part of their audience drawn almost exclusively from the court, only the boldest of them or the most threadbare, such as Shadwell and Settle, could afford to hazard fortune with the new party. Consequently there came into being, at length, the ill-assorted but brilliant alliance of Dryden, Behn, Durfey, and Otway, all serving under the Tory standard. The Whig writers looked askance: "You brag of your Poets and Orators, and that all the witt lies on your side; be it so, we will not strive with you about it, we pretend to honesty and justice, that shall make amends for our ill Language and Verses."[7] There followed from both camps threats of imminent destruction and the confused tumult of armament.

You've seen how two domestick Curs will grin,
Yet fearing with each other to ingage,
Will throw old *Challenges* about in din
And stifle the revengeful heat in rage. . . .

Thus act the two *Disturbers* of the Reign,
The whining *Whig*, and *Tory* of the Town,
Each dread the *Bugbear* jealousies, they feign
And skirmish with the *Windmil* of their crown.

Republick *Whig*, whose true *Protesting Arm*
With so much art a Thunderbolt can fling,
As unto *Majesty* can ne're do harm,
Yet will dissolve a *Charles,* and save a *King*. . . .

His right hand grasps the Sword of *Reformation,*
His left a large *Geneva Bible* sways,
Whose awful *Bosses* threaten *Desolation,*
And *Date* to the Gigantick *Tory's* days.

Here his Device, 'tis first triumphing *Death,*
A *Priest* of his Formalities disrob'd,
A panting *Prelate* gasping for new Breath,
A broken *Crucifix* and shatter'd *Globe,*

Arm'd thus he boldly marcheth out, and sees
His Bravery applauded by the Croud,
Whilst *Herald*-like *Courants* and *Mercuries,*
Proclaim revengeful Challenges aloud.

Alarm'd at this the sprightly Tory flies
   With Martial expedition to the Fight,
Hurling hot Flakes of Passion from his eyes,
   As just resentment of his injur'd right.

Splendid as the Morn he doth advance,
   Each Play commits a Flourish to his care,
Whilst scraps of *History* tagg'd with *Romance*,
   Like *Pantaloons* doth dangle here and there.

And now the noysie skirmish doth begin
   Each at a distance dare maintain the Fight,
And arm'd with their *offensive Scribles* grin
   Yet have no true *Iambick teeth* to bite.[8]

To the outward eye, the state of drama had grown intolerable. The audiences were entirely lost in plot and counterplot, as if they were not already the maddest ever given to playwrights,

And every Fop's a Politician grown.[9]

An episode characteristic of the time reveals the lengths to which they were driven. The great Duchess of Portsmouth, one of the most devoted habituées of the theater, was deeply embroiled in the politics of the court party. Never unduly popular, she now became a storm center, and the visits to the theater of "the *French* whore," as Nelly distinguished her, were fraught with consequences.

On Munday night last [we are informed by a contemporary newspaper], happened a great disorder in the Duke's Play-house, some Gentlemen in their Cupps entring into the Pitt, flinging Links at the Actors and using several reproachfull speaches against the Dutchess of P. and other persons of Honour, which has occasioned a Prohibition from farther Acting, till his Majesties farther pleasure.

The "Gentlemen in their Cupps," went thence to Leicester-fields and made a sermon against popery and arbitrary government to the multitude, then set on the "Rabble to assault the Fortress of a certain Lady of Pleasure then residing in those Fields; which they attaqued with so much zeal, that in a little time all her Glass windows were beaten inn."[10]

London was in tumult, and the rewards of the playwrights, if possible, more uncertain than ever. The routine of the fop had been upset, his daily ritual of attendance at the theater discomposed by alley engagements and loud talk at the coffeehouses. It was after a long and disconsolate reckoning of empty benches that Aphra Behn reiterated what was substance of innumerable prologues of these particular years:

> The devil take this cursed plotting Age,
> 'T has ruin'd all our Plots upon the Stage;
> Suspicions, New Elections, Jealousies,
> Fresh Informations, New discoveries,
> Do so employ the busie fearful Town,
> Our honest calling here is useless grown.[11]

It was incumbent upon the playwrights to fall into step or else to pass from the picture. Elkanah Settle was one of the earliest to make use of political material, in his *Pope Joan* of July, 1679. But Otway and Lee followed closely. The *Caius Marius* of the former was acted, according to the evidence of the prologue, during the illness of Charles in September, 1679. But it had been long in gestation:

> For know, our Poet, when this Play was made,
> Had nought but Drums and Trumpets in his Head,
> H'had banish'd Poetry and all her Charms,
> And needs the Fool would be a Man at Arms.[12]

Since laying aside the sword, Otway had found time sufficient for a thorough overhauling of his tragedy in the light of the new politics.

Caius Marius was an adaptation; and the play of all plays that he had chosen to adapt to the terror of the Popish Plot was Shakespeare's *Romeo and Juliet*. Otway had discovered a parallel latent between Montague and Capulet and Whig and Tory. But since Montague and Capulet were not so formidable as Marius and Sulla, nor so expressive of the terror, with one bold stroke he shifted his entire plot back to the early Roman republic. Old Capulet, Romeo, County Paris, Mercutio, all adopted Roman dress if not Roman characteristics, and thus they dropped the more easily into Whig and Tory politics,—which were felt somehow by the Restoration to be inherently classic in design.

It is doubtful whether as yet Otway perceived his position in the great controversies. At first to the public in general those controversies appear to have been religious rather than political, if that division may be made. Shaftesbury still flourished within the king's council as the champion of Protestantism, now in, now out, like Marius, but in any event a man feared or blessed everywhere as the champion of religious freedom. His opposition to the royal prerogative, the old political basis of heroic drama, was not at this time uppermost, his support of Monmouth not quite clear in its implications, and his radicalism not yet suggestive to the court mind of massacres as bloody as those of Oates' imagining. To have presented a facsimile of him, therefore, in the person of the elder Marius would have been farsighted and daring beyond example. Yet such has been the suggestion: that Otway antedated his portraits in Antonio and Renault by this earlier one. Some fraction of the fury of Marius is suggested in four lines. If not applicable to Shaftesbury, they do at least show the hysteria regarding the whole situation that possessed the English people. Marius says,

> Whom-e're I smile on let thy Sword go through,
> Oh! can the Matrons and the Virgins Cries,
> The Screams of dying Infants, and the Groans
> Of murther'd men be Musick to appease me?[13]

Indeed a frontal attack, such as this, upon Shaftesbury was out of the question. His position in respect to the underlings of Dorset Garden was not understood. It was a time when fears of a Jesuit and French massacre were universal, save only in those quarters closest to Charles himself, and Charles could ill afford to tell all that he knew. Shaftesbury, on the other hand, was able honestly to assume the pose of patriot, and he was so considered by many who ultimately were to be his enemies. *Caius Marius*, then, may be termed the staging of a general situation, rather than any display of personal bias. At the time Otway was neither violently Whig nor Tory.

Almost at the moment of Otway's feeler toward politics, about September, 1679, Lee produced his *Caesar Borgia*.

When an Universal Consternation spreads through the Kingdom [said he in his dedication], and the peace which every man enjoys, becomes dreadful to him; when mens minds in this dead calm of State are as busie, as 'tis fear'd, the hands of some wou'd be in the Tempest of a Battel, to see a Poet plotting in his Chamber quite another way, painting fast as vigorous Fancy can inspire him, drawing the past World, the present, and to come, in a narrow space, is an Image not unworthy of a grave man's Contemplation.[14]

It is to be feared that Lee was not so far above the storm as his words might imply. In the same epistle to Pembroke he added that "ev'ry daring Poet that comes forth, must expect to be like the *Almanack* Hero, all over wounds. For my own part I have been so harshly handl'd by some of 'em, that my courage quite fail'd me." His epilogue also indicates that the hot-heads had discovered political implications in his plot:

> Well, then You be his Judges; what pretence
> Made them roar out, this Play would give offence?
> Had he the Pope's Effigies meant to burn,
> And kept for sport his Ashes in an Urn,
> To try if Reliques would perform at home
> But half those Miracles they do at *Rome*,
> More could not have been said, nor more been done,
> To damn this Play about the Court and Town.

From evidence at hand we know that the complaints came to the attention of the Lord Chamberlain. The author of *Rome's Follies; or, The Amorous Fryars,* a Whiggish play acted privately during the first month of 1682, expressed strong doubts concerning his own play with a comparison to Lee's: "the subject being not a little Satyrical against the Romanists, would very much hinder its taking, and would be far more difficult to get play'd than *Caesar Borgia* was." Lee resembled Dryden in not having quite deciphered the trend of events. Just as the laureate, in his *Spanish Friar,* had joined the hue and cry after the Jesuits, Lee somewhat earlier heavily stocked his play with dissolute cardinals and papal massacres. It was at a time when Charles was not anxious to expose his hand, but when nevertheless Lee's vision of a Catholic Paradise of Fools could hardly prove palatable:

> And look how the ball'd *Fryers* in Russet-gowns
> Croak like old Vultures, how the flutt'ring *Jesuits*,
> In black and white, chatter about the Heav'ns!
> *Capuchins, Monks*, with the whole Tribe of Knaves!
> Then let me burst my spleen! Look how the Tassels,
> Caps, Hats and Cardinals Coats, and Cowls and Hoods
> Are tost about—the sport, the sport of winds—
> Indulgences, Dispences, Pardons, Bulls, see yonder!

Priest, they fly—they're whirl'd aloft. They fly,
They fly o're the backside o' th' world,
Into a Limbo large, and broad, since call'd the Paradise
Of Fools.[15]

By what Lee had to say, not only here but in the papal murders and in his ultra-violent epilogue, we may judge how slight was the organization that held together the court party. It had not yet received the cue from Charles to pass over the so-called Popish Plot with as little emphasis as might be, nor had the forces yet rallied to the succession of Catholic James.

For the rest, this political tragedy was a *mélange* of atrocity culled by the playwright from Guicciardini and from Dacres' translation of Machiavelli, and then concocted after an Elizabethan recipe.[16] Machiavelli again assumed the mask of Iago, moving far from the world of French romance. The play itself was altogether Jacobean in its joy of poisoned gloves and sudden strangulation. Above all it was nicely tuned to the scale of pulpit outcry. It was upon such nocturnal fears of Rome that Lee had been nurtured. He was to be a Tory by policy, but he was a Whig by blood. Even in his saner years, his family tradition was all in favor of these fanatical paroxysms.

At this point, we may glance ahead to observe once more his father, Richard Lee, as he crossed the stage melodramatically before his final curtain. Political differences were beginning to clarify toward the end of 1679. It is to be recalled that Shaftesbury, in his search for a Protestant candidate to dispute the succession of the Catholic Duke of York, had fixed upon James, Duke of Monmouth, an illegitimate son of Charles by Lucy Walters, and that the pretensions of the latter so flourished during 1680 with the city party as to force Charles to move his unruly parliament down to Oxford, out of range of the London mob. The angry Whigs forthwith prepared to press Monmouth's claims by any or the most extraordinary means. At this juncture it was that Richard Lee appeared upon the scene with a stroke rivaling the maddest conceptions of his son. It was launched in a broadside under an imposing title: "A True and Perfect Relation of Elizabeth Freeman of *Bishops-Hatfield* in the County of Hertford, Of a Strange and Wonderful Apparition Which Appeared to Her several times and Commanded Her to declare A Message to his Most Sacred Majesty. January 27.1680[/1]."[17] The story ran as follows:

That on *Monday* Night, being January 24. she sitting by her Mothers Fire-side between Five and Six of the Clock in the Evening, with a Child in her Lap, she heard a Voice behind her, which mildly said, Sweet-heart: Whereupon she turning her Face back, saw an Appearance of a Woman, as she conceived, all in White, covered with a white Vail, so that she saw no Face, but a very white Hand was laid on the back of her Chair, and said to her, *The 15th day of May it is appointed for the ROYAL BLOOD to be Poisoned: and further said, Be not afraid, for I am sent to tell thee: and so vanished.*

The next night the appearance was more glorious and the command harsher. *"Tell King* Charles *from me, and bid him not remove his Parliament* [i.e., from London to Oxford] *and stand by his Council."* The third night she commanded simply, "Do your message," and was recognized forthwith as the mother of Monmouth. This so terrified the maid of Hatfield that she rushed to her rector. The Rev. Richard Lee was learned in politics and apparitions, also the law. He drew in Sir Joseph Jorden, a justice of peace and earnest Whig, and with him attested the truth of all that was related. The king's chaplain, or someone else near to royalty, communicated the message to Charles, causing perhaps some ribaldry, but nothing more, for Charles and his court packed shortly off to Oxford and tarried there some weeks in great prosperity. On the other hand, the Whig and Tory press continued agog for some time with the maid of Hatfield. It was the last appearance upon the political scene of Richard Lee,[18] coming at the moment when his melodramatic son prepared to stride down front. A short while thereafter the younger Lee was engaged with Dryden in composing altogether the most sensational play of this period of political tumult.

The efforts through 1680 to impeach the Duke of York did most to crystallize opinion, for now interest in the succession tended to overshadow that of the Popish Plot. Stricter party lines were formed, and one of our poets, at least, discovered more definitely where lay his allegiance. It has been said of Otway that the great burst of composition which came from him around 1680 was because of some change in his private affairs: repentant Rochester was no more, and Mrs. Barry once again within range of his hopes. Unhappily for this theory, every bit of poetry associated with this prolific period came at least three months prior to the death of the noble convert. Nor as yet had Barry discovered any sign of a change of heart. It was rather that the poet had obviously resolved to forget the past and to devote himself whole-heartedly to the business of gaining a livelihood. Politics acted as the spur. Genuinely loyal by instinct and heritage to an order perhaps not deserving of such loyalty, he now bent himself to the production of a number of powerful political plays and poems.

Of these the first considerable piece was *The Poet's Complaint of his Muse; or, A Satyr against Libells,* in small compass a complete revelation of the temper of Thomas Otway and of the Tory party. The poem divides into two distinct parts: the autobiographical first, and those passages dealing with the dragon Libel and the exiled James added almost as an afterthought. It had appeared opportunely after the discovery of the Meal Tub Plot, when there had suddenly arisen a new plot madness. The whole history of this year, with its charges and countercharges remains in confusion. In October, 1679, a sham Protestant Plot in answer to the more celebrated Popish Plot was suddenly fathered upon Shaftesbury and Monmouth by a new perjurer, Dangerfield. His accusations included a projected attempt upon the life of the King himself and ultimate seizure of the government, and because of their basis of half truth they were attended by tremendous outcry. It was in nowise comparable, however, to the excitement that followed the recoil of the charges upon their Catholic sponsors, through the treachery of Dangerfield, and the discovery, at the bottom of Mrs. Cellier's meal tub, of evidence incriminating them in a plot to murder Shaftesbury and discredit the Whigs. Thus a few hotheads in their midst had sought to emulate the success of Titus Oates with disastrous results. Out of the welter one thing emerges clearly. Libel under this fresh impulse had grown to the proportions it assumed during the French Revolution. The understrappers, Ferguson, Shadwell, and Settle, were in full cry after Tory reputations, and the Tory scribblers had at length been stirred to reprisals.

The Poet's Complaint was perhaps the most famous of these reprisals,[19] at least before *Absalom and Achitophel* had dulled it by contrast. Though now it seems sadly deficient both in point and proportion, in 1680 party factiousness caused it to be hailed as a masterpiece. The leaders of the opposition were passed in review: First, Shaftesbury himself—

A Wight, of whom Fame's Trumpet much does sound—
Shaftesbury, the friend of the whorish GOOD OLD CAUSE,

> By his contrivance to her did resort
> All who had been disgusted at the Court.
>> Those whose Ambition had been crost,
> Or by ill manners had Preferments lost.

He had

> Promis'd strange *Liberties,* and sure Redress
> Of never-felt, unheard-of *Grievances:*
> Pamper'd their Follies, and indulg'd their Hopes.
> With *May-day* Routs, *November* Squibs, and burning *Paste-board*
> *Popes.*[20]

Thenceforward the poem descended through the ranks even to Settle and Shadwell, concluding at last with an interminable panegyric to James, Duke of York, and his heroic-unheroic naval victories over the Dutch.

Some two years later a review of the poem issued from the truculent muse of Thomas Shadwell. It is without value as literary criticism, but it does reveal the wide rift that had opened between the two former friends. Said Shadwell:

> Sure thou wast drunk, when in Pindarick strain,
> 'Gainst *Libels* didst thy dull Muse complain:
> But why didst term it *Satyr? Satyr* tart
> And piercing Verse, that wounds unto the heart;
> But thou got dully drunk ore a Pint Pot,
> Forget'st thy Subject like a drunken Sot,
> And 'stead of *Satyr* didst unto the praise
> Of those that beat the *Dutch* a Poem raise;
> The drowsy, heavy *Hollander* as well
> May chant his Poems, and his Fortunes tell,
> Their Fleet as good, their men as strong as ours,
> The difference lies but in the Governors,
> Theirs only win by Guns, by Ships, by might,
> Ours grew Politicians in the fight. . . .
> Kind hearted *Ot—y,* that does Garlands give
> To beaten Seamen, while thyself dost greive
> Languish and Pine and no man will allow
> Nought; but wreath of Hemp t'adorn thy brow. . . .[21]

The savage last reward here suggested was hardly less liberal than actual fortune. Time had removed most of Otway's earlier patrons; now, in his quest of one still unspoiled to whom he might dedicate his *Poet's Complaint,* he had discovered Thomas, Earl of

Ossory, heir to the great Duke of Ormond. Ossory he hardly knew at all, and his address to him was in that tone of proud humility that so ill fitted him for the business of dedication. He began with an apology: "Though never any man had more need of excuse for a presumption of this nature than I have now; yet, when I have laid out every way to find one, your Lordships goodness must be my best refuge; and therefore I humbly cast this at your feet for protection; and myself for pardon." The pardon he may have received; the protection is dubious. The evil star of Otway was still so much in the ascendancy that the early months of 1680 saw not only the death of Plymouth, his patron of soldiering days, but also of this latter earl. However, some reward in due course may have come to him. Only a few months after the death of Ossory, the playwright drew a full-length portrait of the young earl's father.[22] It was in the person of one of Otway's noblest characters, the aged and loyal Acasto of *The Orphan,* in all probability inserted into the play out of gratitude for favors recently bestowed.

Before proceeding farther, we may consider *The Orphan* for a moment as a political play, for into the comparative quiet of its domestic tragedy, occasionally penetrated the uproar of the outer world. It is Acasto who gives utterance to its political philosophy. Like Ormond the victim of endless wrongs and in retirement that he may escape the chicanery of the court, this loyalist nevertheless finds it in his heart to speak well of his king:

> He is so good, praise cannot speak his worth;
> So merciful, sure he ne're slept in wrath;
> So just, that were he but a private man,
> He could not do a wrong.[23]

Acasto's is the devout absolutism of Otway's earlier characters, a throwback to heroic drama. But its immediate expression was otherwise motivated. The splendid isolation of Ormond was entirely admirable to the young poet, whose world was out of joint when it cast him into the rôle of politician. Thus Otway's own voice is not infrequently heard through the speech of his character:

> Avoid the politick, the factious Fool,
> The busie, buzzing, talking, hardn'd Knave;
> The quaint, smooth Rogue, that sins against his Reason;
> Calls sawcy loud Suspicion, publick Zeal,
> And Mutiny the Dictates of his spirit.[24]

Obviously *The Orphan* is no political play, even though these Tory outbursts are not infrequent. Indeed the prologue contains a renunciation of politics as they were currently practiced:

> He ne're with Libel treated yet the Town,
> The names of Honest men bedawb'd and shown,
> Nay, never once lampoon'd the harmless life
> Of Suburb Virgin, or of City Wife.

And with a conciliatory gesture toward the critics of the pit, Otway seems in this tragedy to have determined to hazard his reputation solely upon theatrical values. As we shall see, the effort was rewarded with immense success, almost in spite of the times.

Nathaniel Lee's second political venture followed in December, 1680. But *Lucius Junius Brutus* was still tarred by Lee's congenital Whiggishness; and, according to Gildon, it was, therefore, "forbid after the third days acting by my Lord Chamberlain *Arlington,* as an Antimonarchical Play, and wrote when the Nation was in a Ferment of *Whig* and *Tory,* as a Compliment to the Former."[25] Bowman informed Oldys that its life was six performances,[26] a supposition hardly plausible, it would seem, under the circumstances, but nevertheless accurately verified by the *Term Catalogue.*[27] At any event, the play was banned by an order of December 11, directed to the Duke's Playhouse: "Whereas I am informed that there is Acted by you a Play called Lucius Junius Brutus . . . wherein are very Scandalous Expressions & Reflections upon yᵉ Government these are to require you Not to Act yᵉ said Play again."[28]

Though never perhaps so arrant a Whig as his father,[29] Lee in his *Brutus* had allowed himself to be ridden by obsessions. There appears to be a reference, in the conjuration of the enemies of Rome, to the supposed pact entered into by the Jesuits, the French, and the Irish. The play, too, was dedicated to the mildly Whiggish Buckhurst, who now was maturing into a gentleman of affairs. If certain Tory sympathies were to be discovered in the burlesque by Nokes and Jevon upon the many-headed monster of Aldersgate, they were more than offset by utterances which tended to bring into disrespect the doctrine of divine right. Most to the Whiggish point was the speech of the hero:

> Laws, Rules, and Bounds, prescrib'd for raging Kings,
> Like Banks and Bulwarks for the Mother Seas,

> Tho 'tis impossible they shou'd prevent
> A thousand dayly wracks and nightly ruins,
> Yet help to break those rowling inundations,
> Which else would overflow and drown the World.[30]

This, in all likelihood, was the speech which was responsible for the banning of the play.

From his earliest years, Lee had been ridden by a hobby. *Nero* had openly reflected upon kingly libertinism, but the remarks had apparently been judged of too slight consequence to warrant a rebuke. By the time of *Theodosius,* when political conditions had become more involved, Charles may have discovered that his young liegeman was inclined to take the bit and run away with it. The play abounded in much rhetoric, concerning the power of women in kingly courts, that was only too applicable to the Whitehall of 1680. Pulcheria, of the tragedy, was more the ruler than her soft, inglorious, yet kindly brother, who "for his Mistress had vow'd to leave the World." The same Theodosius had been challenged to cast aside his Persian effeminacy and to lead his hosts against the gathering foes, advice perhaps unseasonable to the ears of King Charles. On the other hand, it might have been taken as more of the recognized coinage of heroic romance and drama, wherein Love conquered all.[31] And the poet, in that "woman's play," had been happy enough to cultivate by a dedication the good will of the Duchess of Richmond (*La belle Stewart*), a favorite of Charles in spite of her resistance to his heroic love. Her extraordinary fondness "for Heroic Poetry was not the least Argument to show the Greatness of her mind, and fulness of Perfection." At this juncture, Charles may be pictured as smiling amiably upon the lady, and then turning to observe the conflict between his foolish brother and the Earl of Shaftesbury. There the matter might have rested, had not Lee inherited from his sire an unquenchable urge to correction. The sermon to the king reëchoed throughout *Lucius Junius Brutus* of December, the same year. Line after line was only too apropos, both to the Popish Plot and to court conditions. Thus Brutus, from his disguise of madness, uttered this sweeping rebuke:

> What, for a King's Son to love another man's Wife!
> Why, Sir, I've known a King has done the same.[32]

And Teraminta, the heroine of the piece, by her whole course of action was one continuous preachment:

> No, my dear Lord, my honor'd God-like Husband,
> I am your Wife, and one that seeks your Honor:
> By Heaven I would have sworn you thus my self.
> What, on the shock of Empire, on the turn
> Of State, and universal change of things,
> To lye at home and languish for a Woman!
> No, *Titus*, he that makes himself thus vile,
> Let him not dare pretend to ought that's Princely;
> But be, as all the Warlike World shall judge him
> The Droll of th' People and the scorn of Kings.[33]

In the pride of composition, Lee appears to have surveyed his play and to have found it profoundly philosophical, supremely truthful. As he remarked:

> He loos'd the Muse that wing'd his free-born Mind.[34]

And in his dedication he proceeded with some further comment: "I arm'd and resolv'd not to be stirr'd with the little Exceptions of a sparkish Generation that have an Antipathy to Thought." His play, quite aside from its freedom of speech, did have more quotable lines than almost any of the period, including some by Dryden. Nevertheless thought was little esteemed by a court to whom it generally implied either an unbecoming seriousness or else open rebellion. Crowne had ventured to think and had been written down a bore; and now Lee, beside being overmuch concerned with duty, had imposed upon his play a too liberal study of the complicated philosophies of Lear and Hamlet. Whereupon, Charles, with a kingly abhorrence of sermons, let the snuffer descend upon our young poet. Nor was Lee suffered to issue from eclipse until such time as his doctrines had been subject to a thorough overhauling. Royalty itself could hardly take exception to his next efforts.

Chapter XI

"SHAKESPEARE AND OTWAY"

Dread o'er the scene the ghost of Hamlet stalks,
Othello rages, poor Monimia mourns;
And Belvidera pours her soul in love.

THOMSON, *The Seasons*[1]

To treat either Lee's *Lucius Junius Brutus* or the *Caius Marius* of Otway solely as a political play would be a distortion of all dramatic values. To neglect that aspect would be to sin equally against the notable contributions made by politics to the evolution of heroic and sentimental tragedy. In these two plays, however much we may dislike the perversion of Shakespeare in the latter, the drama of the Restoration was upon the verge of greatness,—touched by a vitality missing as long as it dwelt in the twilight of French romance. And now, as though to accelerate the revival, the dramatists of 1680, led by Otway, were rediscovering the undrained sources of inspiration that lay in Shakespeare. That which had fitfully appeared in such plays as *All for Love* now became a well-defined movement. There was nothing abject, however, in the new worship; Dryden and Rymer could criticize the Elizabethan as well as they could praise. This was an age, in its leaders at least, given to sharp judgment within its own peculiar standards.

It was no great shock, therefore, to the sensibilities of 1679 when Otway decided to accommodate to current theatrical practice the tragedy of *Romeo and Juliet*. After Otway's version had appeared, the calm conviction obtained for over half a century of its vast superiority; and *Romeo and Juliet* in its untampered form dropped from the stage until 1744.[2]

At this point in our study, when the two playwrights are discovered in forced collaboration, it may be well to consider the relationship between them. "Shakespeare and Otway"—the names were to be inseparably linked together by the critics of the ensuing century.[3] What similarity, if any, is there between them? Is there the slightest justice in the hyperbole, or was it a complete misdirection of the critical faculties, that bestowed upon Otway such pride of position?

Otway himself recognized in Shakespeare much that was eternal. To that part he rendered homage and acknowledged his debt. His was tribute the more uncalled for, inasmuch as few persons of that time were able to discriminate between the lines of Shakespeare and those of Otway; and, even if they had been, the quiet adoption of another's poetical offspring was then held to be as normal as the bearing of one's own. It is in the misapprehension of these facts that so many of our modern critics have erred: Roden Noel, for instance, who dismissed *Caius Marius* with the comment that it was a "barefaced, and indeed avowed plagiarism . . . though one or two scenes are his own, and have some merit."[4] Dr. Johnson was more temperate when he noted simply without comment that much of the play was borrowed from Shakespeare.[5] His was the common attitude before Shakespeare had been apotheosized. The poet, it would seem, made in his prologue an acknowledgment that was honest beyond example. We may glance at it as the apologia of a lesser artist, face to face with the calm superiority of a greater:

> Our *Shakespear* wrote too in an Age as blest,
> The happiest Poet of his time and best;
> A gracious Prince's Favor chear'd his Muse,
> A constant Favour he ne'r fear'd to lose.
> Therefore he wrote with Fancy unconfin'd,
> And thoughts that were Immortal as his Mind.
> And from the Crop of his luxuriant Pen
> E're since succeeding Poets humbly glean.
> Though much the most unworthy of the Throng,
> Our this-day's Poet fears h' has done him wrong.
> Like greedy Beggars that steal Sheaves away,
> You'll find h' has rifled him of half a Play,
> Amidst this baser Dross you'll see it shine
> Most beautifull, amazing, and Divine.
> To such low Shifts of late are Poets worn
> Whilst we both Wit's and *Caesar*'s Absence mourn,
> Oh! when will He and Poetry return?

Whether in our eyes the apology excuses the crime is immaterial. We should rather examine the exact nature of his deed of violence, and his practice of the now scorned art of adaptation.

First as to the story. We find in Otway's version that a number of the more powerful enemies of the elder Marius, among them Metellus, have resolved to forestall his seventh election to the consulate by putting up Sulla, and that in reprisal Marius has denounced all the Metelli, even including the fair Lavinia (Juliet), the beloved of his son Marius Junior (Romeo). At this the tribune Sulpitius (Mercutio) admonishes the young lover to renounce his infatuation and gird himself against the approaching enemy. In the second act Sulla is revealed as a glorified County Paris, whose love is unacceptable to Lavinia. Her father, Metellus, proves as obdurate as old Capulet, and she seeks sympathy from her nurse, a most redoubtable Restoration bawd. Young Marius leaps the garden wall, woos, and wins. Meanwhile Metellus orates in the forum, after the design of Shakespeare's Roman plays, and wins the suffrage of the mob. A sudden reversal, however, brings him to flight and terror, and thus abruptly we are in the midst of the Popish Plot. By this time the rites of young Marius and Lavinia have been solemnized. Nurse Nokes has enacted his famous scene with Sulpitius, so beloved of the Restoration audience. And, after the bridegroom has published his marriage, there are threats, forgiveness, and the vaunting heroism of 1670. The complications that follow are entirely outside Shakespeare: Lavinia resolves upon flight to her husband, in order to escape marriage to Sulla; Marius Senior flees across the *campagna* to escape his foes; she and he are both near capture—hairbreadth escapes, infinite heroism, amazing nobility. Then, once more upon familiar ground, we have the episode of the potion. Lavinia awakens just as Marius Junior in desperation drinks the last dregs of his poison, and the two sink to death to the accompaniment of much Otwavian elegy. Marius Senior recognizes finally that his guardian genius has departed, and he forswears his course of destruction. The play ends with the death of Sulpitius. Apparently the Restoration playwright was not so fearful as the Elizabethan that unless he killed Mercutio, Mercutio would kill the play.[6]

Even the most cursory examination of *Caius Marius* should reveal that Otway was responsible for the major portion of it; yet criticism has been hesitant in granting him even that half to which he himself laid claim. It is only just, therefore, to make a quick audit upon this account. The play was composed as a tragedy of love with Tory inclinations. But no matter which part came first in point of composition, the final effect leaves the love of Marius Junior and Lavinia almost in the position of a subplot. From the original play of *Romeo and Juliet*, Otway carried over

many speeches without alteration; others quite as often he changed
violently in order to develop un-Shakespearean aspects of love,
tragedy, or comedy. Finally, when all the lines are assembled
which at the utmost stretch may be traced to Shakespeare, there
are found approximately 750 against the 2,100 that were original.
The proportion of scenes is about the same, and not the weak
minority assigned to Otway by Noel. The play contains, then, an
important residuum of Otway's own composition, that through
prejudice has been largely neglected by critical commentary.

For his Roman plot, Otway followed Shakespearean precedent
in turning straightway to Plutarch.[7] This common source, and
much study on Otway's side of Shakespeare's *Julius Caesar* frequently lends to this portion of his play a strongly reminiscent
sound. The voice of Shakespeare, sometimes of his specific characters, lingers as an overtone, even when the voice of Otway is
most evident. Thus on occasion we discover the accent and personality of Cassius:

> O *Romans,* he's the Thorn that galls us all.
> Our harass'd State is crippled with the weight
> Of his Ambition: We're not safe in *Marius*
> Do I not know his Rise, his low Beginning,
> From what a wretched despicable Root
> His Greatness grew? Gods! that a Peasant's Brat
> Born in the utmost Cottages of *Arpos,*
> And foster'd in a Corner, should by Bribes,
> By Covetousness and all the hatefull means
> Of working Pride, advance his little Fate
> So high, to vaunt it o're the Lords of *Rome!*[8]

The two influences of Shakespeare and Plutarch throughout this
play were in endless collaboration. But it is a relation so complicated as to require a special chart to show the various contributions, and, even then, no chart can demonstrate what drafts
were brought from other plays than *Romeo and Juliet,* the endless
shift of speeches from scene to scene and character to character,
or those added in the Shakespearean plot that were entirely of the
Roman. It is all an ingenious cross-word puzzle.

The omissions from *Romeo and Juliet* so far have been entirely
neglected, yet they are equally important as negative evidence
upon a whole state of mind and a theory of the drama. It is first
to be observed that the punning wit of the Montague and Capulet

servants, along with that of Peter and Mercutio, went generally
into the discard, probably less because it was inappropriate than
abstruse and tiresome. Prince Escalus and Tybalt departed as unnecessary to the plot. The speeches of Lady Capulet, when at all
to the point, were bestowed upon her lord, and she dropped by the
way. County Paris was lost entirely in Roman Sulla; and the loss,
so far as Dorset Garden was concerned, was more than compensated
by the heroism of the latter. In each of these changes we witness the
student of classic French drama striving toward greater simplicity.
Elsewhere, the importance of mere chance was diminished by an age
that plumed itself upon its rationality. Hence the major theme of the
two "star crossed lovers" was allowed to lapse. By the same compul-
sion departed the airy grace of the palmer scene. As Shakespeare
had written it, it would have been out of place; it was seas apart
from the sex fencing of Mirabel and Millamant. Likewise, the age
found the puppy love of Romeo for Rosaline unacceptable. To
laugh at love in serious drama was *lèse majesté;* to show young
Marius unfaithful to love in the first act would have been to challenge damnation from all the ladies of pit and balcony. Nor would
the Friar's counsel of moderation have been much more to their
fancy. Thought was not esteemed. His function, therefore, became
twofold: to administer the potion and to die. These were all omissions calculated to speed the plot or to adapt it to the tastes of the
time. There remained, if Otway had not chosen to tamper further
with the lines, a residue of poetry and passion that was the glory
of *Romeo and Juliet.* That the greatness of the play remained
therein Otway seems to have perceived. Though it did not matter
to him or to his audience if he lowered immeasurably the philo-
sophic content, so long as he was able to supply what passed as a
vision of true heroic love.

Throughout, an increasing emphasis devolved upon Mercutio
and the Nurse. By evidence of the prologue, Underhill achieved
immense popularity in the former rôle; while, in the latter, Nokes
established for himself a niche in the history of English acting.[9]
He was the supreme actor of the Jolly Jumbles, the Aldos, the
assorted pimps and panders of contemporary humor, and the part
was ready made for him. It must be said that the Nurse, even before Otway debased her, had in her make-up something of the
bawd. For Nokes the lines were drawn more heavily, and a characteristic garrulity was added, more Restoration than Elizabethan:

'Ods my Life, this Dad of ours was an arrant Wag in his young Days for all this. Well, and what then? *Marius* is a Man, and so's *Sylla*. Oh! but *Marius*'s Lip! and then *Sylla*'s Nose and Forehead! But then *Marius*'s Eye agen, how 'twill sparkle, and twinckle, and rowl, and fleer? But to see *Sylla* a horse back! But to see *Marius* walk or dance! such a leg, such a Foot, such a Shape, such a Motion. Ah-h-h—Well, *Marius* is the man, must be the man, and shall be the Man.[10]

Strangely enough, in Sulpitius—the Latin derivative of Mercutio—there appeared a startling addition of decency, either to befit his Roman toga or to eliminate innuendo too elusive for an age used to its bawdry in strong, undiluted portions. A greater loss from Mercutio was his faculty of begetting poetry of "nothing but vain fantasy." The caprice of Mab's coach and coachman now dissolved away as something too wanton,—her queenship becoming the instrument of blunt satire against mooning lovers and the subject of incredible enfeeblement both of verse and thought:

> Oh! the small Queen of Fairies
> Is busy in his Brains; the *Mab* that comes
> Drawn by a little Team of smallest Atoms
> Over mens Noses as they lie asleep,
> In a Chariot of an empty Hazel-nut
> Made by a Joyner-Squirrel: in which state
> She gallops night by night through Lovers brains;
> And then how wickedly they dream, all know.[11]

Most Restoration of commentary! It was only when Otway abandoned the fruitless pursuit of Elizabethan fancy and spoke in his true voice that he became worth the reading:

> Sometimes she hurries o're a Souldier's Neck,
> And then dreams he of cutting forrein Throats;
> Of Breaches, Ambuscado's, temper'd Blades,
> Of good rich Winter-quarters, and false Musters.
> Sometimes she tweaks a Poet by the Ear,
> And then dreams he
> Of Panegyricks, flatt'ring Dedications,
> And mighty Presents from the Lord knows who,
> But wakes as empty as he laid him down.
> Sh' has bin with *Sylla* too, and he dreams now
> Of nothing but a Consulship.[12]

Thus we arrive at the subject in hand, and no witling need have noticed the momentary distraction of the fairy creature.

But more important to the general evolution of the playwright was the part taken by the hero and heroine. Romeo may be termed Shakespeare's most Otwavian hero in the sense that he is the most headlong, the most a creature of his emotions, and generally the most unintelligent. From him Otway derived Marius Junior, a hero perhaps more distressed by indecision than Romeo, but like Romeo more glorious in word than in deed. It required only slight alteration to fit him easily into the typical scheme of things. So likewise in the case of Juliet, there existed the clear suggestion for an Otwavian heroine. The latter was ever to be more dynamic than her lord, and now she carried over unchanged a "bounty boundless as the sea, a love as deep." Lavinia required the addition only of a certain pervasive sentimentality to make her blood sister to Don Carlos' Queen, Monimia, and Belvidera. The addition was ready at hand. "I come," she cried,

> To bear a part of everything that's thine,
> Be't Happiness or Sorrow. In these Woods,
> Whilst from pursuing Enemies you're safe,
> I'll range about, and find thee Fruits and Springs
> Gather cool Sedges, Daffadills and Lillies,
> And softest Camomill to make us Beds,
> Whereon my Love and I at night will sleep,
> And dream of better Fortune.[13]

In such a speech we may hear the characteristic inflection of Otway. Just as he had evolved his hero and heroine through a series of careful studies after various models, his poetical style had likewise taken the coloring of whatever poet he had studied last. Completely maladroit in his earliest effort, when experimenting with heroics, he had afterward acquired unwonted restraint when dealing with the measure of Racine. Now his verse was shot through with a new luxuriance, even though it could not approach Shakespearean depth of thought or lyric beauty. At times his tragedy moved against a natural background of the Sussex downs as lovely in its kind as that of Shakespeare's Warwickshire. But he reached farther, seeking to make his tragedy richer in allusion and verbal play. His periods attained greater fulness; his vocabulary consciously became more sonorous; and at this point, some years after Lee had made the change, he shifted to blank verse. His was more than the mere rejection of rhyme. The verse of

Alcibiades had invariably been end-stopped, and so fearful had it been of any interruption in the strict jog trot of its couplets that it had resorted to innumerable proclitics and enclitics:

> Already y'ave disarm'd *Timandra*'s charms,
> Me-thinks I see you rev'ling in her Arms!
> Let's then o' th' Wings of Love and honour fly
> To th' field, and meet th' insulting Enemy.[14]

Don Carlos first made use of substitutions, together with occasional enjambed couplets, triplets, and half lines. In this respect *Titus and Berenice* showed little progress. But now, following the precedent of Shakespeare, Otway's verse evidenced greater freedom: the caesura became fluent, substitution more frequent, and an occasional Alexandrine appeared for the sake of variety. His most notable discovery, by reason of the liberation from rhyme, was an entirely individual use of the feminine ending. If it relaxed the fiber of his verse, it gave in compensation that falling cadence so indispensable to the perfect utterance of a Monimia or a Belvidera. His apprenticeship to the couplet had failed to knit his line, and now with blank verse his inclination was in the way of a mellifluous cadence, admirably suited to his purpose, even though at times it should dissolve away to mere formlessness.

With this derivative tragedy of *Caius Marius* was completed the experimental period of Otway's career. His had been a meandering course, ranging from the heroic, through the French, finally to the full flood of the Shakespearean. Throughout, we have witnessed the unfolding of Otwavian sentiments, characters, and style, and now upon the threshold of 1680 he was at last ready to put all his experience and heart into the composition of a masterpiece, no longer troubled by the constraints of apprenticeship.

"Of this play [*The Orphan*][15] nothing new can easily be said." Such was the declaration of Dr. Johnson nearly a century and a half ago, and thereupon he set down so compact a summary of criticism as almost to defy addition. He remarked further that "it is a domestick tragedy drawn from middle life. Its whole power is upon the affections; for it is not written with much comprehension of thought or elegance of expression. But if the heart is interested, many other beauties may be wanting, yet not be missed."[16] This statement is proposed as a text to what follows, with certain additions, however, in regard to the source and to the development of Otway's genius that have not hitherto been noticed.

The plot of *The Orphan* is briefly told. It is the story of twin rivals for the love of their father's ward, Monimia. The elder, Castalio, wins her, but unhappily through conflicting emotions of love and friendship—the age-old themes of Restoration tragedy—conceals his marriage from his brother, Polydore, endeavoring at the same time to dissuade him from his unwelcome attentions to the bride. Polydore by chance overhears him making what he judges to be a guilty assignation with Monimia, and resolves to substitute himself for his more fortunate brother. This he accomplishes through the aid of his page, the dark night, and the secrecy which the situation imposes; while Castalio, enraged at the failure of Monimia to answer his signal, passes the night in railing at womankind. Finally, when in his triumph Polydore discovers the situation to Monimia, her horror and his that follows provoke him to a quarrel with Castalio in which he runs upon his brother's sword. Monimia drinks poison, unable to endure the stain upon her love and honor, while Castalio stabs himself. What a deal of trouble, added an early commentator, would have been spared by a few farthings worth of candlelight!

The plot otherwise contains a few characters of minor importance, of whom Acasto, the foster father, and Chamont, the brother of Monimia, are outstanding. But centered as it is in an easily managed triangle, *The Orphan* moves with unusual directness and intensity. As Johnson remarked: "Its whole power is upon the affections." In composing a domestic tragedy, Otway merely pressed to a logical conclusion that interest in the human heart which Racine anticipated but disguised under high-sounding titles. The same might be said of Otway's earlier tragedies. The characters of *Don Carlos* were of the highest rank, the prologue expressed a conventional interest in the historical implications, but then—in actual composition—Otway forgot all this in his preoccupation with the tragic-tender emotions of the Queen, Carlos, and Philip. *Caius Marius* divided interest between the timely issues of politics and the sentimental problems of young Marius and Lavinia. Even *The Orphan,* of all his plays obviously the truest to the domestic type, did not break abruptly from greatness of station. To Otway's audience that tradition was continued in the character of Acasto, representing the powerful Duke of Ormond. The play was more of a domestic tragedy than its predecessors, but it was not uncompromising in type. Strict bourgeois tragedy, even though influenced by Otway, was to wait until the advent of Lillo.[17]

With politics and great station as a decoy, Otway moved to the capture of all hearts, more specifically those of the "fair sex." He never deviated from the advice of Lady Squeamish to her cousin Sir Noble Clumsey: "Oh Cousin, if you undertake to write a Tragedy, take my counsel: Be sure to say soft melting tender things in it that may be moving, and make your Ladies Characters virtuous what ere you do."[18] It is doubtful whether any play of the Restoration was better constructed in this respect than *The Orphan*. The heroine is all soft and tender,—the creation of Otway more truly than even Belvidera, whose intelligence sometimes rules her heart. Castalio thus characterizes her:

> O thou art tender all!
> Gentle and kind, as sympathizing Nature!
> When a sad story has been told, I've seen
> Thy little breasts with soft Compassion swell'd,
> Shove up and down, and heave like dying birds.[19]

Castalio himself is passionate, wild, a delight to the fair, and without thought of consequence. As much a slave to passion as Monimia, he is even less capable of facing his problem intelligently. Polydore appears to be the most rational person upon the stage, with a kind of libertinism well cogitated by the beaux of the time. He is own brother to Don John, moving with purpose until the blight of the feminine point of view descends upon him also. At the play's end, after the full implications of his lawless act have been discovered to him, Polydore is as irrational as any of the others. He is filled with self-pity and the flabby emotionalism that characterizes so frequently the tragedy of Otway. The three following lines—expressive presumably of Polydore's repentance—contain a world of commentary upon the state of the Restoration theatergoing mind:

> Horrors shall fright me from those pleasing harms,
> And I'll no more be caught with Beauties Charms,
> But when I'm dying take me in thy Armes.[20]

Sentimentality could plumb no lower depths.

It is not too much to say that until *Venice Preserved* Otway produced hardly a single rational human being. Monimia, Chamont, Acasto, the two brothers have all at various times been summoned into the court of the alienist. But it is perhaps very well, at least for the state of tragedy, that these characters were not more foresighted. Had they been endowed with any degree of intelligence they would have worked out their solutions very simply. It may then be said of Otway, more than of any other tragic writer, that his drama arose from the weaknesses of his characters. His tears were for beings strong in emotion and pitifully imperfect in judgment,—children in the clutch of circumstances of their own creation yet completely out of their control. Great tragedy could never develop out of such material, nor until it contained at least one character of sufficient mentality to grapple with the situation.

"It is not written with much comprehension of thought or elegance of expression." Or, as Noel added, it is not rich in the poetry of repose and contemplation.[21] Otway impresses one as a man laboring with his thought. Though many of his verses found their way into the *Elegant Extracts* of the later eighteenth century,[22] they were the descriptive passages, the emotional bits, or the reverberations of Shakespeare. Where he does verge upon a philosophy of his own, it is in reflection of his trials as a harassed playwright. There are examples everywhere in which Otway gropes after profundity without achieving it,—as, for instance, when Polydore lets his mind rove in the mood of Hamlet:

> To live, and live a Torment to my self,
> What Dog would bear't that knew but his Condition?
> We have little knowledge, and that makes us Cowards,
> Because it cannot tell us what's to come.[23]

Or when Castalio cries in imitation of Lear:

> Ye Gods, we're taught that all your works are Justice,
> Y'are painted merciful, and Friends to innocence,
> If so, then why these plagues upon my head?[24]

Or finally when Chamont, the man of action, is beset to find out the hidden mystery of things, like Lear on his way to prison:

> Take care of good *Acasto*, whilst I go
> To search the means by which the Fates have plagu'd us.
> 'Tis thus that Heaven it's Empire does maintain
> It may Afflict, but man must not Complain.[25]

Such parallels are endless. It is the case of an unphilosophical but imaginative and sensitive poet turning repeatedly to Shakespeare for guidance through the domain of thought.

These are not great poetry, "but if the heart is interested many other beauties may be wanting, yet not be missed." Otway had brought his art to the point where it was almost unfailing in command over the emotions. Why the three words, "Ah! poor Castalio," taken by themselves could move the hardened Barry to tears is beyond conjecture, but so she insisted "more than once."[26] The explanation for the rest of the world lies of course in their context, not in any singular beauty they possess. At times, however, Otway had a moving simplicity that was its own explanation. It may be aptly demonstrated by the death speech of Monimia, wherein for the time Otway almost ceased to be derivative, and yet even here is heard the voice of Hamlet and Othello:

> When I'm laid low in the Grave, and quite forgotten,
> Maist thou be happy in a fairer Bride;
> But none can ever love thee like *Monimia*.
> When I am dead, as presently I shall be;
> (For the grim Tyrant grasps my heart already)
> Speak well of me, and if thou find ill tongues
> Too busie with my fame, don't hear me wrong'd;
> 'Twill be a noble Justice to the memory
> Of a poor wretch, once honour'd with thy Love.
> How my head swims! 'Tis very dark: Good-night.[27]

The single speech summarizes all that criticism can say of the tender qualities of Otway. His was an art heaven-sent to the greatest actress of the time, an art granted to few playwrights, and one as mysterious as it was rare. The greatest of Otway's contemporaries, Dryden, attempted to explain it, without, however, giving an altogether satisfactory answer.

To express the passions [said he], which are seated in the heart, by outward signs, is one great precept of the painters, and very difficult to perform. In poetry, the same passion and motions of the mind are to be express'd; and in this consists the principal difficulty, as well as the excellency of that art . . . not to be obtain'd by pains or study, if we are not born to it; for the motions which are studied, are never so natural as those which break out in the height of a real Passion. Mr. *Otway* possess'd this part as thoroughly as any of the Ancients or Moderns. I will not defend everything in his *Venice Preserved;* but I must bear this testimony to his memory, that the passions are truly touch'd in it, though perhaps there is somewhat to be desir'd, both in the grounds of them, and in the height and elegance of expression; but nature is there, which is the greatest beauty.[28]

Thus far we have been concerned only with the various aspects of Johnson's appraisal. Source-hunting lay largely outside his domain. It has justification, nevertheless, when it reveals the creative quality of the poet's mind; and under such terms it is proposed to examine this play. The original source of *The Orphan* was early traced by the inveterate source-hunter Langbaine to a slight novel attributed to Roger Boyle, Earl of Orrery. It is called *English Adventures,* and one of its three parts recounts *The History of Brandon.*[29] Here Otway found a tragedy almost perfectly shaped, rapid and restrained to the point of barrenness, and developing the entire situation save only the tragic *dénouement.* For the latter Otway appears to have derived suggestions, if any were needed beyond current practice, from the casual slaughter at the end of *Hamlet.* But while the alterations were fewer than in *Don Carlos,* the additions were more numerous. Chamont may have been drawn from Laertes, though he is more reminiscent of Beaugard in *The Souldiers Fortune,* a play produced at almost the same time. The criticism directed against Chamont by Voltaire, that he is an objectionable huffer,[30] is quite as applicable to Beaugard. The two seem to have represented the ideal of the poet in his military adventures. There were other additions less debatably from Shakespeare. Thus Otway turned to *Cymbeline*[31] for the scene in which Acasto attempts to dissuade his sons from a career at court. While suggested in *The History of Brandon,* it had its dramatic model in a scene wherein Belarius had employed the same line of reasoning upon the two youths, Guiderius and Arviragus, even to the point of anticipating most of Acasto's invective. And it becomes the more certain that Otway utilized this material when we discover that from *Cymbeline* he borrowed the name Polydore, which had there served as a pseudonym for Guiderius.

The clue for Monimia came indirectly from Racine's Monime, the heroine of *Mithridate.* Various French critics, arguing upon the obvious similarity of the names, have discovered in *Mithridate* the principal source of Otway's tragedy.[32] As a matter of fact the adoption of the name was probably suggested by Monime's being also an orphan with twin brothers as rivals for her love. Other than that there is no debt of material, while the *English Adventures* accounts for the plot of *The Orphan* much more satisfactorily. The direct debt was that of Otway to his young compatriot, Nat. Lee, who had taken over from Racine the name Mithridates and a few characters and out of them had compounded an original play. Otway's indebtedness to Lee was not so much in the appropriation of a name here and there as in the management of whole scenes. What he took he made his own and, in most cases, an improvement upon the original. The suggestions were mostly from the fourth act of Lee's play, wherein a father virtually ravishes the intended bride of his son. Legally no incest, morally it is as much a crime as that of Polydore, and equally subject to the torments of conscience. Otway read and reread the earlier play. The dialogue that follows between Mithridates and the ravished Semandra is very close to the one between Polydore and Monimia. The injured Ziphares may stand as the precursor of the injured Castalio. From Ziphares it was that Otway seems to have had the hint for his celebrated curse of womankind and his endless malediction after injury. Finally, were it not for the danger of pressing these resemblances too far, we might easily discover in Semandra the original of Monimia. Semandra added perhaps that futility to the character of Monimia that sets the latter apart from the rest of her sisters in tragedy. "Like a widowed turtle mourning," Semandra anticipated all the more usual qualities of this the least active of Otway's heroines.

It stands thus. Otway took the mildly tragic story of Brandon, as he found it in *English Adventures,* and shaded it, with the silent collaboration of Lee, to a profounder hue. But it was not until his own imprint was upon it that it partook of any of the characteristics of a great story. Even then, as Hazlitt demonstrated, it did not possess the finest tragic power possible. His criticism of *The Orphan* summarizes all that needs to be added to the judgment of Dr. Johnson. Speaking in his *Lectures on the Dramatic Literature of the Age of Elizabeth,* Hazlitt searched to their depths the problems of Otway's theory of drama and the working of his mind. His conclusion explains why Otway has dropped into relative obscurity, even though it was once thought fit to join his name with Shakespeare's in the superlative of compliments.

In the Orphan [said Hazlitt], there is little else but this voluptuous effeminacy of sentiment and mawkish distress, which strikes directly at the root of that mental fortitude and heroick cast of thought which alone makes tragedy endurable—that renders its suffering pathetic, or its struggles sublime. . . . Yet there are lines and passages in it of extreme tenderness and beauty; and few persons, I conceive (judging from my own experience) will read it at a certain time of life without shedding tears over it as fast as the "Arabian trees their medicinal gums." Otway always touched the reader, for he had himself a heart. We may be sure that he blotted his page often with his tears, on which so many drops have since fallen from glistening eyes, "that sacred pity had engendered there." He had susceptibility of feeling and warmth of genius: but he had not equal depth of thought or loftiness of imagination, and indulged his mere sensibility too much, yielding to the immediate expression of emotion excited in his own mind, and not placing himself enough in the minds and situations of others, or following the workings of nature sufficiently with keenness of eye and strength of will into its heights and depths, its strongholds as well as its weak sides.[33]

Chapter XII

THE DISEASE OF THOUGHT

Say anything to make me mad, and lose
This Melancholly, which will else destroy me.
LEE, *Caesar Borgia*, 1680[1]

THROUGH the years 1679 and 1680 Nat. Lee had been urged by
the same stimuli as Otway—politics and poverty—to redouble
himself to the business of play writing. He knew as well as his fellow upon how flimsy a basis his very existence rested, but unlike
Otway he outrageously flattered his audience for its good will, at
the very instant that he nullified the flattery by likening his profession to that of the "vizard mask":

> Old Writers should not for vain glory strive,
> But like old Mistresses, think how to thrive;
> Be fond of ev'ry thing their Keepers say,
> At least till they can live without a Play. . . .
> She in resistless flattery finds her ends,
> Gives thanks for Fools, and makes ye all her Friends,
> So should wise Poets sooth an awkward Age
> For they are Prostitutes upon the Stage.[2]

With such complete and deserved cynicism toward his chosen profession, Lee, by contrast, presents the amazing spectacle of a pro-
gressive elevation in the ideals of his art. At this time he was to
compose his finest tragedies. Similar environments in the case of
the two poets were operative to produce similar results. One has
the feeling of watching an experiment in biology, to such an extent
did the age of Charles II predetermine the growth of poets. Each
had a strongly marked personality, hitherto held in abeyance, and
now the moment had come most favorable to its expression.

Lee's *Theodosius* of September had been followed by his *Lucius
Junius Brutus* of December, 1680. Both plays, as we have seen,
had been influenced by the political frenzy, but they showed in
other ways a new vitality. After the criticism directed against his
earliest flights into the heroic, Lee was somehow able to modulate
his trumpeting in *Mithridates*. With the advent of *Theodosius*,
though still employing material out of French romance,[3] he was

playing an entirely different tune. In his Epistle Dedicatory there were premonitions of approaching change:

It has been observed against me [said he], that I abound in ungovern'd Fancy; but I hope the World will pardon the Sallies of Youth: Age, Despondence, and Dulness come too fast of themselves. I discommend no Man for keeping the beaten Road; but I am sure the Noble Hunters that follow the Game, must leap Hedges and Ditches sometimes, and run at all, or never come in to the fall of the Quarry. My comfort is, I cannot be so ridiculous a Creature to any Man as I am to my self: for, who should know the house so well as the Good Man at home? who when his Neighbours come to see him, still sets the best Rooms to view; and if he be not a wilful Ass, keeps the Rubbish and the Lumber in some dark Hole, where no body comes but himself, to mortifie at melancholy Hours.[4]

In his next dedication—that of *Lucius Junius Brutus,*—Lee no longer advanced the excuse of youthful ardor, but appeared with a complete critical argument for restraint. It was derived, very likely, from the great Dryden at Will's or from some other seat of metheglin and profundity. Addressing Buckhurst, he exposed these wares with the exact intonation of his master. He demonstrated the incredible preparation to be bestowed upon the plot of a Roman tragedy by any poet hardy enough to challenge antiquity:

When *Greece* or old *Rome* come in play, the Nature, Wit, and Vigour of foremost *Shakespear,* the Judgment and Force of *Johnson,* with all his borrowed Mastery from the Ancients, will scarce suffice for so terrible a Grapple. The Poet must elevate his Fancy with the mightiest Imagination, he must run back so many hundred Years, take a just Prospect of the Spirit of those Times without the least thought of ours; for if his Eye should swerve so low, his Muse will grow giddy with the Vastness of the Distance, fall at once, and for ever lose the Majesty of the first Design. He that will pretend to be a Critick of such a Work, must not have a Grain of *Cecilius,* he must be *Longin* throughout or nothing.

And so our poet was as careful as his English ancestry permitted in the just observance of the pseudoclassical unities, the decorums and decencies of classic expression, and the high seriousness. But to continue:

There must be no Dross through the whole Mass, the Furnace must be justly heated, and the Bullion stamp'd with an unerring Hand. In such a Writing there must be Greatness of Thought without Bombast,

Remoteness without Monstrousness, Virtue arm'd with Severity, not in Iron Bodies, Solid Wit without modern Affectation, Smoothness without Gloss, Speaking out without cracking the Voice or straining the Lungs.

So unaccustomed was Lee, however, to this restraint that we discover him not a little concerned over the final product. "I show'd," said he, "no passion outward, but whether through an Over-Conceit of the Work, or because perhaps there was some Merit, the Fire burnt inward, and I was troubled for my dumb Play, like a Father for his dead Child."[5] An inhibition, such as this, of all that was most natural in Lee—his fury and bombast—seems to have been fraught with the direst consequences.

The affliction that descended upon Lee in 1680 was that of thought; and its pursuit of him was furious until 1684 when it finally drove him to Bedlam. To combine thought and Restoration tragedy was questionable for anyone; for Lee it was madness. Nevertheless, he threw down his challenge: "On this I arm'd, and resolv'd not to be stirr'd with the little Exceptions of a sparkish Generation, that have an Antipathy to Thought."[6] But, as a matter of fact, is not thought more proper for the Study than the Stage? Such was the suggestion of Dryden in his Preface to *Oedipus*. Thought is an intangible thing when one goes to seek it. Frequently, in these plays of Lee, it appears as mere external decoration, instead of growing naturally from situation or character. Thus we have gratuitous rules of conduct for King Charles, or the free expression of unorthodox religious principles, or occasional bits of profundity derivative of Lear or Hamlet. One passage was drawn from the *Essays* of Francis Bacon, which the youth had perhaps discovered upon his father's bookshelves:

> Bru. But is not death a very dreadful thing?
> Tit. Not to a mind resolv'd. No, Sir, to me
>   It seems as natural as to be born:
>   Groans, and Convulsions, and discolour'd faces,
>   Friends weeping round us, blacks and obsequies,
>   Make it a dreadful thing; the Pomp of death,
>   Is far more terrible than Death itself.
>   Yes, Sir, I call the Powers of Heav'n to witness,
>   *Titus* dares dye, if so you have Decreed;
>   Nay, he shall dye with Joy, to honour *Brutus*,
>   To make your Justice famous through the World,
>   And fix the Liberty of *Rome* forever.[7]

The speech contains the secret of Lee's new approach. Hitherto one subject alone had been considered fit material for Restoration tragedy, and that, perhaps, the least proper according to classic canons. It was Crowne who remarked:

I confess since Love has got the sole possession of the Stage, Reason has had little to do there; that effeminate Prince has softned and emasculated us the Vassals of the Stage. The Reason why the Off-springs of the Moderns are such short-liv'd things, is because the Genii that beget 'em are so given to women; they court nothing but the Ladies Favours, with them they waste all their strength, whenas the lusty Ancients who fed on the wholesom Diet of good sense, and used themselves to the strong manly exercises of Reason, have been the Fathers of vigorous Issue, who have lived longer than the oldest Patriarchs, and are like to live as long as there are men. I who am a Friend both to Love and good Sense, endeavoured to reconcile 'em, and to bring Reason into favour, not with hopes to Rule; I desired only to procure him some little Office in the Stage, but I find it made an uproar, Love would not endure such an innovation, it threatned his settled Government; and Reason is not at all popular; the Ladies knew not what to make of his Conversation, and the men generally sleep at it; that I see but little hopes of his preferment; which I am sorry for, since what future being I shall enjoy, I shall owe solely to him. . . . The whinings of Love, like a pretty new Tune, please for a while, but are soon laid aside, and never thought of more; the same Notes perhaps may help to compose another, but the old Air is altered, and for ever forgotten.[8]

Years before, Corneille had set himself resolutely against the ubiquitous rule of love, and as unavailingly, judged by the results upon his own stage. He had seen that tragedy required some more dignified subject—"quelque grand intérêt d'État, ou quelque passion plus noble et plus mâle que l'amour, telles que sont l'ambition ou la vengeance, et veut donner à craindre des malheurs plus grands que la perte d'une maîtresse."[9] And many years later Dennis pronounced that the ancients were too sensible to waste their time in talking when in love.[10] It was a battle that the more sensible critics waged for years to no avail. Voltaire's criticism of the English stage stated the problem fairly:

That love might be worthy of the tragic scene, it should become the necessary knot of the play and not be brought in to fill up the vacancies of your tragedies and ours, which are, both, too long. It must be a passion truly tragic, considered as a weakness, and resisted by remorse.

Either love must be the cause of crimes and misfortunes, in order to show the danger of such a passion, or virtue must get the better of it, to prove that it is not irresistible. Otherwise it will be more properly adapted to eclogues and to comedy.[11]

Voltaire's remarks were as completely alien to the spirit of heroic and sentimental tragedy as those of Saint-Évremond, who had anticipated him in protest against this lovesick tragedy. "We imagine," he said, "we make Kings and Emperors perfect Lovers, but in truth we make ridiculous Princes of them; and by the complaints and sighs which we bestow upon them, where they ought neither to complain or sigh, we represent them weak both as they are Lovers, and as they are Princes."[12]

More completely even than Lee, Otway had up to this time made Love almost his whole subject, even in *Titus and Berenice,* where the clue from Racine had been otherwise. The most perfect apotheosis of the soft emotion, with no distracting problems of fate or patriotism, came in *The Orphan.* But it was Lee, with his true Renaissance instinct everywhere to excite admiration and with his large dependence upon the love epics of La Calprenède and the De Scudérys, who had plunged most desperately. Love, as practiced during the Restoration, was not one of the colossal virtues. Perhaps it was from the very inconsistency of theory and practice that his heroics of the passion took their Icarus flight and precipitate descent. In 1680, on the other hand, he wrote greater tragedy because he departed from the letter of the romance and dared be original in respect to Love. *Theodosius* witnessed the modest beginning. It placed large emphasis upon other emotions, to which La Calprenède had barely alluded. Thus the Princess Pulcheria displays a kind of new patriotism and is filled with a pride of state that she would have her brother emulate. And when finally she is subdued by Love, it is by blunt speech and downright honesty,—good Roman virtues struggling in the breast of the young poet. Theodosius himself is subject to a conflict of larger issues, hardly suggested in the romance, of weakness and nobility in love. He, however, dwells still upon the one theme, and hence is far less of a departure from the romantic manner than Pulcheria and her lover, Marcian. The others, Varanes and Athenais, are conventional. Nat. Lee in composing *Theodosius* was still the ladies' playwright.

In *Lucius Junius Brutus* he ventured farther. In the title rôle he

created a character with no vestige of the soft sentiment, and that
despite the fact that his original, in the *Clélie* of Mlle de Scudéry,
was possessed by an intemperate love for Lucrece.[13] Brutus as a
"whining slave" reaches the nadir of romance. Lee displayed a new
common sense in developing a conflict between parental affection
and an all-absorbing patriotism. A father sacrifices his son's life as
an example to the state. The larger issues of 1680 in English
politics had directed the poet into new channels. To Nat. Lee love
had hitherto been conventional, for so far as we may discover he
had been schooled by no actual experience in that passion. But
now the danger threatening England lent actuality to his life. The
sole love interest in the play was thwarted by the central problem
of its hero Brutus, and throughout it suffered self-effacement before the larger motives of honor and patriotism. The play gave a
new emphasis to the romance and a new tone. The true reason
that it contains less rant and more "inward fire" than *Gloriana*,
for instance, was the discovery by Nat. Lee of something at last
to warrant heroics.[14]

By various earlier references to the character of the hero, we
may judge that Lee had been pondering upon him for some little
time as a possible subject for a tragedy. As he remarked in his
Epistle Dedicatory to Buckhurst:

I must acknowledge, however I have behav'd my self in drawing,
nothing ever presented it self to my Fancy with that solid Pleasure, as
Brutus did in sacrificing his Sons. Before I read *Machivel*'s Notes upon
the place, I concluded it the greatest Action that was ever seen throughout all Ages on the greatest Occasion.[15]

Lee hardly would have been so impressed four years earlier, when
comparative peace of politics and spirit was his.

Accompanying this new tragedy of patriotism were vestiges,
however, of the older manner. The play had been derived largely
from a French romance. Sentiment was by no means defunct; in
fact it would dominate the stage for a century or more. Richard
Duke, of Trinity College, Cambridge, totally unaware of what was
transpiring in the young poet's head, wrote a prologue to *Brutus*
containing the same set invocation to the fair:

> Women for ends of Government more fit, ⎫
> Women shall rule the Boxes and the Pit, ⎬
> Give Laws to love, and influence to Wit. ⎭

And while, in their new environment, neither Titus nor Teraminta, the lovers of the play, could think the world well lost for love, Lucrece, who haply was introduced and heightened from the *Clélie* for sensational effect, acted in full agreement with the earlier tragedy of sex. No strokes were spared in painting her adventures. Lee's attitude toward Lucrece was so symptomatic of the Restoration stage that we may pause for a moment to attend upon the comment of John Dennis.

> A Rape [said he], is the peculiar Barbarity of our *English* stage. . . .
> I would fain know from you . . . for what Reason the Women, who will sit as quietly and passively at the Relation of a Rape in Tragedy, as if they thought that Ravishing gave them a Pleasure . . . will start and flinch . . . at the least approach of *Rem* to *Re* in Comedy, unless that Approach happens to be made in the House of Bondage. I have been sometimes apt to entertain a Suspicion, that 'tis not the luscious Matter which disturbs them in Comedy, but the secret implicit Satire upon the Sex. For a Woman in Comedy never grants the last Favour to one to whom she is not marry'd, but it proclaims the Man's Triumph and her Shame. It always shews her Weakness and often her Inconstancy, and sometimes her Fraud and Perfidiousness. But a Rape in Tragedy is a Panegyrick upon the Sex: For there the Woman has all the Advantage of the Man. For she is suppos'd to remain innocent, and to be pleas'd without her Consent; while the Man, who is accounted a damn'd Villain proclaims the Power of Female Charms, which have the Force to drive him to so horrid a Violence.[16]

We need only recall Lee's reported advice upon the subject to guess with what fervor he now described the rape of Lucrece. The force of his Renaissance fancy still ran strong in him.

The curious result of all these affairs of violence, whether in Beaumont and Fletcher or in their successors two centuries later, was that the woman was conceded but one alternative. Monimia accepted death as the inevitable consequence of her stainless sin; and Lucrece, when confronted by her husband, cried out as though she were leprous:

> Away, and do not touch me:
> Stand near, but touch me not. . . .
> Ah, *Collatine!* Oh Father! *Junius Brutus!*
> All that are kin to this dishonor'd blood,
> How will you view me now? Ah, how forgive me?[17]

To which Collatine, with that large liberality of the husbands and lovers concerned in these transactions, found it in his heart to respond:

> Oh, you avenging Gods! *Lucrece*, my Love,
> I swear I do not think thy Soul consenting:
> And therefore I forgive you.[18]

It is not surprising that Lee was unable to break from this sentimentality. Lucrece found her only answer in suicide, and the vengeance of Rome was set in motion against her ravisher. Upon such causes did the Restoration mind decide the fate of kingdoms. But in the newer mode of Lee the play was allowed to move forward in a rational manner, once this necessary deed of violence was consummated.

Rationality was so alien, however, to the nature of mad Nat. Lee, that its appearance seems to have been the prelude to impending dissolution. In his tragedies of 1679 and 1680 those references to madness, which had been frequent enough before, rose to the point of obsession. Hitherto they might have been traceable to the influence of Elizabethan tragedy, as one of those horrors that youthful art might well fasten upon. The Emperor Theodosius reiterated the theme again and again, the more surprising in him inasmuch as otherwise he was essentially normal. "O ye eternal Pow'rs," he exclaimed,

> That guide the World! why do you shock our Reason,
> With acts like these that lay our thoughts in dust?
> Forgive me, Heav'n, this start, or elevate
> Imagination more, and make it nothing.[19]

The speech has a vaguely Shakespearean ring. So too the utterance of Brutus, who, after the fashion of Edgar and Hamlet, had chosen for himself the "vizor of madness":

> O *Brutus! Brutus!*
> When will the tedious Gods permit thy Soul
> To walk abroad in her own Majesty,
> And throw this Vizor of thy Madness from thee?[20]

But it was in *Caesar Borgia*—perhaps the most thoughtful of Lee's plays—that the passages were multiplied. The hero himself was a study of battling passions, of great nobility and depths of depravity,—a figure Jacobean in outline. That, however, does not

NATHANIEL LEE THE MAD POET.

From an engraving by Watts after the painting by Dobson. Repro-
duced by courtesy of The Victoria and Albert Museum.

explain the whole man. If, as has been remarked, one of the chief
signs of approaching insanity is the obsession of it, then both
Borgia and his creator hovered upon the borderline. It was in this
latter play that were uttered the lines taken by the eighteenth-cen-
tury editors of Lee as most descriptive of the poet himself:

> Like a poor Lunatick that makes his moan,
> And for a time beguiles the lookers on;
> He reasons well; his eyes their wildness lose,
> And vows the Keepers his wrong'd sense abuse:
> But if you hit the Cause that hurt his Brain,
> Then his teeth gnash, he foams, he shakes his Chain,
> His Eye-balls rowl, and he is mad again.[21]

Was the madness of Nat. Lee incipient in 1680? If so, the strict
research of medical science, untinged by speculation, would discover the cause in his dissolute living, and in the hazardous nature
of his profession. Yet in Otway existed all these causes of discord
with several others and he never wavered from rationality. His
senses, from the outset, were more firmly hinged. They found their
relief in the retreats of sentimental tragedy or in an outburst of
sneering satire. Lee was in most respects more intelligent, certainly
more thoughtful than Otway; nevertheless in mid-career he allowed
sentimentality to fail him while he hurried in the pursuit of
thought. Laughter seems never to have been long in his power.
Thus handicapped he was to hover for some few years yet upon
the borderline of sense and genius; then his unbalanced mind was
to snap. "I am apt to think," said he,

> it but a leap of fancy,
> A jading of the mind, which, quite tired out
> With thoughts eternal toil, strikes from the road.[22]

Chapter XIII

THE COLLABORATION OF LEE AND DRYDEN

> Some, to whom Heav'n in wit has been profuse,
> Want as much more to turn it to its use;
> For Wit and Judgment often are at strife,
> Tho' meant for other's aid, like man and wife.
> 'Tis more to guide than spur the Muse's steed,
> Restrain his fury than provoke his speed:
> The winged courser, like a gen'rous horse,
> Shows most true mettle when you check his course.
>
> POPE, *An Essay on Criticism*

IF ever a play was calculated as the symbol of an entire movement in literature, it was Dryden's rococo *State of Innocence; or, The Fall of Man*. With Milton's consent the laureate had tagged *Paradise Lost* with couplets, transformed it into an opera resplendent in all the machinery of Drury Lane, adorned it with song, dance, and a hectoring devil, and then sent it forth to seek its fortunes. Though some hitch at this point seems to have forestalled actual production, it stands imperishable and unchallenged in its first edition of 1677. At the time of its publication Nat. Lee was engaged in the composition of his *Rival Queens*. He paused long enough to cast an astonished glance at Dryden's play, saw therein the image of Tasso, and straightway humbled himself in voluble admiration. The poem he addressed to the laureate upon this occasion doubtless cemented the long and productive friendship of the two poets. Hardly less than *The State of Innocence* itself, this epistle was proof positive of the time's complete derangement of critical values:

> Forgive me, awful Poet, if a Muse,
> Whom artless Nature did for plainness chuse,
> In loose attire presents her humble Thought,
> Of this best POEM, that you ever wrought. . . .
> To the dead Bard, your fame a little owes,
> For *Milton* did the Wealthy Mine disclose,
> And rudely cast what you cou'd well dispose:
> He roughly drew, on an old fashion'd ground,
> A Chaos, for no perfect World was found,

Till through the heap, your mighty Genius shin'd;
His was the Golden Ore which you refin'd.
And to a place of strength the prize convey'd;
You took her thence: to Court this Virgin brought
Drest her with gemms, new weav'd her hard spun thought
And softest language, sweetest manners taught.
Till from a Comet she a star did rise,
Not to affright, but please our wondring eyes.[1]

The address concluded with an exordium that Dryden press forward to even greater tasks. The latter answered with an epistle to Lee's *Rival Queens;* and the compact was sealed. The two poets were almost a perfect complement to one another: Dryden, for all his temporary excursion into the heroic drama, keenly critical, unimpassioned, and finely balanced; Lee, a fury of emotion trembling at times upon the brink of madness. To the end of his life, Dryden seems to have regarded Lee with the affection of an elder brother,[2] nor did he ever display toward him any of those twinges of jealousy which disfigured his relations with Otway.

Two years passed with no visible product of this friendship, but finally, during August or September, 1678, appeared an adaptation of Sophocles' *Oedipus,* their joint work, and perhaps that greater undertaking which Lee had urged. It had been in preparation for some time, but before it reached the stage it was subject to considerable dissension between the two playhouses. The King's Company complained that Dryden had withdrawn his tragedy, even though obligated to give them the right of first rejection:

> Mr. Dryden has now, jointly with Mr. Lee (who was in Pension with us to the last day of our playing, and shall continue) written a play called *Oedipus,* and given it to the Duke's Company, contrary to his said agreement, his promise, and all gratitude, to the great prejudice and almost undoing of the Company, they being the only poets remaining to us.[3]

Whatever the merits of the case, the shift brought to Lee the services of a more powerful company, and this had the greatest effect upon his subsequent development. The change, of course, was not immediately felt. *Oedipus* had been composed for Mohun and Hart, in a style perhaps more characteristic of the Restoration stage than as though it had been for Betterton and his colleagues. It was altogether a product as amazing as Dryden's adaptation of Milton, since it had superimposed upon Sophocles and Seneca the turgid eloquence of Nathaniel Lee. "I writ the First and Third Acts of *Oedipus*," said Dryden, "and drew the *Scenery* of the *whole Play*."[4] It hardly required such a statement to fix the exact responsibility. We need turn only to the opening of the second act to recognize that mad Nat. was upon the boards emulating Lear:

> Sure 'tis the End of all things! Fate has torn
> The Lock of Time off, and his head is now
> The gastly Ball of round Eternity!
> Call you these Peals of Thunder, but the yawn
> Of bellowing Clouds? By *Jove*, they seem to me
> The World's last groans; and those vast sheets of Flame
> Are its last Blaze! The Tapers of the Gods,
> The Sun and Moon, run down like waxen-Globes;
> The shooting Stars end all in purple Gellies,
> And Chaos is at hand.[5]

If Lee drives in triumph over the major portion of the tragedy, we nevertheless perceive throughout the ministering hand of Dryden: in the fine irony, for instance, of Oedipus' unwitting pursuit of himself, and in the brilliant critical apparatus of the preface.

The deviations from Sophocles were scarcely hazardous in 1678. Few of the critics had the faintest apprehension of the true nature of classical tragedy, and the dilettante of the pit, with his vocables concerning pity, terror, fable, and decorum, had progressed only so far as the bare words. The audience was ready to accord an enthusiastic reception to a play so plainly labeled as classic. One easy recipe for success was to take a standard Restoration tragedy, disguise its nature by high-sounding titles and by critical opinions for the smatterers to clutch at, and then lend it the prestige of a Dryden. *Oedipus* could not escape vast commendation. Its Preface was a masterpiece that embroiled the wits in endless citation of Aristotle, Horace, Lucullus, and Julius Caesar! Then, with a passing allusion to Seneca, in whom rather than in Sophocles their spiritual debt largely rested, Dryden concluded with an attack upon Corneille, to whom they were obliged for a most characteristic subplot.[6] His design seems to have been to throw a screen about the Latin and French sources, and to bring forward unduly the Greek.

The French-man [said Dryden], follow'd a wrong Scent; and the *Roman* was absolutely at cold Hunting. All we cou'd gather out of *Corneille*, was, that an Episode must be, but not his way: And *Seneca* supply'd us with no new hint, but only a Relation which he makes of his *Tiresias* raising the Ghost of *Lajus:* which is here perform'd in view of the Audience, the Rites and Ceremonies so far his, as he agreed with Antiquity, and the Religion of the Greeks: But he himself was beholden to *Homer's Tiresias* in the *Odysses* for some of them: and the rest have been collected from *Heliodore's Aetheopiques,* and *Lucan's Erectho.*[7]

Such erudition concealed the fact that Dryden and Lee's *Oedipus,* with its shreds and patches from Sophocles, Seneca, and Corneille, was after all another scorching tragedy of somewhat Jacobean flavor.

The heavy artillery of criticism fortified an otherwise doubtful position. It is all very interesting, while some parts—such as the succinct comparison of ancient and modern tragedy—warrants quotation.

Sophocles indeed is admirable every where: And therefore we have follow'd him as close as possibly we cou'd: But the *Athenian* Theater, (whether more perfect than ours, is not now disputed) had a perfection differing from ours. You see there in every Act a single Scene (or two at most) which manage the business of the Play, and after that succeeds the *Chorus,* which commonly takes up more time in Singing, than there has been employ'd in speaking. The Principal person appears almost constantly through the Play; but the inferiour Parts seldome above once in the whole Tragedie. The Conduct of our Stage is much more difficult, where we are oblig'd never to lose any considerable character which we have once presented. Custom likewise has obtain'd, that we must form an under-plot of second Persons, which must be depending on the first, and their by-walks must be like those in a Labyrinth, which all of 'em lead into the great Parterre: or like so many several lodging Chambers, which have their out-lets into the same Gallery.[8]

Here was set down the plot pattern of nearly all Restoration tragedy: a multitude of characters skilfully distributed between two main plots, the whole design interrelated with many ingenious complications. In another age Gildon, one of the first professional critics, praised *The Orphan* for its just attention to the unity of action,[9] but Otway's play was almost unique in that respect. The tragic writers of the Restoration strove rather more than their Elizabethan predecessors to bind their various plots together artistically; and in general they frowned upon the union of a tragic major with a comic minor plot, though that injunction also was more often than not disregarded. These were matters understood by the veriest fledgling; but to the idea of dual plots in general he had been so accustomed that it rarely occurred to him to protest.

The minor plot of *Oedipus*, as has been remarked, was suggested by the introduction of a romantic love story into Corneille's version. The reason advanced by the French playwright was that the ladies would otherwise have been fearful of the blinded Oedipus and disobliged by the omission of a love interest. The ladies of the Palais Royal appear to have been as omnipotent as those of the Duke's Theatre. No such deterrent as horror, however, could weigh heavily upon the ladies of England; and hence we may suppose that it was the necessity of a love interest alone that brought the subplot into the English *Oedipus*,—that, and the prevailing taste for complexity of "fable."[10] The actual verbal resemblances to the French were not numerous, and those mainly in Dryden's second act. Eurydice's desire to give her life for the salvation of her people was imitative of the action of Dircée. That was a theme more French in character than English, seeking for greater nobility than that which might arise from mere selfish love. Otherwise the likenesses—where they exist—are of importance chiefly as showing the kinship of spirit that existed between the two stages.

In the more startling insertion of a love motif into the major plot of Oedipus and Jocasta, the collaborators were less squeamish than the Greek or the French authors. A certain perversion of national taste—clearly recognizable from Elizabethan times—delighted in all sorts of unnatural relations. Such was the passion of Polydore for Monimia in *The Orphan*, and the endless father-and-son or brother-and-brother rivalries of *Don Carlos, Mithridates,* and *Caesar Borgia*. Nowhere does this habit of mind become so repulsive, however, as in the incestuous plot of *Oedipus*. Where the Greek had dismissed the guiltless-guilty characters with the curse of destiny upon them, and had provoked Jocasta to suicide from the fatal revelation, Lee and Dryden were inclined to palliate the crime to the extent of a recall for one final scene of mad love. The English dramatists made much of the fact that Jocasta would have buried the secret, and that Oedipus himself, enslaved by the love god, trembled upon the brink of compromise.

But these were changes dictated no less by an urge to horror than by the rule of love. The original influence of Senecan tragedy, so important to the shaping of English drama in its earlier stages, here was flowing in a powerful secondary tide. Crowne had uncovered much to his liking in the bloody banquet of Thyestes. Now Lee and Dryden drew from Seneca the terrible last entry of Jocasta, and found occasion elsewhere to enlarge upon the blinding of Oedipus. To an audience already hardened by the blinding of Gloucester, mere retelling, unaccompanied by action, would have been without effect. This original weakness of the Greek tragedy was remedied in the last act by a welter of destruction and violent stage direction. Thus the *"Scene Draws, and discovers* Jocasta *held by her Women, and stabb'd in many places of her bosom, her hair dishevel'd; her Children slain upon the Bed."*[11] Various other admixtures of sensationalism were not so immediately derivative from Seneca. The incantation of Laius, it is true, was in straight descent from the Latin, but all the attendant premonitions, the dreams, prodigies, and somnambulism came to Dryden and Lee by way of *Macbeth, Hamlet,* and the Roman tragedies of Shakespeare.

This gallimaufry—classical, Latin, French, Elizabethan—won the immediate suffrage of the age.[12] One contemporary, it is true, discovered that Lee in his part had out-Heroded Herod:

> A sixth, whose lofty Fancy towers
> 'Bove Fate, Eternity, and Powers
> Rumbles i' th' Sky, and makes a bustle;
> So, Gods meet Gods i' th' dark, and justle.[13]

But most competent critics announced that the two playwrights had surpassed themselves. Langbaine judged *Oedipus* "one of our best plays"; and Gould wrote that:

> . . . *Oedipus* (of which, *Lee,* half is thine,
> And there thy *Genius* does with Lustre shine)
> Does raise our *Fear* and *Pity* too as high
> As, almost, can be done in *Tragedy.*[14]

Dennis, on the contrary, displayed a good sense that was denied many of his critical betters, though it may be said that his superiority manifested itself when the tide had commenced to run the other way. His dialogue may be set down, herewith, as sound criticism of the entire horror school of tragedy:

BEAUMONT: Now I have always taken our *English Oedipus* to be an admirable Play.

FREEMAN: You have had a great reason to do so; and it would certainly have been much better, if Mr. *Dryden* had had the sole management of it. . . .

BEAU. Well the Authority of *Aristotle* avails little with me, against irrefutable Experience. I have seen our *English Oedipus* several times, and have constantly found, that it hath caus'd both Terrour and Pity in me.

FREEM. I will not tell you that possibly you have mistaken Horrour for Terrour and Pity. . . .[15]

The critic proceeds with a demonstration that the misfortunes of Oedipus were so undeserved as to destroy these nobler emotions. It was a line of attack subsequently pursued with some success by Dr. Johnson.

The great difference between raising horror and terror [added Warton], is perceived and felt from the reserved manner in which Sophocles speaks of the dreadful incest of Oedipus, and from the manner in which Statius has enlarged and dwelt upon it, in which he has been very unnaturally and injudiciously imitated by Dryden and Lee, who introduce this most unfortunate prince not only describing but arguing on the dreadful crime he had committed.[16]

So long as it pleased the current race of critics, however, it was immaterial what should be the judgment of posterity. The world was to revolve some few times yet, before it should be in a more temperate clime. Powell took up where Betterton had left off, and his interpretation and the applause he received was thus characterized:

> When *Oedipus* rends forth his Eyes with Tears,
> Each sorrowing Beauty almost puts out hers. . . .
> He foams, he stares, he storms a madding Note,
> And all the Fury thunders in his Throat.[17]

And after Powell had discontinued, it was discovered by Addison that other actors were at hand to carry on the burden. Said he,

The Poets that were acquainted with this Secret [of Rant] have given frequent Occasion for such Emotions in the Actor, by adding Vehemence to Words where there was no Passion, or inflaming a real Passion into Fustian. This hath filled the Mouths of our Heroes with Bombast; and given them such Sentiments, as proceed rather from a Swelling than a Greatness of Mind. Unnatural Exclamations, Curses, Vows, Blasphemies, a Defiance of Mankind, and an Outraging of the Gods, frequently pass upon the Audience for tow'ring Thoughts, and have accordingly met with infinite Applause. . . .

As our Heroes are generally Lovers, their Swelling and Blustring upon the Stage very much recommends them to the fair Part of their Audience. The Ladies are wonderfully pleased to see a Man insulting Kings, or affronting the Gods, in one Scene, and throwing himself at the Feet of his Mistress in another. . . . *Dryden* and *Lee,* in several of their Tragedies, have practised this Secret with good Success.

But to shew how a *Rant* pleases beyond the most just and natural Thought that is not pronounced with Vehemence, I would desire the Reader when he sees the Tragedy of *Oedipus* to observe how quietly the Hero is dismissed at the End of the third Act, after having pronounced the following Lines, in which the Thought is very natural, and apt to move Compassion.

Whereupon Addison quotes a speech that by the division of the play may be assigned to Dryden, and then continues: "Let us then observe with what Thunder-claps of Applause [Oedipus] leaves the Stage, after the Impieties and Execrations at the End of the fourth Act; and you will wonder to see an Audience so cursed and so pleased at the same Time." And Addison transcribes the following lines by Lee:

> O that as oft I have at *Athens* seen,

(Where, by the way, there was no Stage till many Years after *Oedipus.*)

> The Stage arise, and the big Clouds descend;
> So now, in very deed, I might behold
> This pond'rous Globe, and all yon marble Roof,
> Meet, like the Hands of Jove, and crush Mankind.
> For all the Elements, &c.[18]

The public had taken the bit between the teeth, and the critics might rage as they pleased.

When we observe [cried the Hon. George Granville, from his high post], how little notice is taken of the noble and sublime Thoughts and Expressions of Mr. *Dryden* in *Oedipus,* and what applause is given the Rants and Fustian of Mr. *Lee,* what can we say, but that mad men are only fit to write, when nothing is esteem'd Great and Heroick but what is non-intelligible![19]

Chapter XIV

PENITENT PROTEUS THE SECOND

Our Play's a Parallel: The Holy League
Begot our Cov'nant: Guisards got the Whigg:
Whate're our hot-brain'd sheriffs did advance,
Was, like our Fashions, first produc'd in *France*.
DRYDEN's Prologue to *The Duke of Guise*, 1683

THE gyration of Lee's political faith from 1679 through 1682 was symptomatic of the chaos in the public mind. By all antecedents he was a Whig; by his position of henchman at the Duke of York's Theatre he was a Tory; the uncharted tides and courses of the parties threatened to leave him a derelict and a menace to both, but chiefly to the Tories. Because of his association with Dryden in the production of the violently partisan *Duke of Guise*, and to his composition of a laudatory epistle to James, Duke of York, upon his return from banishment, the essentially Whiggish character of Nat. Lee has escaped notice, just as has the fact that Dryden for some while balanced precariously, before he launched the powerful Tory poem of *Absalom and Achitophel*.

In *Some Reflections upon the Pretended Parallel in the Play Called The Duke of Guise*, the Whiggish *character* men, Hunt and Shadwell, went to extraordinary length to single Lee's participation in the play from that of Dryden. Was it that they sought to sow dissension between the two, or did they seek to reclaim a lost brother?

> I cannot believe [said one of them], the first Author [Lee] of himself guilty of such evil Intentions, because I have heard better things of him; but the *old Serpent Bayes* has deluded him, as he would have done of the Reputation, if any had been gotten by it; for so as I am told he did endeavour to do in Discourse with all his own Friends, when he joyn'd with him in *Oedipus*, which deserved applause: and since he hath found that this hath gotten little or no Esteem in the Town, he renounces all he can of it, and endeavours to cast the greatest *Odium* upon his Partner.[1]

The accusation may have had some truth in it; for Lee's first essay upon the subject of the Guisards and popish politics was reported to have leaned heavily to the side of the Whigs.

This play [*The Duke of Guise*] at first (as I am inform'd by some who have a nearer communication with the Poets and Players than I have) was written by another [Lee], intending to expose the unparallel'd Villany of the *Papists* in the most horrid *Parisian Massacre*. And *Bayes* himself, as I am also told, expressed then an intention of writing the Story of the *Sicilian Vespers*, to lay open the treacherous, inhuman, bloody Principles of the *Disciples of that Scarlet Whore*.[2]

Popish massacres, we may note, were much sought after as Whiggish propaganda, when one-half London trembled nightly at the threat of universal destruction.

Dryden countered with vilification of Hunt and Shadwell, and, more to the immediate point, with some allusion to Lee's earlier play, *The Massacre of Paris*. His remarks help to establish the chronology of Lee's plays. Alluding to the charge that he had perverted the latter's intention, Dryden asked:

Which of the two *Sosia's* is it now that speaks? If the *Lawyer* [Hunt], 'tis true, he has but little *Communication* with the *Players:* if the *Poet* [Shadwell], the *Players* have but *little Communication* with *him*. For 'tis not long ago, he said to some body, *By G—, my Lord, those* Tory-rogues *will act none of my Plays* [a statement of Shadwell's that was true enough, for after the Tory catcalls to his *Lancashire Witches*, the bars of the theaters were against him until the revolution of 1688]. Well [continued Dryden], but the Accusation, that this Play was once written by *another*, and then 'twas call'd the *Parisian Massacre:* Such a Play, I have heard indeed was written; but I never saw it. Whether this be any of it or no, I can say no more, than for my own part of it. But pray, who denies the unparalleled villany of the *Papists*, in that bloody *Massacre?* I have enquired, why it was not Acted, and heard it was stopt, by the interposition of an *Ambassador*, who was willing to save the Credit of his Country, and not to have the Memory of an Action so barbarous reviv'd. But that I tempted my Friend to alter it, is a notorious *Whiggism* to save the *broader Word*.[3]

The most difficult problem of chronology in the writing of Lee's plays thus goes some way toward a solution. *The Duke of Guise* was scheduled for production in July, 1682, but was banned until the November following.[4] Even more serious delay attended the production of *The Massacre of Paris*, which was held in abeyance until 1689, when the Protestant succession allowed it to be acted and printed. And *The Princess of Cleve*, another of Lee's plays with some political tincture, was not published until long after its production of 1681 or thereabouts. When in 1689 it did appear, it had been subjected to considerable revision. They were a triad of plays closely related, despite their apparent divergence in spirit; and doubtless they were even more in agreement at their first composition. Parts of the Tory *Duke of Guise* and the non-partisan *Princess of Cleve*—probably not so non-partisan in the unaltered form—arose from the Whiggish *Massacre of Paris*. Lee explains the matter in his preface to *The Princess of Cleve*.

This Play [said he], when it was Acted, in the Character of the Princess of *Jainville* had a resemblance of *Marguerite* in the Massacre of *Paris*, Sister of *Charles* the Ninth, and Wife to *Henry* the Fourth, King of *Navar:* That fatal Marriage which cost the Blood of so many Thousand Men, and the Lives of the best Commanders. What was borrowed in the Action is left out in the Print, and quite obliterated in the minds of Men. But the Duke of *Guise*, who was Notorious for a bolder Fault, has wrested two whole Scenes from the Original, which after the Vacation he will be forc'd to pay. I was, I confess, through Indignation, forc'd to limb my own Child; which Time, the true Cure of all Maladies, and Injustice, have set together again. The Play cost me much Pains, the Story is true, and I hope the Object will display Treachery in its own Colours. But this Farce, Comedy, Tragedy, or meer Play, [*The Princess of Cleve*] was a Revenge for refusal of the other, [*The Massacre of Paris*].[5]

From this and other evidence it is possible to date our plays. When *The Princess of Cleve* was first acted,[6] it was introduced by a prologue and epilogue of Dryden's composition, in the former of which was an allusion as of recent date to Achitophel. Possibly this has been accorded too much weight in assigning the play to 1681/2. Achitophel, as a pseudonym for Shaftesbury, was already in common use as early as 1680; and Dryden merely seized upon it to stamp it with the royal mint. Of greater significance is the allusion—already examined in another connection—to the Earl of Rochester:

> JACQU. . . . And tell me now the bus'ness of the Court.
> VID. Hold it *Nemours* for ever at defiance . . .
>   Since he that was the Life, the Soul of Pleasure,
>   Count *Rosidore*, is dead.
> NEM. Then we may say
>   Wit was and Satyr is a Carcass now.[7]

The elegy that follows, so casually introduced by Lee, loses all significance if we are to suppose that it languished unsung for eighteen months after the death of the great man. Rochester died July, 1680; and *The Princess of Cleve* appears to have been staged in August or September following. That would place the abortive *Massacre,* from which he derived material for the other two plays, around the end of 1679. The early date is rendered more plausible by Dryden's recollection of it in 1682 as of the not immediate past, and by its dramatic character. It is perfectly in tone with *Caesar Borgia,* Lee's first excursion into the byways of papal intrigue and English terror.

The Massacre of Paris was the true composition of the son of Richard Lee. It originated in the clergy, for though Davila's history was its principal source, the immediate inspiration was doubtless Bishop Burnet's *Relation of the Barbarous and Bloody Massacre,*[8] a rehash of old horrors published in 1678 under the impulse of the events of that year. Lee expressed more openly in his play what was the implicit parallel of the tract. Nurtured as he had been from infancy upon lurid pulpit eloquence that associated France, the papacy, and the devil in copartnership, the frenzied youth would have flourished thirty years before, in the heyday of the roundheads, or ten years after, during the Protestant ascendancy. But in 1679 no censor with even the vaguest knowledge of Charles's bias could allow its production. At a more seasonable time the play had its *première* before Queen Mary and her attendant court. Then it was called the Protestant Play, and drew tears of pity if not of terror. "There were more weeping eyes in the church," said a writer searching for a comparison, "than there were at the first acting of Mr. *Lee's Protestant Play.*"[9] In 1680, however, while the damper was upon him and his politics were still unregenerate, Lee could only write his "Farce, Comedy, Tragedy, or meer Play" as a solace to his feelings.

What was it exactly in the *Massacre* to cause its banishment for ten years, or until control passed definitely to the Whigs and Protestantism? One can only conjecture upon the author's intention. Was the queen-mother of the play, Catherine de Medici, to be taken as the image of some powerful foreigner—Portsmouth or the Catholic queen perhaps—who had come to England to rule the king to his destruction? There had been the gravest charges of poisoning brought against Charles's pitiable consort by Titus

Oates; and in this play the queen-mother was slowly poisoning the king. The other menacing foreigner, Louise de Querouaille, Duchess of Portsmouth, was at the time upon the point of indictment as a common nuisance. Lee was fond of the theme of a king surrounded by his court of women. Did he here harp upon the same subject, in his portrait of Charles IX of France under the malevolent influence of the queen-mother?

> Imagin then the King, like *Adam* laid
> Among the Sweets of Paradise to rest,
> While to his listning Soul this Second *Eve*,
> Full of the Devil, and design'd to damn us,
> Thus breathes her Counsels fatal to the World:
> What ever Paths you trod before your Reign,
> 'Tis Blood and Terror must your Throne maintain:
> Scorn then thy Slaves; nor to thy Vassals bow; ⎫
> Fix the Gold Circle to thy bended Brow, ⎬
> By Murders, Massacres; no matter how. ⎭
> For Conscience, and Heav'n's Fear, Religion's Rules,
> They're all State-Bells, to toll in pious Fools.[10]

The policies of this "Italian hag" were those feared by all true-blue Protestants of England. There were covert revelations here of an unholy compact of murder sealed in the chamber of a "great person," perhaps with the weak connivance of the king himself. The speaker of the lines above, Coligny in the play, may perhaps be taken as Lee's vision of Shaftesbury, the defender of the faith and the opponent of royal prerogative to a young playwright not yet gone heretic Tory. It was to Coligny that the queen-mother alluded, when the king grew overfearful of universal massacre:

> If, Sir, you fear it,
> Why give it o're, and let the Admiral reign. . . .
> Let Knaves in Shops prescribe you how to Sway,
> They read your Acts, and with their hardned Thumbs
> Erase them out, or with their stinking Breath
> Proclaim aloud they like not this or that.[11]

The lines reflect the sullen class hatred that had arisen in London between the city and the court. If Lee did not intend all this, it is a serious indictment of his intelligence. Indeed the whole tragedy of *The Massacre of Paris* by its very nature was designed to foment pit and gallery into a brawling mob. It is little wonder that the

French ambassador, and behind him Charles the Second, found occasion to protest.

The Princess of Cleve "was a Revenge for the Refusal of the other." As a play it need not detain us, for all the acute analysis of sentiment and character evaporated from Mme de La Fayette's novel once it was turned to the purposes of Restoration comedy. It was a production comparable to Otway's *Friendship in Fashion*, irreligious and cynical, but lacking however the power of the latter. Nemours lays about him, as Lee remarked, "like the *Gladiator* in the Park,"[12] and Margaret, introduced from the *Massacre*—where she was a figure of all nobility—enters here in company with a bawd and a cuckold. Only the Princess of Cleve herself retained that gentle tragedy which Lee might have been expected to take over from the original. The unfortunate poet had been transformed out of recognition during the mad March days of 1680. Banned the stage for his expression of political doctrine, he no longer found in himself or in his audience the patience to revive the old heroic formula, once so heartily in favor. Bawdry and intermingled wisdom now failed him; and his play thus had nothing left to recommend it. *The Princess of Cleve* fell flat in 1680, if one may judge by the lack of evidence; nor has it been revived since.[13]

This tragi-comedy marked an interlude during which Lee was allowed to take stock of his past and future. There followed *Theodosius* and *Lucius Junius Brutus*, untroubled at least by French violence or papal intrigue, though the latter was sufficiently affected otherwise to warrant its suppression. So it might have rested, had not the Oxford parliament of March, 1681, radically changed the world of dramatists and politicians. The triumph of Charles, rendered possible by heavy subsidies from Louis, made king-baiting unfashionable. Addresses of loyalty replaced the covert criticism of the preceding years, and there was a rebirth of fervent nonresistance rivaling that of Filmer and Hobbes. The Tory coffeehouses grew boisterous; Oates went into eclipse to the accompaniment of prodigious tossing of healths to the Duke of York. Dryden settled himself once and for all in the Tory party, becoming its most vigorous satirist; Crowne quieted his Protestant clamor; Settle showed in his prologue to *The Heir to Morocco* that he was ready to bolt the Whigs; and Lee, generally bewildered by the course of events, began to write addresses, complimentary epistles, and to participate in a new play upon the Tory platform.

First came his address to *Absalom and Achitophel*, unsigned at its first appearance, November, 1681, and hence not hitherto associated with Lee. But the conclusive evidence is at hand in Tonson's attribution of it, early in the next century.[14] A strange production, it would be negligible save for one superlative couplet in description of Dryden:

> As if a *Milton* from the dead arose,
> Fil'd off his Rust, and the right Party chose.

Here and elsewhere in the poem Lee proclaimed himself a Tory, though not of the more assertive variety. He made no assault upon the personalities of Dryden's satire, and, in fact, devoted the greater part of his energy to an unexampled panegyric of Monmouth and his wife! The reason will shortly appear. Meanwhile it may be noted that he urged Dryden to continue as he had gone. The lines deserve repetition:

> 'Tis Gracious all, and Great: Push on your Theam,
> Lean your griev'd head on *David*'s Diadem.
> *David* that rebel *Israels* envy mov'd,
> *David* by God and all Good Men belov'd.[15]

The praise of Charles allowed Lee a graceful retreat: his was a loyalty to the King with no accompanying disloyalty to the party. But early in 1682 he joined in the grand chorus at the return of the Duke of York from Scotland,[16] and after that followed with a play that on the face of it was so completely Tory as to obliterate all memory of earlier peccadilloes.

After *The Duke of Guise*[17] had been dropped into the opposing camp, the tumult was so great that Dryden, as collaborator, was impelled to write a considerable dedication to explain his play and prologue, and a long *Vindication* to explain his explanation. The Whiggish town had by no means associated the two poets as equal sharers in the venture, and certainly not as equal turncoats. There were several violent retorts, of which one was addressed to Monmouth. It drew no distinctions:

> Thus thou kind Duke wert in Effigie kill'd
> By Poets too in Tragedy unskill'd:
> And Story wrested to an Impious Case
> Of the Sons Death before the Fathers Face.
> Men that would Write for any Factions use
> Or Int'rest, can a full Third Day produce.[18]

In Dryden's *Vindication* was an account of the genesis of *The Duke of Guise:* "I must do a common Right both to Mr. *Lee* and *my self,* to declare publickly that it was at his earnest Desire, without any Solicitation of mine, that this Play was produced betwixt us." This was in answer to the charge that the "old Serpent Bayes" had tempted Lee into a betrayal of his earlier allegiance.

After the writing of *Oedipus* [continued Dryden], I pass'd a Promise to joyn with him in another; and he happen'd to claim the performance of that Promise, just upon the finishing of a Poem, when I would have been glad of a little respite before the undertaking of a second Task. The Person that pass'd betwixt us, knows this to be true; and Mr. *Lee* himself, I am sure, will not disown it: so that I did not (*seduce him to joyn with me*) as the malicious Authors of the *Reflections* are pleas'd to call it; but Mr. *Lee's Loyalty* is above so *ridiculous* a *Slander.* I know very well, that the Town did ignorantly call and take this to be *my Play;* but I shall not arrogate to myself the Merits of my Friend. *Two Thirds* of it belong'd to *him;* and then to *me* only the *First Scene* of the Play; the whole *Fourth Act,* and the *first half,* or somewhat *more* of the *Fifth.*[19]

The tragedy was in distress upon its first appearance, for the Whigs refused to recognize it except as a very present parallel.

Ther is a play hear to be acted [said a letter of July 26, 1682], that makes a great business, for the Duke of Munmouth has complained of it, and they say that nothwithstanding it is to be acted sometime nixt week. They call it the Duke of Guise, but in the play the true story is cheinged to the plott I hear.[20]

Dryden has narrated the course of its difficulties:

Upon a wandering Rumour (which I will divide betwixt *Malice* and *Mistake*) that some Great Persons were represented or personated in it, the Matter was complain'd of to my Lord *Chamberlain;* who, thereupon, appointed the Play to be brought to him, and prohibited the Acting of it till further Order; commanding me, after this, to wait upon his Lordship; which I did, and humbly desir'd him to compare the *Play* with the *History,* from whence the Subject was taken, referring to the *First Scene* of the *Fourth Act,* whereupon the *Exception* was *grounded,* and leaving *Davila* (the *Original*) with his Lordship.

(Dryden afterward defended this part as coming from an earlier play of his own against the Covenanters.)

This was before *Midsummer;* and about two Months after, I receiv'd the Play back again from his Lordship, but without any positive Order whether it *should* be Acted or *not;* neither was Mr. *Lee,* or *my self* any way solicitous about it: But this indeed I ever said, That it was intended for the *King's Service;* and *His Majesty* was the best *Judge,* whether it answer'd that End or no; and that I reckon'd it my duty to submit, if his Majesty, for any Reason whatsoever, should deem it unfit for the *Stage.* In the *interim,* a strict Scrutiny was made, and *no Parallel* of the Great Person design'd, could be made out. But this Push failing, there were immediately started some terrible Insinuations, that the *Person* of his *Majesty* was *represented* under that of *Henry the Third;* which if they could have found out, would have concluded, perchance, not only in the stopping of the *Play,* but in the *hanging up* of the *Poets.* But so it was, that his Majesty's *Wisdom* and *Justice,* acquitted both the *One,* and the *Other;* and when the *Play it self* was almost *forgotten,* there were Orders given for the *Acting* of it.[21]

The composition of *The Duke of Guise* appears to have been in process during the first months of 1682. It was scheduled for production July 18, held in abeyance until the atmosphere had cleared, and finally was produced at the end of November. What in July had been too dangerous an attack upon Monmouth and Shaftesbury's party to be openly tolerated, by December had become fit for the King, Queen, and the maids of honor to attend. "It *succeeded,*" said Dryden, "beyond my very *hopes,* having been frequently Acted, and never without a considerable Audience."[22] By the discovery of a plotted insurrection—the last desperate hazard of the Whigs—and the subsequent flight overseas of Shaftesbury, November, 1682, the atmosphere had thoroughly cleared in the course of a few months.

It is nevertheless something of a question whether Nat. Lee was not led unwittingly into the political fury of *The Duke of Guise.* Otherwise his was almost too complete a *volte-face,* a break too abrupt with all his antecedents. To understand wherein he erred one needs be in possession of a history of the time. The play tells how a council of sixteen, under the leadership of Guise, planned to rule Paris, and thus the crown, by the aid of the Parisian mob:

> Our City Bands are twenty thousand strong;
> Well Disciplin'd, well Arm'd, well season'd Traitors;
> Thick rinded heads, that leave no room for *Kernel;*
> Shop Consciences, of proof against an Oath,
> Preach'd up, and ready tim'd for a Rebellion.[23]

The speech was Dryden's. To the audience, of which some part may be presumed of the city party, this was all Tory diatribe against Monmouth's supposed association to rule England through the mob force of London.[24] Navarre, of the play, whose succession the conspirators sought to prevent, obviously was intended as York. Their ringleader, Guise, was Monmouth. He was drawn with a certain sympathy: Dryden had been patronized by his duchess; Lee had lines out for future favors; and, besides, it was not the mode of the court to attack the handsome and reckless son of Charles. With this in mind, the poets wove into the story of Guise a love interest, in which Marmoutier endeavored to save the duke from his traitorous associates, just as the Duchess of Buccleuch was supposed to have exerted her influence to detach Monmouth from the clutches of Shaftesbury. It was the cue of the time to fix all blame upon Shaftesbury for the turmoil of these years, and to let Monmouth as far as possible escape uncriticized. The unlicensed return of Guise to Paris, however, with its consequent threat of mob action, had its parallel in the similar return to London of Monmouth. In the former case the results were tragic; and the implication was obvious for the latter.

This much must be said: that the most vigorous blows were dealt in those scenes of the first and fourth acts for which Dryden alone was responsible. The first scene, indeed, was so tractarian that it seems little more than a versified pamphlet. Lee was delegated, as master of the feminine heart, to write the scenes of passion between Guise and Marmoutier. He composed, also, the spectacular conjuration of Malicorn and all the blood and thunder of the *dénouement*. These scenes were fairly harmless. But what no one seems to have observed is the impoverishment of his portion of the play. His verse was failing and his imagination losing its vigor. The scenes of love were bloodless adaptations from those of Otway's *Venice Preserved*, while two other scenes were ill digested by the "brain sick poet" from his own *Massacre of Paris*. In contrast to Dryden, who in his reincarnation as Tory simply carried forward the offensive he had undertaken in *Absalom and Achitophel* and *The Medal*, Lee was seeking in this play an outlet for his urge toward play writing and a few guineas reward therefor. It seems that he was much less of a Tory than his association with Dryden would lead us to believe. A silenced Whig like his father, he had been painlessly returned into the good graces of the court, and thus once more walked in the paths of righteousness.[25]

Chapter XV

INTERLUDE

I mind not grave Asses, who idly debate
About Right and Succession, the Trifles of State;
We've a good King already: and he deserves laughter
That will trouble his head with who shall come after:
Come, here's to his Health, and I wish he may be
As free from all Care, and all Trouble, as we.
OLDHAM, *The Careless Good Fellow*, 1680

WHILE Lee was embroiling himself in the political whirlpools of Dorset Garden, his unhappy colleague was in search of some quiet haven from the storm. Otway's unwonted burst of productivity—of which *The Poet's Complaint, The Orphan,* and *The Souldiers Fortune* were the most notable result—came abruptly to an end after March, 1680. His epilogue to this period of his life, like the comedy it accompanied, was the protest of a savagely misused man of genius, and, like most of his prologues and epilogues, composed with a sincerity rare in kind at the end of the seventeenth century. The poet narrates how he had "led abroad his mourning muse" and how she had commenced to sing:

> Wretch, write no more for an uncertain fame,
> Nor call thy Muse, when thou art dull, to blame:
> Consider with thyself how thou'rt Unfit
> To make that Monster of Mankind, a Wit:
> A Wit's a Toad, who swell'd with silly pride,
> Full of himself, scorns all the World beside;
> Civil would seem, though he good manners lacks,
> Smiles on all faces, rails behind all backs. . . .
> So who e're Ventures on the Ragged Coast ⎫
> Of starving Poets, certainly is lost, ⎬
> They rail like Porters at the Penny-Post. . . . ⎭
> Like *Trincalo*'s and *Stephano*'s, ye play
> The lewdest tricks each other to betray.
> Like Foes detract, yet flatt'ring friendlike smile, ⎫
> And all is one another to beguile ⎬
> Of Praise, the Monster of your Barren Isle: ⎭
> Enjoy the prostitute ye so admire, ⎫
> Enjoy her to the full of your desire, ⎬
> Whilst this poor Scribler wishes to retire, ⎭

Where he may ne're repeat his Follies more,
But curse the Fate that wrackt him on your Shore.[1]

It was a final malediction to wit uttered when Otway was in high
hopes of a reprieve. His opportunity came from the direction
whence it might have been expected. Gallant Otway, "who never
could say an unpleasant thing to the ladies," had early turned
toward this friendly audience with a petition for its good will:

'Tis thence he Chiefly favour would implore;
And, Fair Ones, pray oblige him on my Score.[2]

The sex had not been altogether unmindful of his plea. If Otway
was unsuccessful in the adventures of love itself, he was not so in
drawing their more disinterested tears, nor in many of his most
pleasant relations outside the playhouse. Now, in his time of despondency, the hand of Eleanor Gwyn reached down with aid and
comfort. It was the more sensible because she herself had undergone some of his tribulations. Nelly had lost none of her half-
humorous sympathy with the nether world, and the nether world
responded in kind. As "Protestant whore,"[3] her own title of distinction, she had recently received a dedication from Mrs. Behn,
extolling her goodness, the greatness of her mind, and, above all,
her beneficence in bestowing upon the world "two Noble Branches
of the Royal Stock." By the testimony of "chaste Aphra," her
conquests were known "to the utmost Limits of the Universe."[4]
At this time it was that Nelly, looking abroad for a tutor for her
ten-year-old son by Charles, had turned to the scene of her lesser
triumphs, and had selected Otway for the position. The fact is set
down in an unpublished and unpublishable satire of the period:

Then for that Cub, her Son, and Heir,
Let him remain in *Otway's* Care,
To make him, (if that's possible to be,)
A viler Poet and more dull than he.[5]

He undertook his duties at about the time of the completion of *The
Souldiers Fortune*. The evidence is in one of the few existent bits
of memorabilia of his brief transit: a power of attorney from Nell
Gwyn to receive her pension, witnessed on June 1, 1680, by
Thomas Otway.[6]

The poets generally throve by the amorous adventures of
Charles II. In fact it is a matter of speculation how far English

literature would have suffered by a general exodus of its kings'
mistresses. Otway's friend and fellow poet, Richard Duke, of
Trinity, Cambridge, was tutor to a child of the King by the Duchess of Portsmouth.[7] But Duke had at least one degree to his credit,
while Otway apparently quitted Oxford without any. Was it
through the great promotion of the latter to his tutorship that, this
same year of grace, 1680, he received a degree of Master of Arts
from Cambridge?[8] "I have heard at *Cambridge*," remarked Giles
Jacob, "that he went afterwards to St. *John's College* in that University, which seems very probable from a Copy of Verses of Mr.
Duke's to him, between whom there was a fast Friendship to the
death of Mr. *Otway*."[9] There were various respites during his
theatrical career, but none seems so likely for attendance at Cambridge as this of 1680, when he was tutor for the offspring of Nell
Gwyn. He received his degree perhaps through the mediation of
his powerful new friends,—just as Dryden, more deservedly it is
true, was recipient of a degree for political reasons. Honorary degrees had even so early a well-defined habit of issuing forth from
the universities.

Here, at any rate, was granted an interlude in the mid-career of
Otway, when it seemed that he had discovered a momentary peace
of mind. There followed, upon the banks of the Cam, days the more
idyllic after the storm and bluster of London. Their story is recounted in three poems: an epistle from Otway to Duke, with an
answer in English and one in Latin. Apparently they were written
early in 1682, since they refer to events of that year:

> The sprightly Court that wander up and down,
> From Gudgeons to a Race, from Town to Town—[10]

This and what follows would seem to contain a reference to the
descent of Catherine of Braganza, the sad-eyed queen of Charles,
upon the peace of academe.[11] With her came Nelly, perhaps in her
capacity of maid of honor, and various other royal mistresses.
Now—

> All, all are fled.

Duke apparently had visited Otway in London. He knew Lee,—at
any rate to the extent of lending him a prologue to *Lucius Junius
Brutus;* for a time he had hobnobbed with wit and politics,—while
Shaftesbury's *mobile* swaggered about with medals struck in honor

of his acquittal. That was shortly after November, 1681, and now, back in Cambridge, he begged Otway to be:

> True to thy Word, afford one Visit more,
> Else I shall grow, from him thou lov'dst before
> A greasie Blockhead Fellow in a Gown,
> (Such as is, Sir, a Cousin of your own;)
> With my own Hair, a Band and ten long Nails,
> And Wit that at a Quibble never fails.[12]

It was the terror of a man who perceived scholarship descending upon him. Charles Otway, of the Yorkshire branch of the family, by this time was a forbidding example of righteous living. Of the other acquaintances, whom Otway had found at Cambridge, hardly more than the names have survived:

> When to our little Cottage we repair,
> We find a Friend or two, we'd wish for there,
> Dear *Beverly*, kind as parting Lovers tears,
> *Adderly*, honest as the Sword he wears,
> *Wilson*, professing Friendship yet a Friend
> Or *Short*, beyond what Numbers can commend.
> *Finch*, full of Kindness, gen'rous as his Blood,
> Watchfull to doe to modest Merit good;
> Who have forsook the vile tumultuous Town,
> And for a Taste of Life to us come down.[13]

Otway recalled the names of those who apparently were his friends of the "idle court" upon its expedition. They help to fill out the circle of his acquaintance. Short, a man of letters in medicine, court physician, later was to be in jeopardy from his charge that the King was poisoned. He was a good Catholic, and it was dangerous in those times to be a good anything. To him it was that Duke and various other poets addressed some of their labors, and his death was to be elegized in broadside by a nameless friend, perhaps of this same group.[14] Adderly was a common enough name; this seems to have been one Richard Adderly, a captain of the King's Guard, "honest as the sword he wears." He too may have been something of a man of letters, for a certain anonymous R.A. contributed freely to one of Mrs. Behn's miscellanies. Wilson, of whom nothing appears beyond the complete disguise of his name, was probably William Wilson who entered with Duke into Trinity in the year 1671. Years later he was mentioned by Dennis as the one-time friend of Otway, when at a dinner with Duke, and Loggan the painter he had joined in a rousing health to Captain Wycherley.[15] All these friends of Otway were wits about town, and all, by evidence of the epistles, tossed off innumerable bumpers and verses in this time of conviviality. James Beverly and Henry Finch, of Corpus and Christ's respectively,[16] were two popular members of the group: the former remains little more than a name, the latter was of the same "generous blood" as the second Earl of Nottingham. Duke thus recounts how with Beverly he had toasted the health of the flown revelers—Otway and Finch:

> Then thee we name; this heard, cries *James,* "For him,
> Leap up, thou sparkling Wine, and kiss the Brim;
> Crosses attend the Man that dares to flinch;
> Great as that Man deserves, who drinks not *Finch."*
> But these are empty Joys, without you two,
> We drink your Names, alas! but where are you?[17]

Lest it be thought, however, that the friendship of Duke and Otway was only pot-tossing, we may add the reminiscence of the latter. Sometimes, said he,

> upon a Rivers Bank we lye,
> Where skimming Swallows o'er the Surface fly,[18]

or again,

> We two together wander'd through a Grove,
> 'Twas green beneath us, and all Shade above,
> Mild as our Friendship, springing as our Love.[19]

By all contemporary testimony, Otway had the power of making many friends, but to Richard Duke alone he seems to have delivered himself without reservation. There is something of the confessional hinted in the final lines of his poem, where the tragedy of the writer for a moment was allowed to obtrude itself. The benevolence of Nell Gwyn was a tenuous thing at best. These years of turmoil had not been too easy for kings' mistresses. Portsmouth was reduced to a bare £20,000 a year, and there is no telling to what extremes of penury poor Nell was sunk. Her collections were coming in with an increasing difficulty. In short, when Otway wrote the epistle, his brief respite from poverty and unrequited love was nearly over:

Gods! Life's your Gift, then season't with such Fate,
That what ye meant a Blessing prove no Weight.
Let me to the remotest Part be whirl'd
Of this your play-thing made in Haste, the World;
But grant me Quiet, Liberty and Peace,
By Day what's needful, and at Night soft Ease;
The Friend I trust in, and the She I love,
Then fix me; and if e'er I wish Remove,
Make me as great (that's wretched) as ye can,
Set me in Power, the wofull'st State of Man;
To be by Fools mis-led, to Knaves a Prey:
But make Life what I ask, or tak't away.[20]

If in these verses there was the hint of fatality, in others almost as certainly written by Otway to Duke, there was its complete revelation. Shortly before the death of the playwright, in Dryden's *Miscellany* of 1684 appeared an anonymous and hitherto unnoticed *Letter to a Friend*.[21] The coincidences that it directly followed the *Epistle to R.D. from T.O.*, as though it had been forwarded in the same packet, that its opening lines were in striking reminiscence of the prelude to *The Poet's Complaint*, and finally that it was shot through with evidences of his style—such, for example, as the falling cadence of his verse—seems clearly to identify the poem as the work of Otway.[22] The fact that its authorship was unacknowledged at the time need not surprise us, for frequently the signature was omitted to the latter poems of a group, and in this case the absence was very likely but a part of that conspiracy of silence which seemed to surround the love of Otway for Mrs. Barry. In any event, the poem is so completely autobiographical and consistent with the known facts of his life as to deserve reprinting. The reader may judge for himself upon its authenticity:

A LETTER TO A FRIEND.

A Youth once free and happy, now a slave,
Found a retreat within a peacefull Cave;
Where no intruders durst his hours molest,
(But the dear Passion still inflam'd his Breast)
And where abandon'd to his restless pains,
He weeps alone, and feels his weighty Chains
From thence—
To a dear Friend (such as are hard to find)
Known true and just, and longing to be kind,

Who always shar'd his pleasures and his pain,
In these sad terms writ the tormented Swain.

My onely Friend, learn my unhappy Fate,
That I'm undone by Love, oppos'd by Hate;
Your pity e'er I ask I'm sure to gain,
But cruel *Cynthia*'s never must obtain.
You are not ign'rant of Her Charms I know,
Too well by Her they're known, and thence my Woe:
Yet must I not complain,[23] I own the Fair
Has justly doom'd me to the pains I bear;
For I have long profanely laught at Love,[24]
And oft to make the World despise it, strove.

Wanton till now were all the flames I knew,
With pleasure wing'd my minutes Gaily flew,
When Beauty wounded, Wine soon freed my soul,[25]
My peace came swimming in the healing Bowl;
Or if too weak the Wine against Love's Charms,
I took some Balmy Harlot to my Armes;
Which always did the rageing pains remove,
And cool the stings of any other Love.
In peace and plenty, with still new Delights,
I past my Joyfull Days, and Amorous Nights.

But now in vain that freedom lost I mourn,
My far fled Liberty will ne'er return;
Too strong's my passion, as the Nymph too Fair,
(Ah, lovely Nymph, must I for ever bear!)
In your bright Eyes such Heav'nly Beauty's shine,
You want but mercy to be all Divine;
Lost freedom to regain I dare not try,
That were Rebellion, and I ought to Dye.
Why shou'd your pow'rfull Charms your pride create,
Your pride your onely Fault, my onely Fate?

    Thus oft I've mourn'd the Conquest of Her Eyes,
Since first my Heart was made Her Sacrifice,
And she the panting Victim cou'd despise.
Yet spite of all Her rigorous disdain,
I love my Ruine, and I hugg my Chain.[26]

Reason in vain endeavours to persuade
That I shou'd quit this Haughty, scornfull Maid;

Small Passions often make our Reason yeild,
When Love invades, it well may quit the Feild.

Your hopeless Friend thus languishing remains, ⎫
Enslav'd by one who will not ease his pains;   ⎬
Smiles when he weeps, and Frowns when he complains.[27] ⎭

At this period the letters from Otway to Barry[28] seem to have been composed, and likewise such of his lyrics as were solely concerned with his love. In the former he speaks of having loved from the first day he saw her, "now for seven years."[29] Inasmuch as the *début* of the actress came at the earliest in 1674, this would date the letters around 1681 or 1682. But immediately there arise several inconsistencies with the accepted account. The poet states that during the seven-year interval he had rebelled seriously but once, and that when he saw her become the mistress of another. Now according to tradition, Mrs. Barry appertained to Rochester before Otway ever saw her. The poet was remarkably obtuse if he had not been aware of the fact. Again in the third letter, we read of the intention of the lady *to quit the world,* a phrase generally interpreted as an intention to quit the stage. We are unaware of any such purpose. Indeed it has been argued as unlikely that she should have entertained any such design around 1682, when close to the zenith of her career. This reasoning, however, fails to take into account the lady's flexible character. Though very likely she did hold for Rochester a genuine affection—witnessed by her long cherishing of his picture that Congreve sought to purchase from her heirs[30]—she was not deterred, by the shade of Rochester, from parleys with certain other people of importance. Even so early as the date of the letters, Otway could write of Rochester's child by Barry as "that sweet Pledge of your *first* softest Love."[31] One may be curious about these heirs, John Custis, Gent., and Abigal Shackhouse, both of shadowy origin.[32] Time was to bring her many lovers, and she appears to have profited no less by her avocation than her vocation.

> Her Fifty shillings a week [had] rais'd her price
> Besides her other charming Quallities. . . .[33]

At this distance, it is hazardous to thrust any new figure into the picture, but there was a rival in 1681/2 fairly well characterized by Otway:

My Rival's rich in Worldly Store,
   May offer heaps of Gold,
But surely I a Heav'n adore,
   Too precious to be sold;
Can *Sylvia* such a Coxcomb prize,
   For Wealth and not Desert,
And my poor sighs and tears despise;
   Alas, 'twill break my Heart.[34]

A person similar to this appeared in his first letter: "Give it," he cried, referring to her heart, "Give it to him who would waste his *Fortune* for you, give it the Man would fill your Lap with Gold, court you with Offers of vast rich Possessions, give it the Fool that hath nothing but his *Money* to plead for him."[35] The assumed date of the letter and the character given to the rival would seem to exclude the Earl of Rochester from consideration. Who then was the coxcomb that around 1682 blighted the hopes of Otway for a second time? There is available only Etherege, suggested by Oldys upon very dubious grounds,[36] and the hitherto unnoted figure of St. John, a fop of the first water and in time the father of the famous statesman, Bolingbroke. The basis for connecting him with Barry and Otway is to be found in a couplet alluding to the boundless avarice of the actress—

Which makes her all the Captains Love forgett
And nauseous *St. Johns* to her Arms admitt.[37]

It is all very confusing, though this unexplained reference to the Captain would seem to have some significance. To our knowledge there never entered into her career any other Captain but Otway.

Whatever the cause, whether by the rivalry of St. John or that of some other rich interloper, Otway found his love affairs of 1682 in the same hopeless tangle as those of 1677,—with this essential difference, that in the earlier year he had been capable of setting himself free. His love had developed into an obsession from which he emerged only for brief intervals. The letters themselves contain page after page of prose hovering upon the unhealthy borderline of verse. In fact they could almost as well be written as such, thus:

'Tis me, 'tis only me you have barr'd your Heart
Against. My Sufferings, my Diligence,
My Sighs, Complaints, and Tears are of no power
With your Haughty Nature: yet sure you might

At least vouchsafe to pity them, not shift
Me off, with gross, thick, home-spun *Friendship*,
The common *Coin* that passes betwixt Worldly
Interests.[38]

That language of doting [said Oldys], madness, and despair, however it may succeed upon raw girls, is so seldom successful with such practitioners of the passion of love as Mrs. Barry was, that it only hardens their vanity against their consent, as it was here. For she could get bastards with other men, and 'twas a wonderful condescention in her to let Otway kiss her lips, tho he was as amiable in person and address as any of them.[39]

There may be some legitimate doubt upon the truth of this latter portrait. Time and discontent had begun to leave their mark upon the poet. Only a short while thereafter, Shadwell sketched a likeness of Otway, one actuated by jealousy or even by the hatred of a dispossessed rival, yet reposing upon some solid basis of truth. It is not a pleasant picture:

But who but Fools would praise dull *Otw–ys* strains,
Compos'd with little wit and lesser pains;
Whose fiery face doth dart as hot a ray,
As the fierce warmer of a Summers day,
Whose very looks would drive the Fiends away.
He may so painted with the juice of Vines,
Turn his Invectives to the praise of Wines;
Love is a pitteous God, and Honour's grown,
To such a height it is almost unknown.
Immortal beauty drown'd in quiet lies,
And spends all its charms on its owners Eyes;
But Wine do's now the Poets breast inspire,
Wine, that doth kindle all our youthful fire,
Wine, that makes *Ot—y* write and Fools admire.[40]

Immoderate in all things and as irrational as the world in which he lived, Otway now wrote endless complaints that only substantiated Shadwell's indictment. His life was fashioned upon a single theme:

I Love, I Dote, I am Mad, and know no measure.[41]

Such he was in his thirtieth year, a figure of ineffectual protest, the lines of discontent prematurely furrowed upon his brow and about his mouth, his cheek and jowl inclined to flabbiness, the whole man ill conditioned to play his part in any sort of tragedy. And yet, at this time, he was upon the verge of writing his great summary of life. *Venice Preserved,* some time called the finest tragedy composed since Ford and Webster, was a chief product not only of a man but of a generation whose nerves were either overslack or overtense, rarely in repose.

MISS BRUNTON AS MONIMIA.

MRS. SIDDONS AS BELVIDERA.

Chapter XVI

"VENICE PRESERVED"

There was a time when *Otway* charm'd the Stage,
Otway, the Hope, the Sorrow of our Age;
When the full Pit with pleas'd attention hung,
Wrapt with each accent from *Castalio*'s Tongue,
With what a Laughter was his Soldier read!
How mourn'd they when his *Jaffeir* struck, and Bled!
PRIOR, *A Satire upon the Poets*[1]

THE support afforded to Otway by Nell Gwyn and her little "branch of the royal stock" was summarily withdrawn some time before February, 1681/2; for then it was that he dedicated his greatest play to her rival, the Duchess of Portsmouth. Otway was again in the arena and sadly in need of protection.

Forgive me then, *Madam* [said he], if (as a poor Peasant once made a present of an Apple to an Emperour) I bring this small Tribute, the humble growth of my little Garden, and lay it at your feet. Believe it is paid you with the utmost gratitude, believe that so long as I have thought to remember, how very much I owe your generous Nature, I will ever have a heart that shall be gratefull for it too: Your Grace, next Heaven, deserves it amply from me; That gave me life, but on a hard condition. . . . When I had enemies, that with malitious power kept back, and shaded me from those Royal Beams, whose warmth is all I have, or hope to live by; Your noble pity and compassion found me, where I was cast backward from my blessing; down in the rear of Fortune; call'd me up, plac'd me in the shine, and I have felt its comfort. You have in that restor'd me to my native Right; for a steady Faith, and Loyalty to my Prince, was all the Inheritance my Father left me.[2]

Venice Preserved was the final product of that faith and loyalty, and though time should have demonstrated their ultimate tawdriness, at the present moment they seemed to Otway inheritances of great worth. He was to take the center of the stage, to be applauded not only as the most powerful playwright of his generation but as a brilliant accessory to the Tory triumph. The tragedy had its first production, according to the date upon the original broadside prologue, February 9, 1681/2. It was visited by the king on

the poet's day, the eleventh,[3] when perhaps he was lured thither by
the duchess.[4] Thenceforward it was almost officialized as the Tory
paean of triumph. It was remarked in the next century upon authority best known at the time, that the notorious Nicky Nacky
scenes, with their ribald satire upon Shaftesbury, were suggested
by Charles himself.[5] Certainly the Duke of York joined in the
savage laughter at this discomfiture of his arch-enemy. Upon his
return from exile, when his battle for succession had been won,
James made his earliest public appearance at a production of
Venice Preserved, the afternoon of April 21.[6] For that occasion
Dryden forgot past rivalries and wrote a special prologue to accompany the new epilogue by Otway. Again upon May 31 the
two playwrights pooled their talents to welcome home the duchess.[7]
Both the epilogues were famous in their day, notably that to her
Highness, for she was now beloved by all loyal hearts, carrying as
she did the hopes of the solicitous for a "Royal boy."

Aside from these political considerations, one chief cause for the
play's success was its worth as an acting vehicle. The art of Betterton and Barry in *Venice Preserved* is one of the splendid traditions of the English stage, though how much greater they were than
Garrick, Siddons, O'Neill and the others who have taken luster
from the same play we have no means of judging. But to an audience with hardly any standards of comparison for the wealth of
sentiment and soft passion to be disclosed to them the first impression must have been startling. Overnight Barry became "the great
Mrs. Barry,"[8] and if Betterton's glamor could hardly be increased,
at least there was added in Jaffeir one of his most striking rôles.

Tenderness, friendship, and love, conflicting with rage, terror, and
remorse were painted with the liveliest colours, and shewn in the most
striking attitude by the accomplished Betterton. Smith's person [in
Pierre] was commanding; and the spectators justified, by applause, the
propriety of that line where he calls himself—

A fine, gay, bold-fac'd villain, as thou seest me.

And Bedamar's compliment:

The Poets who first feign'd a God of war,
Sure prophesy'd of thee![9]

But at that precise moment, however, great acting was not rel-
ished by the Whigs. Their undercurrent of hostile criticism, fol-

lowing long years of political dominance, made applause the more exquisite. A disgruntled satire of 1682 bore ample testimony to this part of the triumph. It was concerned with a bookseller, who pressed a copy of *Venice Preserved* upon an unwilling buyer:

> He crys,—S^r. Mr. *Otway*'s last new Play
> With the Epilogue which for the Duke he writ,
> So lik'd at Court by all the Men of Wit:
> I heard an Ensign of the Guard declare,
> That with him *Shadwell* was not to compare,
> He liked that Scene of *Nicky Nacky*, more
> Than all that *Shadwell* ever writ before.
> Was't not enough, that at this Tedious Play
> I lavish'd half a Crown, and half a Day,
> But I must find, Patch'd up at every Wall
> Stuff none can bear, who starves not at Whitehall?
> As Rascals, changing Rags for Scarlet Coats
> Cudgell'd before, set up to cut Whig's Throats;
> So every Blockhead that can please the Court
> Plucks up a Spirit, and turns Poet for't.[10]

It remained only that Otway should keep out of dark alleys and see to it that his nose was not slit. For after Shaftesbury's indictment, the city party was in an ugly mood, and one intolerant of attack by such small fry as Otway. Generally mindful of all this, the poet loosed a parting bolt in his original epilogue:

> Poets in honour of the Truth shou'd write,
> With the same Spirit brave men for it fight.
> And though against him causeless hatreds rise, ⎫
> And dayly where he goes of late, he spies ⎬
> The scowles of sullen and revengefull eyes; ⎭
> 'Tis what he knows with much contempt to bear,
> And serves a cause too good to let him fear:
> He fears no poison from an incens'd Drab,
> No Ruffian's five-foot Sword, nor Rascal's stab;
> Nor any other snares of mischief laid,
> Not a Rose-alley Cudgel-Ambuscade.[11]

The assault had been flung by Otway along the whole Whiggish front. Old issues were revived in prologue and epilogue: the terrorism of the "Popish Plot," when *"an Army composed of all Religious Men and Pilgrims from St. Jago in Spain"*[12] was most certainly believed to have landed in Wales, and when great caches of

arms were "known" to have been secreted in all recusant house-
holds, and in those of half the nobility. The playwright, speaking
for himself, sneered at these nocturnal forebodings of the Whig
party:

> He, of black Bills, has no prodigious Tales,
> Or Spanish Pilgrims cast a-shore in *Wales.* . . .
> Yet here's an Army rais'd, though under ground,
> But no man seen, nor one Commission found.[13]

Now that the Tory tide had risen, the air was full of counterplot.
The play tells of a subterranean conspiracy of the Spaniards
against the state of Venice, and of a vast projected massacre. It
was in part a reflection of the old "Popish Plot" and in part a new
interest added by a Whiggish plot, as yet unjustified by the event.
In some manner, still undisclosed, an association of Whigs men-
aced the state. The seizure of Shaftesbury's papers had revealed
two lists: one of men worthy of promotion, another of those intended for less dignified elevation. Later in the year 1682 a plot of
assassination actually did come to light, though the connivance of
Shaftesbury was never quite proved. All this was to be subject matter for *The Duke of Guise.* Everywhere the surface of England
was felt to be mined, and he who trod abroad had need to look to
his health.

Aside from this general attack upon the Whigs, the most hazardous adventure in *Venice Preserved* was that involved in the famous
Nicky Nacky scenes.[14] In the eighteenth century, when they had
lost political point, they were banned the stage as being abhorrent
to all decency, and today they are repulsive to any but the avowed
specialist in the literature of masochism. But the less squeamish
Restoration was in raptures. "When Leigh and Mrs. Currer performed the parts of doting cully and rampant courtezan, the applause was as loud as the triumphant tories, for so they were at that
time, could bestow."[15] Upon the unfortunate Shaftesbury was de-
bouched all the cloacal garbage of these obscene years: charges
with some modicum of truth, charges with none at all. One must be
unduly credulous to accept even half the filthy libel that circulated
indiscriminate of party or person.

When our poet submerged himself in this business, he had provo-
cation greater than most. His sentimentality from an overdose of
life had turned vinegar. This was the other half of the "tender Ot-

way,"—the half not commonly regarded, virulent and without regard for the decencies. The same mood that had created Sir Jolly Jumble and the nymphomaniacs of his comedy was now turned to tragedy and wrought this impotent old wretch:

> Next is a Senatour that keeps a Whore;
> In *Venice* none a higher office bore;
> To lewdness every night the Letcher ran:
> Show me, all *London,* such another Man,
> Match him at Mother *Creswold's* if you can.[16]

Nevertheless the figure of Antonio fitted into Otway's general design with an exquisite precision. It was with partial perception of this fact that Taine made his famous commentary:

Like Shakespeare again, Otway has found, at least once, the large bitter buffoonery, the crude sentiment of human baseness; and he has introduced into his most painful tragedy an impure caricature, an old senator, who unbends from his official gravity in order to play at his mistress' house the clown or the valet. How bitter! how true was his conception, in making the busy man eager to leave his robes and his ceremonies! how ready the man is to abase himself, when, escaping from his part, he comes to his real self! how the ape and the dog crop out of him![17]

With our knowledge of Otway's underlying purpose of satire, we may somewhat question the conscious universality of the portrait. Taine misses, moreover, an effect that Otway probably did intend: the *chiaroscuro* to which the scenes contribute, their dark contrast to the pure and noble love of Belvidera and Jaffeir. Goethe was more acute in his observation: "The comic scenes are particularly good. It is they alone which account for, and go near to justify the conspiracy; for we see in them how utterly unfit for government the Senate had become."[18] Thus by the sordid person of Antonio was visualized the Whiggish parliament, the same that had protected the liberties of its people by the refusal of grants to the private army of Charles and to his spendthrift court. He was token of all the stored-up hatred of the period. The Tories in one short year had become loudly expressive. The scent of victory was in their nostrils; and they were now permitted to single out Shaftesbury as the symbol of all political decay.

Their declaration of abuses came in a speech by one of the conspirators:

The publick Stock's a Beggar; one *Venetian*
Trusts not another: Look into their Stores
Of general safety; Empty Magazines
A tatter'd Fleet, a murmuring unpaid Army,
Bankrupt Nobility, a harrast Commonalty,
A Factious, giddy, and divided Senate,
Is all the strength of *Venice:* Let's destroy it.
Let's fill their Magazines with Arms to awe them, . . .
Turn out their droning Senate, and possess
That Seat of Empire, which our Souls were fram'd for.[19]

To Dr. Johnson, and his fellow conservatives of the eighteenth century, the speaker passed as merely one more political malcontent in a play possessing hardly a decent character.[20] But this criticism failed to perceive that the theater-going party of 1682 discovered slight villainy in any attempt against the House of Commons. The deification of Pierre as another Brutus reflected a political philosophy that identified liberty with the destruction of so-called representative government and the increase of royal prerogative.

But that likewise might proceed too far. Lest in preaching absolutism, Otway might be suspected of encouraging rebellion, he made the schemes of Pierre abortive—therein of course following the original story—and, with some adroitness, coupled to Pierre's party a second Shaftesbury in Renault. The latter comprehended not so much the supposed debauchery of the Whig leader, as his newest threat of a universal massacre. It was the old Whiggish charge against the Tories, that now had recoiled upon Shaftesbury himself. In the play Renault was made the most bloodthirsty of the conspirators:

Here is a Traitour too, that's very old,
Turbulent, subtle, mischievous, and bold,
Bloudy, revengefull, and to crown his part,
Loves fumbling with a Wench, with all his heart;
'Till after having many changes pass'd,
In spight of Age (thanks Heaven) is hang'd at last.[21]

It must be reiterated that this political *milieu* was of the first importance in the evolution of Restoration tragedy. In contrast to his earlier plays, *Don Carlos* and *The Orphan,* where he had projected his tragic figures against a colorless background of court or coun-

try, Otway in *Venice Preserved* tested the love of Jaffeir and Belvidera in the clash of great events. Before, they had developed
mere wayward sensibility in response to their entirely selfish problems. In 1682, challenged as they were by reality, they became
more intelligent than their prototypes and altogether more capable
of perceiving the consequences of their deeds. To these two, Otway
added a third character, whose philosophy arose at last from the
action of the play and was not derivative to any extent from the
precepts of Shakespeare or of Rochester. Yet the poet easily could
have utilized the writings of the former. The materials were ready-
made in the meditations of Cassius, who seems to have been indirectly the original for Pierre, just as Brutus and Portia may have
likewise been secondary sources for Otway's hero and heroine. The
Shakespearean philosophy would have been utilized in Otway's
formative years, but now life had furnished him with commentary
infinitely more true, because his own.

In this study of the sources of *Venice Preserved*, it is proposed to
develop the manner in which Otway, for the first time in his career,
was able to master his materials. It is the account of a man of great
sensibility, but one weak upon the side of invention, in his efforts
to refashion his borrowings into an inevitable expression of his own
peculiar personality.

The first and most pressing of his creditors, as in *Don Carlos*,
was again the Abbé de Saint-Réal. It is hardly necessary to retell at
this place the story of the latter's *La Conjuration des Espagnols
contre la République de Venise, en l'année MDCXVIII*, nor to recount the indebtedness of *Venice Preserved* to that novel.[22] It was a
tale of conspiracy and sudden death crying for adaptation to the
English political crisis of 1679–82. The Restoration stage had been
avid for plots against the state, whether Grecian oligarchy or the
modern sophy of Persia. Otway was well advised in following the
historical outline of *La Conjuration* so closely, even to the individual speeches of the conspirators. What changes he introduced
were to fortify the Tory position or to suffer the introduction of
major characters into the romantic plot. Thus Bedamar ceased to
be the directing mind of the conspiracy, yielding place to Renault
and Pierre, while Jaffeir, the Provençal malcontent, became Jaffeir
the lover and the deeply injured Venetian. But to fashion a play
from Saint-Réal, Otway needed more than a lurid tale of conspiracy, however appropriate it might be to the events of his own

time. He drew, therefore, upon other funds of inspiration. Of these the debt most immediately noticeable was to Shakespeare.

It is a commonplace to say that *Venice Preserved* is Shakespearean, yet it is this quality of the play, curiously enough, that has not been subject to any considerable investigation. Of course, emotionally unbalanced and irrational as was Otway, he never could be truly Shakespearean. But the influence of the latter is to be noted over the management of scenes and in a reminiscence of speech. The accent and thought is Otway's own. His first impulse, whenever he composed a tragedy, was to turn first of all to *Othello*, and afterward to *Hamlet* and *Julius Caesar* for inspiration. Following precedent, he drew heavily for this play upon the first and third of these. It has been noted that the opening scene of *Venice Preserved* is fashioned after the first act of *Othello*.[23] But the force of the greater genius had ceased to dominate Otway. The aged senator Priuli had lost his daughter to Jaffeir, a guest and favorite in his home. The outline is similar; the inflection is the poet's own. And the same is true of his adaptations from *Julius Caesar,* whence —at least secondhand—he borrowed the interrelation of Cassius, Brutus, and Portia as model for the three leading characters of *Venice Preserved.* Pierre discovers himself as a nobler if less profound Cassius; Jaffeir, a Brutus whose motives of social idealism were overbalanced by the intense personal bias of Otway himself. So throughout. There are various other parallels, but the resemblance is generally one of management rather than phrasing. Otway no longer composed with a book open before him.

The plot of *Venice Preserved* became dynamic with the introduction of Belvidera. It was she that motivated the defection of Jaffeir from the cause of destruction, becoming at once his good and evil genius as she led him to heroic sacrifice and shameful disloyalty. And of this there was not a hint in Saint-Réal. Otway wove Belvidera into his design by the happy inspiration, doubtless from *Othello,* of making her the daughter of one of the Venetian senators. Forthwith, she became subject to the typically Otwavian conflict of great loyalties. Belvidera, however, is a character more active than Desdemona, a composite of various originals. The scene between Portia and Brutus has its counterpart in that between Jaffeir and Belvidera, after the latter has come near to betrayal by Renault. Portia gently chides her lord for his failure to confide in her; Belvidera is explicit in comparing her situation to that of the

Roman matron. Indeed is not this admixture of Roman blood in Otway's heroine partly accountable for her distinctly finer fiber than that of Monimia or the Queen of *Don Carlos?* Neither of them, nurtured as they were in the traditions of heroic tragedy and sentiment, would have expressed themselves thus:

> Look not upon me, as I am a Woman,
> But as a Bone, thy Wife, thy Friend; who long
> Has had admission to thy heart, and there
> Study'd the Virtues of thy gallant Nature;
> Thy Constancy, thy Courage and thy Truth,
> Have been my daily lesson: I have learnt them,
> Am bold as thou, can suffer or despise
> The worst of Fates for thee; and with thee share them.[24]

Otway's women are ever stronger than his men. Belvidera demonstrates to Jaffeir that his projected course of blood and revenge is a perversion of his humanity and his intelligence. She is rational beyond all precedent. But it is noteworthy that the argument which ultimately sways Jaffeir from participation in the plot is one of emotion: his rage at the attempt of Renault upon the person of his wife. It is only the clearer nobility of Belvidera that lifts *Venice Preserved* above the other tragedies of its author.

We may digress for the moment to observe the portion of *Venice Preserved* adjudged by criticism to be Otway's most typical expression. The tragedy is *intense* beyond any of his earlier dramas to a degree that only could have arisen from the poet's own experience. Poverty is its discordant undertone. In the reading of *Venice Preserved*, one constantly recalls the complaint of Lavinia in *Caius Marius*—

> Must I at the uncharitable Gates
> Of proud great men implore Relief in Vain?[25]

—or the wail of Monimia imagining herself in destitution, or finally the stark portrait of the poverty-stricken old hag met by Chamont. But now poverty takes possession and shapes the plot:

> Oh *Belvidera!* double I am a Beggar,
> Undone by Fortune, and in debt to thee;
> Want! worldly Want! that hungry meager Fiend
> Is at my heels, and chases me in view;
> Can'st thou bear Cold and Hunger? Can these Limbs,
> Fram'd for the tender Offices of Love,
> Endure the bitter Gripes of smarting Poverty?[26]

There is in Otway little analysis beyond the bare fact which admitted of no further commentary. To the despoilers of Jaffeir's home appears the lovely Belvidera, and to the speech just quoted comes the answer:

> I'll make this Arm a Pillow for thy Head;
> And as thou sighing ly'st, and swell'd with sorrow,
> Creep to thy Bosom, pour the balm of Love
> Into thy Soul, and kiss thee to thy Rest;
> Then praise our God, and watch thee 'till the Morning.[27]

Human suffering—sentiment. "I once asked Dr. Johnson," said Burney, "if he did not think Otway a good painter of tender scenes? and he replied, 'Sir! he is all tenderness.' "[28] When we read such poetry as that just quoted we are inclined to agree. But frequently the speech rises higher. It is the intensity of *Venice Preserved,* an intensity not to be explained by his source material, that is Otway's new characteristic.

A succession of dramatic scenes follow in the play that ordinarily would suffice half a dozen of its kind. By Otway's insistence upon crowded action he was Elizabethan; by his avoidance of divided interest, where he followed Racine, he was only rivaled among his contemporaries, and that distantly, by Dryden and Lee. He utilized all the heroic conflicts of love, honor, and friendship, imparting to them a fresh vitality and letting them follow one another with amazing rapidity. The violent rage of Jaffeir at Renault was succeeded by Pierre's shock at the canker disclosed in the heart of the conspiracy. There ensued the half-veiled hatred of the dialogue between Renault and Jaffeir, then the midnight conspiracy with its startling emotional crises, the distraction of Jaffeir at the horror of the plot, the life struggle as Pierre matched wits with Renault to save his friend and thus on through the third act with a steady crescendo of power. But Otway held the tension by a subtle variation of mood. Whereas in *The Orphan* he had improvised with little emotional range, here he was a master of modulation. Afterward came the scenes of conflicting love and honor, as Belvidera led Jaffeir to the palace of the Doge.

Was this development of Otway's tragedy entirely because of his deepening perception, or of some unexplained influence which the critics of *Venice Preserved* have left out of the account? The answer lies between the two. But before we consider this influence, it should be reiterated that while in his earlier tragedies his sources tended to master his thought and plot construction—everything in fact save his sentimentality—in this play he had mastered his sources.

It is in the *dénouement* that we have a clue of the utmost importance. *Lucius Junius Brutus,* produced slightly more than a year earlier, had been constructed by Lee for the same triumvirate of actors that interpreted *Venice Preserved:* Betterton, Smith, and Mrs. Barry. They might have had as notable success with the one as the other had not the former tragedy been so summarily dealt with by the censor. Otway found an occasion more auspicious in which to create for them exactly parallel rôles. The two poets by this time were probably more than casual acquaintances. We have out of the early eighteenth century the picture of Otway and Lee arm in arm.[29] It may imply a fairly close association. Otway has been assumed as the author of a prologue to Lee's *Constantine the Great,* a play still to come. Duke contributed prologues to their plays and to no others. Their ways lay together and tradition has associated them. But if we had no other proof of the correctness of this assumption, it might rest upon the barefaced manner in which they borrowed from one another, without animosity or audible complaint. We have seen how *The Orphan* was probably debtor to Lee's *Mithridates. Lucius Junius Brutus* definitely derived material from *Caius Marius* for its mob scenes and for the relations of Teraminta and Brutus. The latter pair have more than a little resemblance to Lavinia and the elder Marius. There was also some appropriation of speeches, hardly necessary to cite, but everywhere Otway lent willingly. Far more poverty stricken than Lee upon the side of invention, he simply bided his time and then called upon his friend for a return in kind. The lendings became almost blood and bone to his great tragedy, especially in its *dénouement.*

It will be remembered that Pierre, caught in the toils by the fatal treachery of Jaffeir and unable to face the shame of the torture wheel, begs his friend to reëstablish himself by stabbing him upon the scaffold. The scene is identical to one at the end of *Lucius Junius Brutus.* Lee handled it thus:

> Titus. Hope, say'st thou! O the Gods! What hope of life?
>   To live, to live! and after this dishonor!
>   No my *Valerius,* do not make me rave;
>   But if thou hast a Soul that's sensible,

> Let me conjure thee, when we reach the Senate,
> To thrust me through the heart.
> VAL. Not for the World.
> TIT. Do't, or I swear thou hast no Friendship for me.
> First, thou wilt save me from the hated Ax,
> The Hangman's hand.[30]

The favor begged by Titus was performed exactly, but in a succeeding scene. With finer dramatic instinct, Otway compressed into one moment all the diffuse speech and action of Lee:

> PIER. Is't fit a Souldier, who has liv'd with Honour
> Fought Nations Quarrels, and bin Crown'd with Conquest,
> Be expos'd a common Carcass on a Wheel?
> JAFF. Hah!
> PIER.   Speak! is't fitting?
> JAFF.   Fitting?
> PIER.   Yes, is't fitting?
> JAFF.   What's to be done?
> PIER.   I'd have thee undertake
> Something that's Noble, to preserve my Memory
> From the disgrace that's ready to attaint it.
> OFFIC.   The day grows late, Sir.
> PIER.   I'll make haste! Oh *Jaffeir,*
> Though thou'st betray'd me, doe me some way Justice.
> JAFF. No more of that: Thy wishes shall be satisfied. . . .

And then for a moment Jaffeir speaks from the irrational mind of the Restoration and Thomas Otway:

> I have a Wife, and she shall bleed, my Child too
> Yield up his little Throat, and all t'appease thee—

Pierre returns him to reason:

>   *Going away*
>   No—this—no more! (*He whispers* Jaffeir.)   Pierre *holds*
> JAFF.   Hah! is't then so?   *him.*
> PIER.   Most certainly.
> JAFF. I'll do't.
> PIER. Remember.
> OFFIC.   Sir.
> PIER. Come, now I'm ready.[31]

Thenceforward the action speeds rapidly to the double sacrifice of Pierre and Jaffeir. The quotation proves one thing beyond doubt:

that Otway was culling over the play of his colleague with all due attention. It goes some little way, therefore, toward validating a more important debt, though one not so accurately registered by verbal reminiscence.

From Lee, rather than from Shakespeare, Otway derived the original character of Belvidera and the outline of her relations with Jaffeir. The love interest was absent from Saint-Réal, and the great nobility of Belvidera was unapproached by any of Otway's earlier heroines. Something he derived, it is true, from Brutus' Portia and a hint here and there from Desdemona. But it remained for Lee's Teraminta to complete the portrait, to put in the living touches, and to fit her finally into the tragedy of politics. It is to be noted, first, that Teraminta's general situation in her plot is fairly similar to that of Belvidera. She too is of a blood alien to that of her husband, and with the revolt of her father-in-law, Brutus, is condemned to exile along with the rest of her kin. We observe, moreover, the complete affinity of the two heroines as Teraminta departs and her husband, Titus, utters his typically Otwavian complaint:

> Perhaps to starve upon the barren plain,
> Thy Virgin Wife, the very blush of Maids,
> The softest Bosom, sweet, and not enjoy'd:
> O the Immortal Gods! and as she went,
> How e're she seem'd to bear our parting well,
> Methought she mixt her melting with disdain,
> A cast of anger through her Shining tears.[32]

Within the last two lines there is revealed a pride not discoverable in Monimia and that, on the contrary, is of the very soul of Belvidera. It is after this that Teraminta returns to Titus, sent by the Tarquins to tempt him from his loyalty to his house, and to urge that he should not war against her blood. Her speech upon this occasion is an earlier draft for one in which Belvidera depicts the scene of her father beset by the ruffians of the conspiracy. Like Jaffeir, Titus is sometime resolute, until, variable as Otway's hero, he weakens before her entreaties. Here, in the character of Teraminta, occurs one of those inconsistencies that places her on a plane lower than that of Belvidera: her whole argument was calculated merely as a test of the greatness of Titus. Then, however, she anticipated Otway's heroine by urging her husband to remain loyal to his ideals. There it was that she made her most notable contribution to the full development of the character of Belvidera.

At this juncture the two stories diverge for a moment, as Titus, less impressionable than Jaffeir, hurls himself into the very center of the conspiracy, in spite of her entreaties, nor was there any assault upon his wife's virtue to alter his resolution. After that, however, the two plots move as one. Titus enters the secret council chamber of the conspirators with the same questions as Jaffeir, is bound by his signature to the general massacre of his kinsmen, and is overwhelmed by abhorrence of the crime he is about to commit. Finally, he likewise withdraws, too late. In the fifth act the plot takes the course already noted, wherein Lee reveals in his Titus a stoicism more nearly akin to that of Pierre than to the weak vacillation of Jaffeir. Lee was always a great lover of the classic virtues, and Otway's wavering character could ultimately play no part in his drama.

Venice Preserved, then, very likely came into being as follows. Otway had noted in Lee's tale of the conspiracy against the Romans a close resemblance to Saint-Réal's *Conjuration des Espagnols contre la République de Venise.* The repentance of Titus, being similar to that of Jaffeir, as narrated in the novel, inspired him to create a hero after the same pattern, to append the same *dénouement,* and to introduce a character such as Teraminta to enrich his plot. With his surer technique he enlarged upon scenes and characteristics that Lee had barely suggested. The debt hardly stopped there. The tenderness of Belvidera was Otwavian; the quality that gave her a new elevation above her elder sisters in tragedy was owing to Lee. What Desdemona with her gentle passivity, Bérénice with her sentiment, Juliet with her absolute surrender, had been unable to accomplish, was done by this half-sketched heroine of Lee. Through her suggestion Otway was suddenly transformed into a tragic dramatist verging upon the first order.

Throughout this study it has become fairly conclusive that Otway was not richly endowed upon the side of invention. Nevertheless one character in *Venice Preserved* appears to have been almost entirely his own; and with that character it seems fitting to conclude any treatment of his dramatic work and philosophy. The figure of Pierre had been tentatively sketched in Marius the Elder and in Polydore. Otway was one to experiment with his types before he was ready to make a finished engraving. Pierre, like Marius,

is the fiery demon of destruction, like Polydore, an exacting friend
and something of a libertine, but beyond either noble and endowed
with the capacity to forgive. One of the soundest of Otway's critics,
Hazlitt, has summarized him thus: "The character is not one of
blunt energy but deep art. It is more sarcastic than fierce, and even
the fierceness is more calculated to wound others than to shake or
disturb himself."[33] Pierre is the one character whom the poet himself would most wish to resemble. Did the poet for a moment perceive the courtesan in Barry when he created Aquilina, and did perhaps Pierre act toward her as Otway would have acted? The
weaker alloy of Otway could hardly be tempered to the firmness of
Pierre, but are we wrong in supposing that, at the end of his brief
career, disillusionment had brought him to the philosophy of the
great man of action? Under the insistence of the sordid present,
and not much concerned with the hereafter, the rector's son of
Woolbeding gave in a speech of Pierre what seems to have been his
ultimate judgment upon religion and its promises:

FATHER.　Why are you so obstinate?
PIER.　Why you so troublesome, that a poor wretch
　　　Cannot dye in peace?
　　　But you like Ravens, will be croaking round him—
FATH.　Yet, Heaven—
PIER.　I tell thee Heaven and I are friends,
　　　I ne'r broke Peace with't yet, by cruel murthers,
　　　Rapine, or perjury, or vile deceiving,
　　　But liv'd in moral Justice towards all men,
　　　Nor am a foe to the most strong believers:
　　　How e'r my own short-sighted Faith confine me.
FATH.　But an all-seeing Judge—
PIER.　　　　　　　　You say my conscience
　　　Must be mine accuser: I have search'd that Conscience,
　　　And find no records there of crimes that scare me.
FATH.　'Tis strange you should want faith.
PIER.　　　　　　　　You want to lead
　　　My Reason blindfold, like a hamper'd Lion,
　　　Check'd of its nobler vigour then, when baited
　　　Down to obedient tameness, make it couch,
　　　And shew strange tricks which you call signs of Faith.
　　　So silly Souls are gull'd and you get money.
　　　Away, no more: Captain, I would hereafter
　　　This fellow write no lyes of my conversion,
　　　Because he has crept into my troubled hours.[34]

Otway left behind no account of a deathbed repentance, such as illuminates the end of Rochester.

Noel speaks of the "intense furnace breath" of his passion. It here glows with the fine honesty of Pierre; elsewhere it is choked with poisonous fumes in Antonio and Renault; it springs to clear blue flame in the passion of Jaffeir and Belvidera; and finally it burns to ashes in the tragic insufficiency of all his heroes and heroines as they sink to the grave. Castalio had whispered:

> Farewell, I now am—nothing.

Monimia:

> How my head swims! 'Tis very dark: Good night—

and now Jaffeir:

> I am sick—I'm quiet.

Chapter XVII

THE SIGN OF CAPRICORN

Qui Pelago credit magno, se fænore tollit;
Qui Pugnas & Castra petit, præcingitur Auro;
Vilis Adulator picto jacet Ebrius Ostro;
Et qui sollicitat Nuptas, ad præmia peccat:
Sola pruinosis horret Facundia pannis,
Atque inopi lingua desertas invocat Artes.
Petron. Arb. Sat. (Motto to The Orphan)

THE production of *Venice Preserved* was the last occasion on which Otway basked in the full warmth of greatness. Thenceforward his course was rapidly downhill. His was the altogether typical presentment of one whose ears were filled with the plaudits of the multitude while his body was famished and neglected. Through the ascendancy of Toryism, Otway had completely displaced Shadwell as public favorite, but that same public watched his decline with a certain dispassionate curiosity. It occupied, altogether, somewhat more than the year prior to the ascent of James, a time when normally the fortunes of Otway should have been approaching their zenith. Instead, his slow starvation was one of the lighter topics of the town, alluded to in several satires, of which two couplets will be enough to argue the callousness of this wit-driven London world:

> Lift up your Heads ye Tories of the Age,
> Let *Otway* tumble *Shadwell* from the Stage,
> *Otway* who long leane Loyalty preserving
> Has shown a wonder and grown fat with Starving.[1]

Starvation, however, is a process that occupies some little time.

After *Venice Preserved* we next hear of Otway through his composition of a prologue for Mrs. Behn's *City-Heiress*. It was produced about May 15, 1682, and visited by his Excellency the Moroccan ambassador with some fraction of his unparalleled suite of 6,017 persons.[2] What the ambassador made of the play or Otway's political prologue passes comprehension. *Venice Preserved* was still a sensation, and hence the addition of a prologue by its author lent considerable prestige to Mrs. Behn's play. The climactic scene of the comedy displayed Sir Timothy Treatall in the act of accepting the crown of Poland, a singular ambition attributed to Tapski, alias Shaftesbury, and treated with some sharpness in the original prologue to *Venice Preserved*. But as Shaftesbury was to be handled severely enough in the play, Otway directed his chief attention to the falling credit of Titus Oates and to the late city feast, projected by the Whigs in celebration of "the providential escape of the nation from the hellish designs of the Papists." It was to the immense edification of the Tories that the banquet fell flat through the interference of the crown. Otway alluded to it thus:

> Sham-Plots you may have paid for o'er and o'er;
> But who ere paid for a Sham-Treat before?[3]

We may judge that the gibe was irksome to the Whigs from an answer that issued shortly from the pen of Shadwell:

> Poetess *Afra* though she's damn'd to day[4]
> To morrow will put up another Play.
> And *Ot*—*y* must be Pimp to set her off,
> Lest the enraged Bully scoul and scoff,
> And hiss, and laugh, and give not such applause
> To th' *City-heresie* as the *good old Cause*.[5]
> You're baulkt worse there then at a City Feast
> To part with stolen half-Crown for—no jest;
> *Sham treats you may have paid for o're and o're,*
> *But who e're paid for a Sham Play before?*[6]

With the remainder of Shadwell's invective we need not concern ourselves. His was a defeated cause that would require some six years yet to restore to former vigor.

The prologue with its repercussions was in part Otway's farewell to politics. Even so soon after his great triumph it was marked by a tone of utter weariness:

> How vain have prov'd the Labours of the Stage,
> In striving to reclaim a vitious Age!
> Poets may write the Mischief to impeach,
> You care as little what the Poets teach,
> As you regard at Church what Parsons preach.[7]

It is worthy of note that hardly a play, save only Crowne's *Sir Courtly Nice*, rose above the level of mediocrity between the settlement of 1682 and the revolution of 1688. Whether this was due to the intolerance of James, or to the fading of genius once the inspiration of great events had passed, or to some other reason, it is certain that various playwrights lapsed into incoherence or withdrew from the stage entirely. Such were Dryden, Southerne, Banks, and Shadwell. But for Otway there could be no such escape. He was allowed only to speculate at length upon the decline of drama. His explanation was entirely sensible.

First of all, the two playhouses, in their struggle against diminishing returns, had found their answer at last by pooling their resources.

> 'Tis said, Astrologers strange Wonders find
> To come, in two great *Planets* lately joyn'd.
> From our *Two Houses* joyning, most will hold,
> Vast Deluges of *Dulness* were foretold.[8]

However, there were no deluges. The market was reduced, and even dulness might not thrive under the new despotism of Betterton. He had fallen heir to numberless rôles hitherto denied him,—rôles that had been dignified by the acting of Mohun and Hart. Now the opportunity was afforded the town to make its comparisons, and the new sport held its attention for some time. As the demand for new plays declined, the dispirited poets, of necessity, turned to every sort of hack work. Their trials were summarized by a contemporary *Satyr on the Modern Translators*:

> Since the united Cunning of the Stage
> Has balk'd the hireling Drudges of the Age:
> Since Betterton of late so thrifty's grown,
> Revives old Plays, or wisely acts his own: . . .[9]
> Those who with Nine Months Toil had spoil'd a Play
> In hopes of Eating at a full Third Day,
> Justly despairing longer to sustain
> A craving Stomach from an empty Brain,
> Have left Stage-practice, chang'd their old Vocations,
> Attoning for bad Plays, with worse Translations;
> And like old *Sternhold*, with laborious Spite,
> Burlesque what nobler Muses better write.[10]

Almost a year after his prologue to *The City Heiress* and with nothing to show for his time, Otway directed from London, January 10, 1682/3, a short poetic epistle to Creech upon his translation of Lucretius.[11] It was a pleasing gesture indicating that Otway was still a man of letters. A new translation of respectable quality was greeted then with greater gusto than any number of original plays or poems. Every gentleman tried his hand at it: it was the hall mark of wit; and the purchase of a new translation, the seal of taste. Thus the literary event of the concluding years of the century was Dryden's *Virgil;* the milder sensation of 1683 was this *Lucretius*. Dryden was absent, but Evelyn, Duke, Otway, and other notable wits joined in addresses to the second edition. Poor Creech, who found his exit in 1700 by way of suicide, seems to have been on some slight terms of intimacy with Otway, supplying Wood with a little of the information we have concerning the poet. But the epistle itself is no proof of intimacy. Otway was celebrated; and it was the custom of the lesser poets, or their publishers, to solicit these testimonials from the great, occasionally even to reward their composers with a guinea or two.

Life continued by reason of these driblets. The whole mob of scribblers was in debt to Jacob Tonson:

> *Jacob* the Muse's Midwife, who well knows
> To ease a lab'ring Muse of Pangs and Throws;
> He oft has kept the Infant-Poet warm,
> Oft lick't th' unweildy Monster into Form;
> Oft do they in high Flights and Rapture swell,
> Drunk with the Waters of our *Jacob*'s Well.[12]

It was Tonson, in chief, who supplied Dryden, Duke, Otway, and the rest with a vehicle for their occasional verse. *The Epistle of T.O. to R.D.* appeared at this time in his first *Miscellany,* 1684, as well as Otway's version of *The Sixteenth Ode of the Second Book of Horace.* From dependence upon Betterton, he had now passed under less kindly direction, being indentured for present and future performance. Three known examples survive of his handwriting, each symbolical of a period of his life: first, the scrawl upon the parish register at Woolbeding; then, the witness to Nell Gwyn's power of attorney: and now, this note to Jacob Tonson dated June 30, 1683: "All Accounts evend between M⸢r⸣ Thomas Ottway Jacob Tonson. The said M⸢r⸣ Ottway does hereby acknowledge himself indebted to Jacob Tonson in the Sum of eleven pounds w⸢ch⸣ hee hereby engages to pay upon demand witness his hand—Tho: Otway."[13] The sole existing letter of the poet, if we may call it such, is this I.O.U. Probably Otway sat down to clear off the loan by his hack-work comedy of September, 1683.

The Atheist; or, The Second Part of the Souldiers Fortune was an afterthought born of necessity, and, like most sequels, a confession of impotence. A cynical, loose-jointed thing, it never became a stock play, it was not mentioned by Downes, copies of it today are exceedingly rare, and it is altogether improbable that Tonson grew unduly fat upon the profits of its sale.

Duke contributed an epilogue recalling the great days when *Venice Preserved* had soared triumphantly over Shadwell's *Lancashire Witches:*

> At a *Whig-Brother*'s Play, the Bawling Crowd
> Burst out in shouts, as *zealous,* and as *loud,*
> As when some *Member*'s stout *Election-Beer*
> Gains the *mad Voice* of a whole *Drunken Shire.*
>   *And yet, even then, our Poet's Truth was try'd,*
> *Tho 'twas a Dev'lish pull to stem the Tyde;*
> And tho' he ne'er did Line of *Treason* write,
> Nor made one Rocket on Queen *Besse*'s night,
> Such was his Fortune, and so good his Cause,
> Even then he fail'd not wholly of Applause.
> He that could *then* escape, *now* bolder grows:
> Since the *Whig-Tyde* runs out, the *Loyal* flows.[14]

Of course all this had no more concern with the plot of *The Atheist* than had 50 per cent of these ephemera with their plays. Otway was a little closer home when, in his most cynical of prologues, he counseled a return of drama to the legitimate subject matter of the stage. Surveying his fellow scribblers rhyming *pit* and *wit, stage* and *age,* and—at the height of genius—*raillery* and *gallery,* he found that they were not alone. He was by his own admission one of the chief of sinners, but he at least did not have "the apish quality of loving his own offspring." His advice to the whole pack of writers was to give over, and for himself he promised that—

> He'll find out Ways to your Applause, more easie;
> That is, write worse and worse, till he can please ye.[15]

The play was dedicated to Elande, a tyro in gallantry, and the son of the great Marquise of Halifax. "Epistles Dedicatory," remarked Otway, "be lately grown so Epidemical, that either sooner or later, no man of Quality (whom the least Author has the least pretense to be troublesome to) can escape them."[16] The tone of this dedication argues that Otway was barely acquainted with Elande. Yet his need of protection had not decreased. The play as usual seems to have undergone a struggle for existence, "having at its first coming into the World met with many Enemies, and very industrious ones too."[17] Unlike the enemies of the scandalous *Friendship in Fashion,* however, these were probably discontented Whigs together with a few recruits from the writer's overcrowded profession. But so far from being in any vital danger, Otway probably required no protection from Elande beyond a solid meal and a guinea or so for ale.

A fair appraisal of the patrons of Otway is briefly given in a rare tract of the next century. It states that he "was more beholding to Captain *Symonds* the Vintner, in whose Debt he dy'd 400£ than to all his Patrons of Quality."[18] The list may be passed in review: Buckhurst, the kindliest of the lot, lost by some mischance in connection with *Friendship in Fashion;* Rochester, friend for long to no man; Plymouth and Ossory, dead by 1680; and Falkland, his old-time friend, nearly as indigent as the poet himself. There remain the Duke of York—a laggard in such matters, the two royal mistresses, Lord Elande, and Captain Symonds. One ponders at length upon the indulgent figure of Captain Symonds.

What, in the meantime, had been the direction taken by young Nat. Lee? Both poets had contributed to the production of *Constantine the Great.* Staged in 1683, it was one of Lee's least satisfactory plays,—a flareback to his earlier heroic manner. The outline was such as he might have utilized in 1676: the villain a rehash of the villains of that time; its hero engaged as a rival to his father in a fatal love affair; its heroine, what we might expect from a younger Lee. There were the fatal lapses of style so marked in *Gloriana* and almost as completely absent from *Lucius Junius Brutus.* In fact one might easily conclude that Lee had delved into his trunk and brought forth an old piece, which either he or someone else close to him had revised. And that such a trunk existed—perhaps still exists—we know from Oldys: "There is or was lately a brother of Nat. Lee's somewhere in or near the Isle of Axholm in Lincolnshire, who has a trunk full of his writings as I have been informed by old Mr. Sam. Wesley the late parson of Epworth in that Isle."[19]

But the conjecture that *Constantine the Great* was resurrected from Lee's past rests upon somewhat more secure grounds. As we examine the first quarto, we find that it is lacking a dedication, that its prologue has been rather conclusively assigned to Otway, and that its epilogue—with even greater certainty—has been given to Dryden. It is obvious, then, that Lee had little to do either with his play's presentation or printing. Why this unaccustomed display of interest by his friends?

The answer is not far to seek. Within a year Lee was to be incarcerated in Bethlehem Hospital for the insane. His mind had been in its decline, as we have observed, for some little while before:

> I remember [says Dryden], poor *Nat Lee,* who was then upon the Verge of Madness, yet made a sober and a Witty Answer to a Bad Poet, who told him, *It was an easie thing to write like a Madman: No,* said he, *'tis very difficult to write like a Madman, but, 'tis a very easie matter to write like a Fool.*[20]

His last certain piece of play composition came in the middle of 1682, when he joined Dryden in *The Duke of Guise;* and even then he had been forced to borrow two scenes from his earlier and unpublished play, *The Massacre of Paris.* The beginning of the end to his hitherto unbounded invention may well be dated from that confession of weakness. *Constantine the Great* was merely its final demonstration.

Lee's sanity seems to have been subject to frequent relapses, which might easily have been observed as early as 1682. Oldys noted that his indulgences "flying up to his face broke into those carbuncles, which were afterwards observed therein and also touched his brain, occasioning that madness so much lamented in so rare a Genius; he was some years in bedlam *by intervals.*"[21] The italics are mine, but the passage is substantiated by a letter from Etherege that speaks of the poet's intermittent confinement. Wycherley, on the other hand, claims never to have held Lee's sanity in any too high regard. Addressing him in Bedlam, he gave a slightly different diagnosis from that of Oldys:

> Your Fancy now, does all your Wants supply, ⎫
> Which once, but by your Frantic Poetry, ⎬
> Kept you still, in much more Necessity. ⎭
> You, but because you starv'd, fell mad before,
> Now Starving, does your Wits to you restore; . . .

You did, before that you were mad, engage ⎫
With Numbers, and in your Poetic Rage,   ⎬
Lash'd (as your Keepers you) the madder Age; ⎭
In Poetry, wou'd have your own mad Way,
In spight of all, your sober Friends cou'd say;
Thought others mad, from your own Madness too,
Because, they did not Talk, Think, Do, like you;
You mutter'd Fustian, to your self before,
'Gainst Friend, and Foe, (to show your Wit) did roar;
Which made your Vain, Poetic Rage, appear
Less reas'nable, as you more sober were;
You had High-flights, above all common Sense
To draw to you your Staring Audience,
Whom you, more to your Pleasure, entertain'd,
The less they did your Bombast understand; . . .
Delighted with your own Hot-headedness,   ⎫
Wou'd never, your own Want of Sense confess, ⎬
Or rave in Verse, for Friend's Entreaty less.[22] ⎭

Finally, Southerne upholds the theory of Lee's intermittent madness by two letters, most of the contents of which, with various anecdotes of the poet, are unhappily lost. But one excerpt speaks of him breaking somebody or other's head "at Will's Coffee house in one of his merry mad fits."[23] We find no way of deciding exactly when his madness first became evident, beyond the suggestion of deterioration that appeared in *The Duke of Guise;* and it is quite improbable that he had his wits sufficiently about him in 1683 to compose *Constantine the Great*.[24] The latter work is insignificant, but it is, nevertheless, sane enough to date from any other year than this.

Something depends upon the authorship of its prologue. If Lee's, it may be included among the chief products of his genius, thus destroying at once the whole validity of our argument. Though the prologue was not attributed to Otway either in the broadside or in the first edition of the play itself, the arguments in favor of his authorship are fairly conclusive: it contained the complete epitome, to date, of Otway's philosophy of protest, one of perfect and savage sanity; and it was assigned to him in the collected edition of his works, published by Tonson in 1713. Tonson should have known the author.

The prologue is tragically in keeping with the lives of both poets. Their ways had fallen together. They were doomed to an equally tawdry exit. If Otway was the author, it is doubly interesting as a valedictory to the stage: one final in his own case, and for a long and tragic interval in that of his friend.

> What think ye meant wise Providence, when first
> *Poets* were made? I'd tell you, if I durst
> That 'twas in Contradiction to Heaven's Word,
> That when its Spirit o're the Waters stir'd,
> When it saw All, and said That All was good,
> The Creature *Poet* was not understood.
> For, were it worth the Pains of six long Days, ⎫
> To mould Retailers of dull Third-Day-Plays,   ⎬
> That starve out threescore Years in hopes of Bays? ⎭
> 'Tis plain they ne're were of the first Creation,
> But came of meer Equiv'cal Generation.
> Like Rats in Ships, without Coition bred;
> All hated too as they are, and unfed.

Otway complains then of the ill-timed competition of titled amateurs:

> The *Poet* and the *Whore* alike complains, ⎫
> Of trading Quality, that spoils their Gains; ⎬
> The Lords will write, and Ladies will have Swains. ⎭
> Therefore, all you who have Male Issue born,
> Under the Starving Sign of Capricorn;
> Prevent the Malice of their Stars in time,
> And warn them early from the Sin of Rhime;
> Tell 'em how *Spenser* starv'd, how *Cowley* mourn'd
> How *Butler*'s Faith and Service was return'd
> And if such Warning they refuse to take,
> This last Experiment, O Parents, make! [25]

But we need not continue with the savage last suggestion set down by Otway, inasmuch as it was dictated by an age more outspoken than our own.

With such general malediction, dramatic values insist upon an exit, and had our playwrights been the directors of their own tragedies, things would have been managed much better. As it was Otway was ordained to go down to an anticlimax of hack work, and Lee to undergo long, tiresome years as an exhibited madman. Under date of September, 1684, Anthony Wood made the following entry: "Nathaniel Lee the playmaker endeavouring to reach high in the expression in his plays broke his head and fell distracted.

Whereupon he was put in Bedlam London, Sept. or thereabouts 1684."[26] Wood's is an explanation similar to that of a contemporary poet:

> But *L—gh* by Reason strove not to controul
> The powerful heat, which o'er-inform'd his Soul.
> He took his Swinge, and Nature's bound surpast,
> Stretchd her, and bent her, till she broke at last.[27]

It was perhaps not good psychology, but adequate enough at the time. Fashionable London appears to have tracked to Bedlam to behold the tenth wonder: such another madman as generations could not duplicate.

> And now, the Rabble to thee does resort,
> That thy Want of Wits may be their Sport.[28]

Various accounts of his more or less lucid intervals began in due course to find their way into books of anecdotes. Tom Brown mentions his composition of a prodigious play of twenty-five acts.[29] Bowman, the player, tells that once going to see him, "Lee shewed him a scene in which says he I have done a miracle for you; what's that? said Bowman. I have made you a good priest, at last."[30] It is also reported "that while he was writing one of his scenes by moonlight, a cloud intervening, he cried out in extasy, 'Jove snuff the Moon,' but as this is only related upon common report, we desire no more credit may be given to it, than its own nature demands."[31] Oldys recalls another of his mad sayings, but does not vouchsafe with whom it passed:

> "I've seen an Unscrew'd spider spin a Thought,
> And walk away upon the wings of angells!

What say you to that, Doctor?' 'Ah, marry, Mr. Lee, that's superfine indeed.' " To which Oldys added: "The thought of a winged spider may catch sublime readers of poetry sooner than his web, but it will need a commentary in prose to render it intelligible to the Vulgar."[32] To all of this were added lesser marvels by Dean Lockier, Roger L'Estrange, and others, but we may pass them by.

Bedlam, as a retreat for a "brain sick poet" was no happier in 1685 than Hogarth represented it in the course of the following century. Yet Wycherley, through some hundreds of incredibly dull lines, argued the relative advantage of Lee's situation. It was all in answer to the purported complaint of Lee, in his intervals, *"that He ought no more to be in* Bethlem *for Want of Sense, than other* Mad Libertines *and* Poets *abroad, or any* sober Fools *whatever."*[33] So too an anonymous author of *A Search after Wit* found Lee's situation better than that of the remainder of this mad world:

> Poor *Mortals!* What different *Fortunes* befal us, ⎫
> Poor *Authors! Hard fate!* so unkindly to *maul* us! ⎬
> Rouse, *Elkanah;* rouse in the Name of *Grimhallaz:* ⎭
> Since thy *Guts* are *still croaking,* and thy *Brains* are still *chiming,*
> *Plague* the *Stage* once again with thy huffing and rhiming.

> Poor *Nat,* thou hast lost both thy *Reason* and *Wit;*
> Yet the *happiest Author* for *Bread* that e'er *writ.*
> Let the *Criticks* fret on;—if they *snarl,* thou can'st *growl;*
> If they *bark,* thou can'st *bite;* if they hiss, thou can'st *howl.*

> Thy *Fortune,* whatever they think of the Matter,
> Is what they *all come to,* or sooner, or later;
> Upon a *mad Subject* to make a *mad Play,*
> And write for a *Third House** without any *Third Day.*   * Bedlam

> So didst thou not once, when *Fortune* was kinder,
> And the Theatre rung with thy *brave Alexander.*
> Scarce Roscius himself could *Goodman* outdo;
> He spoke it as well as 'twas *written* by you.[34]

The happiness of Lee and his fellow Bedlamites, however, was only comparative, for their keepers had stern notions as to the treatment of the insane. Part of the discipline is recounted by Wycherley:

> You, but because you starv'd, fell mad before,
> Now Starving, does your Wits to you restore.[35]

They also deprived him of one of his glories: "He had a fine head of hair, which, when he missed in his lucid intervals, he often regretted, it having been necessary to shave him in his madness."[36] Elsewhere Wycherley describes the whipping to which his keepers subjected him. Finally the irony of Lee's situation became entirely fantastic. We may remember that several years prior to his incarceration he had projected an elaborate study of madness in his *Caesar Borgia.* Now it came to pass that some inspired hack delved into this play and resurrected Lee's most apposite lines. These he patched and tinkered to the new circumstances, and then issued them in *A Satire on the Poets*. It was much as though Lee had composed for himself an epitaph. The lines were only too unhappily descriptive of his state:

> There in a Den remov'd from human Eyes
> Posses'd with Muse, a Brain-sick Poet lyes.
> Too miserably wretched to be nam'd,
> For plays, For Heroes, and for passion fam'd,
> Thoughtless he Raves his sleepless hours away
> In Chains all night and darkness all the day.
> And if he gets some Intervals from pain,
> The fit returns, he foams and bites the chain,
> His Eye Balls rowl, and he grows madd again.[37]

And with that epitaph, we may turn our attention again to Otway.

Starvation and the lash were not of Bedlam alone. Most tragic of pictures is that of Otway bent to the hack translation of a dull French history. It was published the year after his death, a *History of the Triumvirates*, by one Sieur de Broë. It is so deplorably lacking, in the translation, of the slightest touch of personality, style, preface, or dedication, that one may be allowed to question its authenticity. It was produced by a nondescript printer, with whom Otway had had no previous dealings. That in itself may argue that he had been driven to the most desperate of shifts. But it came one year after the poet's death, and, more damaging than that, it was announced, while Otway was still alive, as on the press,—this time translated not by Otway, but "By a Judicious Hand."[38] Either shame had elbowed the poet into anonymity, or else the whole business was the fabrication of the publisher. Like many another production of this and the succeeding century, the history may have been fathered upon greatness when greatness could no longer raise its voice in protest.

Wood remarks that during his last illness Otway was composing a congratulatory poem on the inauguration of King James II.[39] This perhaps was the fragmentary *Pastoral on the Death of his Late Majesty*, published in one of Mrs. Behn's Miscellanies,[40] or it may have been the long poem issued posthumously in 1685, by name *Windsor Castle*. The latter was one of the countless elegies at the death of Charles and panegyrics to the new king. The king was dead. Long live the king! James out of gratitude should have

delighted to honor young Otway. The road to preferment was opening and the poet might have been a credit to the Otways of Yorkshire. But surely it was no lack of prevision of exactly what was in
store for him that brought him to pause from overeagerness and to
write into this poem what must stand as his final marginalia to life:

> And happy that Man's Chance who falls in time,
> E'er yet his Vertue be become his Crime;
> E'er his abus'd Desert be call'd his Pride,
> Or Fools and Villains on his Ruine ride.
> But truly blest is he, whose Soul can bear
> The Wrongs of Fate, nor think them worth his Care:
> Whose Mind no Disappointment here can shake,
> Who a true Estimate of Life does make,
> Knows 'tis uncertain, frail, and will have end,
> So to that Prospect still his Thoughts does bend;
> Who, though his Right a stronger Power invade,
> Though Fate oppress, and no man give him Aid,
> Cheer'd with th' Assurance that he there shall find
> Rest from all Toils, and no Remorse of mind;
> Can Fortune's Smiles despise, her Frowns out-brave:
> For who's a Prince or Beggar in the Grave?[41]

A map of the purlieus of London could doubtless have been
sketched from the movements of the fugitive poet during the last
months of his career. Dennis tells us that *"Butler* was starv'd the
same time that the King had his Book in his Pocket, that another
great wit [Wycherley] lay some seven Years in Prison for an inconsiderable Debt, and that *Otway* dar'd not show his Head for
fear of the same Fate."[42] But while fleeing the bailiffs he was observed with passing interest by the age. A satire, alluding to Lee in
Bedlam and therefore written some time after September, 1684,
tells us that Otway's hunt for sanctuary was widely known:

> *Otway* can hardly *Guts* from *Jayl* preserve,
> For though he's *very fat* he's like to *starve*.

His condition, however, was not wholly unique, for the satirist
calls the roll:

> And Sing-song *Durfey* plac't beneath abuses
> Lives by his *Impudence*, not by the *Muses*.
> Poor *Crowne* too has his *third days* mixt with *Gall*;
> He *lives so ill* he hardly *lives at all*.

> *Shadwell* and *Settle,* who pretend to Reason, ⎫
> Tho paid so well for scribling *Dogrel Treason,* ⎬
> Must now expect a very barren Season; ⎭
> But chiefly he that writ his *Recantation;*[43]
> For *Villain* thrives best in his own *Vocation.*
> Nay *Lee* in *Bedlam* now sees better days,
> Than when applaus'd for writing *Bombast Plays:*
> He knows no *care,* nor feels *sharp want* no more;
> And that is what he ne'r cou'd say before.[44]

"At length," added Anthony Wood, "after he had lived about 33 years in this vain and transitory world, [Otway] made his last exit in a house on Tower-hill (called the Bull as I have heard) on the 14th of Apr. in sixteen hundred and eighty five."[45]

To the melancholy list of starving poets, which he had lately compiled, his own and succeeding generations added the name of Thomas Otway. Oldys thinks his end came at a sponging house. Johnson, in elegant Latinity, finds that "having been compelled by his necessities to contract debts, and hunted as is supposed, by the terriers of the law, he retired to a publick house on Tower-hill."[46] Theophilus Cibber, or one of his assistants in the *Lives,* added the famous details:

He had, no doubt, been driven to that part of the town, to avoid the persecution of his creditors, and as he durst not appear much abroad to sollicit assistance, and having no means of getting money in his obscure retreat, he perished. It has been reported, that Mr. Otway, whom delicacy had long deterred from borrowing small sums, driven at last to the most grievous necessity, ventured out of his lurking place, almost naked and shivering, and went into a coffee-house on Tower-hill, where he saw a gentleman, of whom he had some knowledge, and of whom he sollicited the loan of a shilling. The gentleman was quite shocked, to see the author of Venice Preserved begging bread, and compassionately put into his hand a guinea.

Mr. Otway having thanked his benefactor, retired, and changed the guinea to purchase a roll; as his stomach was full of wind by excess of fasting, the first mouthful choaked him, and instantaneously put a period to his days.[47]

"All this," remarked Johnson, "I hope, is not true; and there is ground for better hope." What that ground was appeared in Spence's *Anecdotes.* Its ultimate authority, John Dennis, we may note was twenty-eight years old at Otway's death, and a young blade about town. He stated that "Otway had an intimate friend (one Blackstone), who was shot; the murderer fled toward Dover; and Otway pursued him. In his return, he drank water when violently heated, and so got a fever, which was the death of him."[48] With the seal of Dr. Johnson and Warton upon it, this version has been universally accepted.

To the present writer the murder of Blackstone seemed possible of verification, and so it proved after some search into the contemporary records. It was advertised thus in *The London Gazette* of April 21, 1684:[49]

> Whereas upon Enquiry made before the Coroner of London, Edward Hubbard, Charles Rawlinson, and . . . Williams, were found guilty of a Murther committed upon the Body of John Blakiston, on Monday the 7th Instant at Night, and the said Williams being committed to Newgate for the same, and Edward Hubbard and Charles Rawlinson being fled, whosoever can give notice of the said Hubbard and Rawlinson, so as they may be apprehended, shall have Ten Pounds paid by Gilbert Marshall, Esq. . . .

The account agrees in some details with that of Dennis, and even the slight difficulty of the spelling of the murdered man's name is cleared away by a reference to Luttrell's *Brief Relation*.[50] Under April 7, 1684, he noted that "Mr. John Blackston was sett upon in the night in Whitefryers and there murdered." Whoever got into Luttrell's account must have been a person of importance enough to have been the possible friend of Otway, and not some mere unknown murdered on the streets of London. In spite of the discrepancy of the two Aprils a year apart, there may have been an element of truth in Dennis' story. Whatever else, John Dennis was not given consciously to the spinning of romance; and his version may reflect a deed of friendship by Otway that somehow through popular tradition became involved in the story of the poet's death. Certainly there seems no good reason to deprive him of his gallant pursuit.[51]

Nor should we doubt the other story of an almost completed masterpiece—a second *Venice Preserved*—left behind by Otway at his death. The earliest hint of it appeared as an advertisement in *The Observator* of November 29, 1686: "Whereas Mr. Thomas Otway some time before his death made four Acts of a Play, whoever can give notice in whose hands the Copy lies, either to Mr.

Thomas Betterton, or Mr. William Smith at the Theatre Royal shall be well rewarded for his pains."[52] It appears that the information was never supplied.[53] "What an invaluable treasure," exclaimed Goldsmith, "was there irretrievably lost by the ignorance and the neglect of the age he lived in!"[54]

In this connection, a neglected account of the death of Otway is here submitted for what it is worth, though, in its acquaintance with obscure facts of the end of Otway's life and the good credit of its assumed author, it should be allowed some degree of credence. It appeared in a comparatively unnoticed work of 1759: *A General View of the Stage,* purported to be by one "Mr. Wilkes." The identity of this person has long remained in obscurity. Lowe, without stating his reasons, attributed the book to Beau Derrick of Bath, but Mr. W. J. Lawrence has conclusively assigned it to Thomas Wilkes of Dublin, who died in 1786 after a long friendship with Garrick and other worthies of the contemporary stage.[55] His proximity to authentic sources of information tends to make the narrative more credible.

It is well known [said he], that by his want of oeconomy [Otway] was often obliged to apply to his friends for support; and he was so much in debt at the time of Venice Preserved being performed, that all the profits of it would not have silenced the clamours of his creditors, had not the Duchess of Portsmouth to whom he dedicated it, made a present of twenty guineas for the compliment. His constant friend, Mr. Betterton, and some others, made him up the like sum, and desired him to retire to Hampshire, as being a cheap country, and to write another Tragedy, which he promised to bring on the Stage the next season. Otway seemingly complied, left his lodgings, and retired to the country, as they thought: his friends were very uneasy at not hearing from him for some time, when in about three months they were informed, that he had been seen in the outskirts of the town in a very mean garb. This they soon found to be true, on the receipt of some petitionary letters for a further supply, which they were too much displeased with him to answer. He had now no resource left but to apply to Mrs. Behn for the loan of five pounds, to enable him, as he termed it, to finish his play, which she generously advanced; but how agreeably was she surprised with the style and pathetical distress of four Acts of it almost finished which he shewed her! In her judgment it was superior to anything he had before written. The story was that of Iphigenia: she advised him to shew it to Mr. Betterton, adding, that she was sure it would compromise all differences.[56] This he modestly declined till he had completed the whole. It is probable that at this time he went to his lodgings on Tower-hill. However, Mrs. Behn acquainted Mr. Betterton with this interview, who immediately made all possible enquiry after him, till about a month afterwards he was informed of his death on Tower-hill. He soon enquired out his lodging, which he found to be with a poor woman in one of the blind alleys there, where he was further informed, that on the night he died, a man, who used to visit him, had come into his room and taken away his papers, with some few books he had remaining. Mr. Betterton did not neglect to make the strictest search after this person, but could never learn who he was that had deprived the world of this invaluable treasure. That Otway did leave a Play is very certain; and it is as certain, that the piece called Heroic Friendship, which was laid to his charge by a certain publisher, had no mark of his genius.[57]

If the writer meant that Otway set to work upon his new tragedy immediately after *Venice Preserved,* with no intervening production, he was of course laboring under the general misconception of the eighteenth century that the poet's greatest work was also his last.[58] Even so, that is no very damaging criticism. On the other hand the account seems to have a certain affinity to Goldsmith's brief narration of 1759 in *The Bee.*[59] The latter adds one or two unnoticed details to the story. It remarks that "when he died (which he did in an obscure house near the Minories) he had about him the copy of a tragedy, which, it seems, he had sold for a trifle to Bentley the Bookseller." We are in something of a maze when we try to make entire consistency out of these various versions, but certainly they do not preclude the truth of Otway's tragic death. Beyond that assurance, Wilkes's account, by its absence of sensationalism and its general agreement with the known facts, seems quite as plausible as any other. Most interesting of all, it suggests the subject of his unfinished tragedy. The character of Iphigenia, with Otway handling it, might well have furnished another sympathetic rôle to the "famous Mrs. Barry." But her reputation was now secure.

"Whereupon," added Wood, "his body was conveyed to the church of S. Clement Danes within the liberty of Westminster, and was buried in a vault there."[60] The entry in the parish register is symbolic of the bare necessity to which time had stripped him:

1685. Thomas Otway, a man, buried 16 April.

"He was a Jovial Companion, and a great Lover of the Bottle, and particularly of *Punch;* the last thing he made before his death, being an excellent Song on that Liquor."[61]

Nathaniel Lee lingered on, equally a curiosity and something upon which to hang a moral. Finally, in 1689, he was discharged from Bedlam forever. The same fitful observance of the decencies —more strongly marked in the theater itself than among its patrons—which gave poor Cademan a lifelong pension after he had been stabbed in the eye by a stage sword, discovered itself in the pension of £10 a year granted Lee, and paid until his death.[62] It was hardly a living wage. He eked it out by the production of two plays which had been either banned or unsuccessful in his earlier existence. One, *The Princess of Cleve,*[63] was refurbished with a new prologue more fit for the house of Orange than the original by Dryden, with a dedication to Buckhurst who was now Lord Chamberlain under the new *régime,* and with a new epilogue defining Wit with unwonted wittiness. "Time," as he remarked in his dedication, is "the true Cure for all Maladies." He forwarded "this Farce, Comedy, Tragedy, or meer Play" to Buckhurst, along with the other item from his past, namely, *The Massacre of Paris.* And in this latter play the Lord Chamberlain saw true Whiggish sentiment. He approved it for production of November, 1689. The "Protestant Play," as Haynes called it, was wept and applauded by Queen Mary and her maids of honor. Years earlier her sister Anne had acted in a court production of his *Mithridates,* and gained thereby the name Semandra.[64]

It all seems a kind of reflex before dissolution. One by one the familiars of Lee had disappeared, though Betterton was to last honorably until 1709—a wonder and an example to Pope, Steele, and Addison—and Mrs. Barry until 1713, alternately to rend all tender hearts by the pity of her voice and to amaze the rest of the world by her rare acquisitive genius. Mrs. Behn found life hard beset by wracks and twinges and quit this world early in 1689. So it came about that Lee wrote the elegy that Otway should have composed. Of this rare poem, so far as known, only one copy exists —in broadside, and that seems never to have been reprinted. Moreover, it is the last word that we have from Nat. Lee, Gent., and one haply not dictated by any hope of reward. As such, if for nothing else, it deserves to be set down at this place:

Death
of
Mrs. Behn

By *Nat. Lee,* Gent.

The Sadness of thy Death extends my Muse,
To rail at Nature, and the Fates abuse:
That doom'd such Wit and Goodness to the Grave
To grieve the Wise, and make the Temperate rave.
Why art thou dead? Or wherefore didst thou live?
Such Pangs for Pleasure after Death to give.
I lov'd thee inward, and my Thoughts were true;
And after Death thy Vertue I pursue.
Thou hadst my Soul in secret, and I swear
I found it not, till thou resolv'dst to Air.
To Air, to Flame, to Beauty, and that Light,
Where Heav'ns perpetual blushing, and more bright.
Melpomene the stateliest of the Nine;
And more Majestick where thy Numbers shine;
Commands my Thoughts a mightier Urn to raise,
And Crown thy Verse with an Immortal Praise.
I mourn thy Death like Nightingales their Young:
My Grief's like thee, too precious for the Throng.
I'll bury it in Smiles, and force my Tears
Back to those Fountains where no Spring appears.
Flatman thy Mate, and that dear part of me;
But I'll expect till all the blest agree
To mount me in their Arms, and draw me near,
Where I shall never shed another Tear.[65]

The death of Lee, like his life, had not a little resemblance to that of Otway. It causes us to regard this age as one in which the pattern dominated the man, and in which the difficulties of rising above environment were almost insuperable. The die was stamped at birth and the click of the machine, trimming, cutting, and discarding, went on with savage uniformity. It was now Lee's turn.

At last in one of the intervals of his liberty, returning one night late from the Bear and Harrow tavern in butcher row, thro Close market to his lodgings in Duke St. overladen with wine, he fell down on the ground as some say (according to others on a bulk) & was chilled or stiffled in the snow & was found dead.[66]

That was during May, 1692. The additional details are again provided by Wilkes:

> Misfortunes and drink were the occasion: he was under the regimen of a milk-diet for the last week of his life; but getting one evening out of his physician's reach, he drank so hard, that he dropped down in the street, and was run over by a coach. His body was laid in a bulk near Trunkit's, the perfumer's at Temple-bar, till it was owned.[67]

Mad Nat. Lee, on May 6, 1692, came to rest like Otway at St. Clement Danes,[68] the pantheon of vagrant poets, where he lies in the churchyard, "next to the tomb of William Pattison."[69]

Only a few years later the witty Tom Brown narrated what yet remains to be told, in one of his *Letters from the Dead*. It seems that Lee and Otway, condemned through five acts to suffer the perversities of the tragic and comic muses, in a sixth attained some belated happiness. With this account we may take leave not only of them but of many other actors in this drama:

> To the Shades of *Elizium* I strait did repair;
> Where *Dryden* and other great Wits o' the Town,
> To reward all their Labours, are damn'd to Write on.
> Loose *Eth'ridge* presume on his Stile and his Wit,
> And *Shadwell* on all the dull Plays he e'er writ;
> *Nat Lee* here may boast of his Bombast and Rapture,
> And *Buckingham* rail to the end of the Chapter;
> Lewd *Rochester* Lampoon the King and the Court;
> And *Sidley* and others may cry him up for't;
> Here *Johnson* may boast of his Judgment and Plot,
> And *Otway* of all the Applause that he got.[70]

On the other hand, it is credibly reported by Hazlitt that "Otway and Chatterton were seen lingering on the opposite side of the Styx, but could not muster enough between them to pay Charon his fare."[71]

Notes

Chapter I

1. *Life and Times of Anthony Wood*, II, 125.

2. J. Foster, *Alumni Oxon.* (Oxford, 1891), p. 1095.

3. Written "by Richard Rhodes, of that house" (Christ Church) (*Life and Times*, II, 2).

4. *Ibid.*

5. G. M. Trevelyan, *England under the Stuarts* (13th ed.), p. 330.

6. Etherege's *Love in a Tub* was acted at "Gildhall," July 8, 1669. Wood paid 2s. 6d. admission (*Life and Times*, II, 165).

7. *The Prologue to the Oxford Schollers at the Act there, 1671*. Signed J.S., conjectured E.S. (Elkanah Settle) (Bod. MS. Eng. Poet e.4, p. 176).

8. The prologue written by Settle to *Cambyses* at Oxford, 1672, and recited by "Betterton in a riding habit" is in the Bod. MS. Eng. Poet e.4, p. 177. According to Wood (*Life and Times*, II, 226) the play was acted July 12, 1671, in the New Tennis Court.

9. *Life and Times*, II, 165.

10. It is told in *The Gentleman's Magazine*, XV, 99, that Otway ran away from Oxford with the players in 1674, but there seems to be little plausibility to the story. As I remarked in *Notes and Queries*, August 15, 1925, the whole article may be discredited. Though it provided a fund of information for biographers in the field of Restoration literature, it apparently was a hoax gathered from two chief sources: Otway's *Poet's Complaint* and Settle's *Tryal of the Poets*.

11. From Everingham, in 1660, he was one of a list of petitioners to obtain tithes and other livings sequestered during the commonwealth (*Hist. MSS. Comm.* 7th Rept. 107b). The life of Humphrey Otway, as well as the facts of his ancestry, I outlined more fully in *Notes and Queries*, January 30, 1926. In the same article I announced the discovery of his wife's will and a daughter, Susanna.

12. *Admissions to the College of St. John the Evangelist*, ed. J. E. B. Mayor, I, 43.

13. J. and J. A. Venn, *Alumni Cantab.* (Camb., 1924), III, 64.

14. J. Peile, *Biographical Register of Christ's College*, p. 384. Information upon the various members of the family is to be found in this work and in Venn.

15. Dugdale, *Visitation of the County of Yorke* (Surtees Society Publ.), XXXVI, 385.

16. An abbreviated genealogical table may be composed through the help of Dugdale, Peile, and Venn:

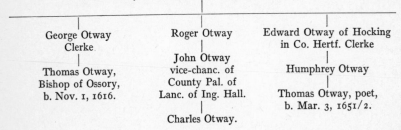

Thomas Otway of Middleton in com. Westmerl . . . . .

George Otway Clerke	Roger Otway	Edward Otway of Hocking in Co. Hertf. Clerke
Thomas Otway, Bishop of Ossory, b. Nov. 1, 1616.	John Otway vice-chanc. of County Pal. of Lanc. of Ing. Hall.	Humphrey Otway
	Charles Otway.	Thomas Otway, poet, b. Mar. 3, 1651/2.

17. Missing before 1670.

18. *Athenae Oxonienses,* ed. Bliss (London, 1813–1820), IV, 168.

19. *The Poet's Complaint of his Muse; or, A Satyr Against Libells* (London, 1680), p. 3.

20. Cf. my article *Notes and Queries,* January 30, 1926, CL, 76. The will mentions her kinsmen Will: Emes, Thomas Emes, Richard Emes, her kinswoman Dorothy Turner, her daughter Susanna Otway, and, besides others, Tho: Musgrave, Rector of Midhurst (successor to her husband), and John Emes of Empshott, executor. It was proved December 7, 1703. *Chichester Registry,* XXX, 643. Cf. *Sussex Arch. Collections,* XXXVI, 117, for a gift to Richard Emes, through Tho: Nepiker, Rector of Bepton.

21. Inscribed "Ex Dono Eliz. Otway. relict. Humph. Otway, Eccl. de Woolbeding Rect. Nov. 13.1703."

22. *Poet's Complaint,* p. 3.

23. *The Orphan* (1680), Act III, p. 37.

24. *Ibid.,* Act. IV, p. 49.

25. *Poet's Complaint,* p. 1.

26. *The History and Fall of Caius Marius* (1680), Act IV, sc. ii, p. 43.

27. *Friendship in Fashion* (1678), Act V, sc. i, p. 53.

28. Act. III, sc. i, p. 28.

29. First appeared in Dryden and Tonson's *Miscellany Poems* (1684).

30. *Poet's Complaint,* p. 2.

31. *Life and Times,* III, 175 (to Creech); III, 206 (to Aubrey).

32. A. K. Cook, *About Winchester College,* p. 303. Another note, *ibid.,* states, "£20 brings them into Winchester."

33. Ed. C. F. Holgate, pp. 7–8. Cf. p. 168.

34. William Emes, perhaps the same person mentioned in the will of Eliz. Otway, afterward prebendary of Chichester (*Winchester Scholars,* ed. T. F. Kirby, p. 188).

35. Holgate, *ibid.*

36. "The Lover's Session" (*Poems on Affairs of State* [1703], II, 159). The prologue was to Otway's *Souldiers Fortune.* In Bod. Rawl. Poet. 159, p. 54 it is remarked:

> "His Prologues are such Stuff,
>   As show plain enough
> He's a poor, detestable Rhymer."

37. *Caius Marius,* Epistle Dedicatory.

38. T. F. Kirby, *Winchester Scholars,* pp. xiv–xvii.

39. Cf. *De Collegio Wintoniensi,* a Latin poem composed *ca.* 1647 and printed with a translation in Cook's *About Winchester College,* pp. 12–29.

40. Quoted by G. F. R. Barker, *Memoir of Richard Busby,* p. 87.

41. Goldsmith, *Works,* ed. Cunningham (1854), III, 127. Goldsmith merely incorporated this criticism almost verbatim from an article by another hand printed November, 1757, in *The Literary Magazine.* Cf. R. W. Seitz, "Goldsmith and the Literary Magazine," *R.E.S.,* V, 1–21.

42. *About Winchester College,* pp. 302–304.

43. *Poet's Complaint,* p. 3.

44. *About Winchester College,* p. 297.

45. *In Praise of Winchester. An Anthology* (London, 1912), p. 83.

46. *Athen. Oxon.,* IV, 168.

47. *Alum. Oxon.,* p. 1095.

48. *Ibid.,* p. 246.

49. *Poet's Complaint,* p. 3.

50. The derivation was first suggested by J. C. Ghosh, *Notes and Queries*, CXLVII, 421.

51. C. Fleet, *Glimpses of Our Ancestors in Sussex* (2d ser.), p. 245.

52. *Venice Preserved* (1682). Epist. Ded.

53. *Glimpses of Our Ancestors in Sussex* (2d ser.), p. 245. He also wrote: "Serius aut citius sedem properamus ad unam" (*The Sedbergh School Register* [1895], p. 72). This latter work contains much information concerning the other Otways.

Chapter II

1. *Cor Humiliatum & Contritum. A Sermon Preached At S. Pauls Church London, Nov. 29.1663. By Richard Lee, D.D. Chaplain to the most Renowned George Duke of Albemarle, his Grace, and Rector of Kings-Hatfield in Hartfordshire* (1663). B.M.

2. *Ibid.*, Epist. Ded.

3. *Ibid.*

4. Printed in broadside with *The Recantation of a Penitent Proteus*. B.M.

5. *Cor Humiliatum*, Epist. Ded.

6. B.M. A broadside exists in the Bodleian (Wood 416. 100) entitled "A Rod for the Fools Back: or, An Answer to a scurrilous Libel, called the *Changeling*."

7. For further details concerning Rich. Lee cf. *Alum. Cantab.*; B.M. Add. MS. 5820, f. 121.

8. Cf. A. Kingston, *Hertfordshire During the Great Civil War and the Long Parliament*, p. 99, for Lee and Hugh Peters; also Skinner, *Life of Monk, passim*.

9. *Cor Humiliatum*, Epist. Ded.

10. *Acts and Ordinances of the Interregnum*, I, II, *passim. Journals of the House of Commons*, III, 136, 630; VI, 403; VII, 258, 462, 466.

11. B.M. *A Catalogue of the Library of Choice Books Latin and English, Of the Reverend and Learned Dr. Richard Lee, of Kings-Hatfield in Hartfordshire, deceased. By the Appointment, and for the Benefit of Mrs. Eliz. Lee* (1685). The titles I have reproduced as in the catalogue, though they are merely descriptive. Anthony Wood bought some of Dr. Lee's books (*Life and Times*, III, 167).

12. *Hist. MSS. Comm.* XIII, Append. VI, 273 (Letter dated 1671).

13. *Critical Essays of the Seventeenth Century*, ed. J. E. Spingarn, II, 282–283. The references, *Hannibal* and *Scipio*, are to characters in Lee's *Sophonisba*, produced April, 1675.

14. *Notes and Queries*, 11th ser., XII, 502; 12th ser., I, 35.

15. Gilbert Burnet, *Some Passages of the Life and Death of the Right Honourable John Earl of Rochester* (1680), p. 26.

16. "20 May 1658 Nathaneill Lee For the Earle of Salisbury. Exhibitioner 22 June 1665; of Trinity College, Cambridge, admitted 7 July 1665, B.A. 1668" (*Alumni Carthusiani*, eds. Marsh and Crisp [1913], p. 27).

17. Langbaine, *An Account of the English Dramatick Poets* (1691). Oldys' copy with his MS notes. B.M.

18. *Alum. Carthus.*, p. ii.

19. For these brothers cf. *Alum. Cantab.; D.N.B.* (Nathaniel Lee); and Leigh, *A List of Eton Collegers*.

20. *Alum. Carthus.*, p. ii.

21. Lee, Nathaniel. Pensioner, July 7, 1665. Tutor, Mr. Pulleyn (Matriculated, 1668; Scholar, 1668; B.A. 1668–9) (Ball and Venn, *Adm. to Trinity College, Cambridge*).

22. *Musarum Cantabrigiensium Threnodia In Obitum Incomparabilis Herois ac*

Ducis Illustrissimi Georgii Ducis Arbaemarlae (*Cantabrigiae, 1670*). The poem is signed Nathanael Lee, A.B. *Trin. Coll.*

Chapter III

1. *Poet's Complaint*, pp. 3–4.
2. J. Spence, *Observations, Anecdotes, and Characters*, ed. E. Malone (London, 1820), p. 101.
3. *The Antiquary* (August, 1884), X, 63.
4. Misson, *Memoirs and Observations in his Travel over England* (London, 1719), p. 219.
5. Cf. *The Counterfeit Bridegroom: Or, The Defeated Widow* (1677). Prologue:
   Who, (while their Wives (good men) are gone to meet ⎫
   Some of you Sirs i'th' Countrey) here can sit   ⎬
   Wonderously pleas'd with our Vacation Treat.   ⎭
6. "Prologue to *The Ordinary*" (*A Collection of Poems* [London, 1673], p. 163).
7. Mrs. Aphra Behn, *Sir Patient Fancy* (1678), Act I, p. 10. The point of view, of course, is that of a playwright.
8. Robert Gould, *Poems, Chiefly Consisting of Satyrs* (1689), p. 164.
9. *The Poems of John Dryden*, ed. Sargeaunt (Oxford, 1925), p. 224.
10. (Arrowsmith?), *The Reformation* (1673), Act II, sc. ii, pp. 23–24. Cf. the prologue to Otway's first play, *Alcibiades*.
11. B.M. Harl. MS. 7003, f. 186.
12. Charles Gildon, *Nuncius Infernalis: Or, A New Account from Below* (1692), p. 16.
13. Aston, *A Brief Supplement to Colley Cibber, Esq., reprinted in An Apology for the Life of Mr. Colley Cibber*, ed. Lowe (1889), II, 300.
14. *Letters Addressed from London to Sir Joseph Williamson*, ed. Christie (Camden Soc., 1874), I, 87, 94, 100.
15. Gould, *Poems* (1689), p. 170.
16. August 28, 1675 (Nicoll, *Restoration Drama*, p. 17 n.).
17. *The Ambitious Statesman* (1679), Preface.
18. *Poet's Complaint*, p. 4.
19. Her name is spelled variously. As a clue to possible pronunciation, it may be noted that she appears as Madame Beane in the advertisement attached to the novel, *The Princess of Cleves* (1679).
20. John Downes, *Roscius Anglicanus*, ed. Knight (1886), p. 34.
21. *The Playhouse, 1699*, Harl. MS. 7315, f. 267. This is the most complete version, in spite of the absence of punctuation. In *A Pacquet from Parnassus, or, a Collection of Papers* (London, 1702), pp. 18–21, it is attributed to T.G. Gent., while in *A New Collection of Poems Relating to State Affairs* (London, 1705), pp. 486–489, the poem is attributed to Mr. A.D——n (Addison?). I have edited the MS version from the other two.
22. He appears in the cast of *Macbeth* (1674) and in *Hamlet* (1676) as Mr. *Lee*. Inasmuch as Cademan—who left the stage in 1673—was in the cast of *Hamlet* the time is satisfactory. Nat. Lee would appear a more likely candidate for the rôle than either John Lee or Anthony Leigh. In *Hamlet* he took the part of Marcellus.
23. *Apology*, ed. Lowe, I, 114.
24. *Rosc. Angl.*, p. 17. Cf. *The History of the English Stage* (London, 1741), p. 90, where the speech is specifically attributed to Lee.
25. Gildon, *The Complete Art of Poetry* (1718), I, 258.
26. *The Life of Mr. Thomas Betterton* (1710), p. 16.

27. Cf. *The Censor* (1717), No. 9; and E. Malone, *The Critical and Miscellaneous Prose Works of John Dryden* (1800), I, i, 515–516.

28. "A Tryal of the Poets for the Bays," *Miscellaneous Works of Buckingham* (1704), p. 44. Dated 1676, in Bod. Rawl. Poet. 159.

29. "The Stage" (attributed to Mr. Webster), *A Collection of Original Poems* (1714), p. 24. F. W. Bateson has demonstrated that the poem is by Francis Reynardson, *M.L.N.*, XLV, 27.

30. *Sophonisba*, Act II, sc. iii, p. 21.

31. *Apology*, ed. Lowe, I, 110.

32. This was republished by Curll, with numerous additions, as *The History of the English Stage* (1741).

33. (Gildon), *The Life of Mr. Thomas Betterton* (1710), pp. 40 ff.

34. *Apology*, ed. Lowe, I, 141–142.

35. Cf. Tilley, "Tragedy at the Comédie-Française (1680–1778)," *M.L.R.*, XVII, 362–380.

36. She created the rôles of Bérénice, Monime, and Iphigénie. Doran first suggested the parallel of the two actresses (*Annals of the English Stage*, ed. Lowe [1888], p. 161).

37. Tilley, *op. cit.*

38. *Apology*, II, 303.

39. *Ibid.*, I, 110 n.

40. *Ibid.*

41. *Ibid.*

42. *Ibid.*

Chapter IV

1. *Don Carlos* (1676), Preface.

2. In his MS *History of the Restoration Stage* (Harvard), p. 227, Collier stated that he had a MS copy of the Prologue to *Nero* with an additional couplet at the end. The speaker is Haynes:

> Dances & songs I love & wit that's new,
> But plot & sense I hate, & so do you.

3. *Essays of John Dryden*, ed. W. P. Ker (Oxford, 1900), I, 157.

4. Shadwell, *The Sullen Lovers: or, The Impertinents* (1670), Prologue.

5. (Arrowsmith?), *The Reformation* (1673), Act IV, sc. i, pp. 47–48.

6. Mrs. Manley, *Lucius, The First Christian King of Britain* (1717), Prologue.

7. *Don Carlos*, Epist. Ded.

8. *Ibid.*, Preface.

9. Act V, sc. i, p. 53. Cf. *Hamlet*, Act IV, sc. v.

10. These innovations were attributed to foreign influence:

> Th' Old English Stage, confin'd to Plot and Sense,
> Did hold abroad but small intelligence,
> But since th' invasion of the foreign scene,
> Jack pudding Farce, and thundering Machine,
> Dainties to your grave Ancestours unknown,
> (Who never disliked wit because their own)
> There's not a Player but is turned a scout,
> And every Scribler sends his Envoys out
> To fetch from *Paris*, *Venice*, or from *Rome*,
> Fantastic fopperies to please at home.

> And that each act may rise to your desire, ⎫
> Devils and Witches must each Scene inspire, ⎬
> Wit rowls in Waves, and showers down in Fire. ⎭
>
> *Tunbridge Wells* (1678), Prologue.

11. Plutarch's *Lives* (Loeb Class. Lib.), IV, 113.
12. *Alcibiades,* Act III, sc. i, p..21.
13. *Misc. Prose Works* (Edin., 1827), VI, 424.
14. Plutarch's *Lives* (Loeb Class. Lib.), IV, 65, 67, 113.
15. *Don Carlos,* Preface.
16. *Nero* (1675), Prologue.
17. *Ibid.,* Act IV, sc. iii. p. 36.
18. *Ibid.,* p. 37.
19. The question of sources is adequately treated in the thesis of Mühlbach: *Die englischen Nerodramen des XVII Jahrhunderts insbes. Lees Nero* (Leipzig, 1910). In *Notes and Queries,* 12th ser., V, 254, 323, Nicoll demonstrated that *Piso's Conspiracy* (1676) was a reprint of May's Elizabethan play of *Nero* rather than Lee's play. Probably it was called forth by the success of the latter.
20. *Nero,* Epist. Ded.
21. In *The Character of the Town-Gallant* (1675) it is remarked of the lesser wit that "he swears that the *Leviathan* might supply all the lost leaves of Soloman, though for anything he has read himself, it may be a treatise on catching sprats." For further references to the popularity of this philosopher, cf. L. Stephens, *Hobbes* (1904), pp. 67–69.
22. B.M. Sloan MSS, 1458, 8888.
23. Tennison, p. 8.
24. Gilbert Burnet, *Some Passages of the Life and Death of the Right Honourable John Earl of Rochester* (1680), p. 38.
25. Act II, sc. i, p. 8.
26. Act III, sc. i, p. 17.
27. Burnet, *op. cit.,* p. 52.
28. John Holland, *An Elegie . . . to the Memory of . . . Rochester Who most Piously exchanged Earthly Honour for Never-fading Glory the 26th Day of July, 1680.* B.M.
29. Cf. p. 199.
30. *The Princess of Cleve* (1689), p. 7.
31. So attributed in Bod. MS. Add. B. 106. f. 34.
32. *The Works of Mr. John Oldham* (1684), pp. 105–106.
33. Act I, sc. ii, p. 8.
34. Oldys' MS notes to Langbaine.
35. "The Tryal of the Poets," *The Works of Buckingham* (1704), p. 43.
36. *The Rival Queens* (1677), Epist. Ded.
37. Nicoll, *Restoration Drama,* p. 307.
38. Act V, sc. iii, p. 49.
39. Act I, sc. ii, p. 11.

Chapter V

1. Leanerd, *The Counterfeits* (1679), Prologue.
2. *Nero,* Epist. Ded.
3. L. C. Warrant, Nicoll, p. 310.
4. *Don Carlos,* Epist. Ded.
5. *Friendship in Fashion,* Epist. Ded.

6. These are technical notes which I was permitted to copy at the National Portrait Gallery from the note book of Sir George Scharf, K.C.B., first director. In *Notes and Queries,* August 15, 1925, CXLIX, 7, I considered the problem of the portraits of Otway, and reached the conclusion that of the seven assumed portraits of the poet, this one attributed to Soest and the frontispiece by Du Guernier to the 1712 collected *Otway* are probably the most authentic. A mezzotint from the Soest —falsely attributed to Lyly—is the frontispiece of this book. It is attributed to Faithorne, and has never been reproduced until now. Mary Beale's portrait, which is well known in the engraving by Houbraken, and the portrait attributed to Riley, used as a frontispiece to the Mermaid *Otway,* possess a certain veracity. I may add to my article that the Victoria and Albert Museum contains a charming wash portrait, resembling the Soest, that Proctor's *Effigies Poeticae* (1824) has an excellent engraving of the picture by Riley, and that the original of the latter is at Bretby Castle in Derbyshire. Cf. *D.N.B. Errata.* Summers utilized the material without much change in his *Otway,* I, ciii.

7. *Friendship in Fashion,* Epist. Ded. This same dedication was printed by accident before the first edition of Mrs. Behn's *Sir Patient Fancy.*

8. *Memoirs of the Count Grammont,* ed. Vizetelly (1889), II, 120–121.

9. "Rochester's Ghost," *Poems on Affairs of State* (1703), II, 131.

10. *The Rival Queens,* Epist. Ded.

11. Prior, "A Satire upon the Poets," *Dialogues of the Dead and other Works in Prose and Verse,* ed. A. R. Waller, p. 57.

12. *Ibid.,* Lee dedicated his *Caesar Borgia* to Pembroke.

13. *Sophonisba* (1676), Epist. Ded.

14. Undated letter of Nell Gwyn published in *Notes and Queries,* 4th ser., VII, 3.

15. (1680), Act I, sc. i, p. 12.

16. *The Souldiers Fortune* (1681). John Banks imitated Otway in dedicating his *Innocent Usurper* (1694) to Bentley, citing his precedent: "I have herein follow'd the steps of no mean Author, who before me, made you a tribute of his best Comedy."

17. *The Careless Lovers* (1673), Epistle to the Reader.

18. Bod. MS notes to D. E. Baker and I. Reed, *Biographia Dramatica.*

19. Settle, *Ibrahim The Illustrious Bassa* (1677), Prologue.

20. Gildon, *The Laws of Poetry* (1721), pp. 37–38. Cf. Thaler, *Shakespeare to Sheridan,* p. 40.

21. *Caius Marius,* Epilogue.

22. *Theodosius* (1680), Epist. Ded.

23. *A Comparison Between the two Stages* (1702), pp. 8–10.

24. *The Laws of Poetry* (1721), pp. 37–38. Quoted by Thaler, p. 30.

25. Prior, *Dialogues of the Dead,* ed. Waller, p. 56. In *The Poetical Remains of Buckingham* (1698) this poem is printed with considerable variation.

26. *Three Original Letters . . . on the Cause and Manner of the late Riot at the Theatre Royal* (1763). Quoted by Thaler, p. 50 n. Cf. Davies, *Dramatic Miscellanies* (Dublin, 1784), III, 150.

27. The poem is printed in Dryden's and Tonson's *Examen Poeticum* (1693), p. 168. Lee's nadir of taste came perhaps after his reputation was well established. Appended to a broadside, a copy of which is in the B.M., is our poet's certificate: "I have perused these verses, and find them composed according to the rules of poetry, and therefore think them fitting to be printed. Nath. Lee." N.D. My hazard would be that the printer had his doubts and called upon the poet, with the stated result. The poem is reprinted *Notes and Queries,* 1st ser., I, 149.

28. *To the Duke On His Return* (1682). The broadside in the Huntington Library has Luttrell's date of acquisition, May 29, 1682.

29. One such is given as by Otway in *The Works of Buckingham* (1704), pp. 96–98, and reprinted in Summers' edition of Otway, III, 215. I have long been doubtful of its authenticity, for the following reasons: it is attributed to Otway in a work otherwise full of false claims, it is without any trace of his style, and it was written for the Theatre Royal to which he never contributed, to our knowledge, another piece of writing.

30. *Theodosius* (1680), Epist. Ded.

31. *Don Carlos,* Preface.

Chapter VI

1. *Alcibiades* (1675), Epilogue.

2. L. C. Warrants, Nicoll, p. 307.

3. *Sophonisba,* Epist. Ded.

4. Langbaine, *An Account of the English Dramatick Poets* (Oxford, 1691), p. 321.

5. *Sophonisba* (1676), Act IV, sc. i, p. 50.

6. Cf. note 13, p. 223.

7. *Gloriana* (1676), Epist. Ded.

8. For the relations of this play to its source, the *Cléopâtre* of La Calprenède, cf. Auer, *Ueber einige Dramen Nathaniel Lee's* (Berlin, 1904).

9. *The Spectator,* ed. G. A. Aitken (London, 1898), I, 202–203.

10. *Apology,* ed. Lowe, I, 105–106.

11. *Gloriana,* Act II, sc. i, p. 10.

12. *Ibid.,* Act IV, sc. i, p. 39.

13. *Ibid.,* Act I, sc. i, p. 1.

14. Prologue.

15. *Mithridates* (1678), Act III, sc. ii, pp. 30–31.

16. *The Spanish Fryar* (1681), Epist. Ded. Dryden qualifies his statement by adding that these are not the true beauties of drama.

17. *Mithridates,* Epist. Ded. The sources in Shakespeare have been traced to *Richard III, Titus Andronicus,* and *Julius Caesar* (Haupt, *Quellenstudien zu Lee's "Mithridates, King of Pontus"* [Kiel, 1916]).

18. Cf. H. W. Hill, *La Calprenède's Romances and the Restoration Drama* (Diss., Univ. of Chicago), pp. 53–54.

19. *Parthenissa, That most Fam'd Romance. Composed by The Right Honorable The Earl of Orrery* (London, 1676). Cf. pp. 197 ff. For earlier editions cf. Esdaile.

20. Lee's *Theodosius* was indebted to La Calprenède's *Pharamond; Lucius Junius Brutus,* to Mlle de Scudéry's *Clélie; The Princess of Cleve,* to Mme de La Fayette's *La Princesse de Clèves.* For translations cf. Esdaile, and for the indebtedness of other playwrights to French romance, Nicoll, pp. 86–87.

21. *The Rival Queens* (1677), Act IV, pp. 48–49. Cf. *Curtius,* trans. Digby (1725), II, 61: "As for my part, I believe what your Unkle said in *Italy* to be true, that he had to do with Men, and you with Women."

22. *Rival Queens,* Act IV, p. 45.

23. *Cassandra* (London, 1652), Pt. II, Bk. II, p. 219. For other parallels cf. Hill, *op. cit.,* pp. 103–115.

24. *Cassandra,* Pt. II, Bk. I, p. 207.

25. *Rival Queens,* Act I, sc. i, p. 4.

26. "The Stage," *A Collection of Original Poems* (1714), p. 27.

27. *Miscellanea Aurea* (London, 1720), pp. 37–38. Attributed to T. Killigrew, who was a minor contributor. The main body of the work I find has numerous resemblances to that of J. Dennis.

28. H. McAfee, *Pepys on the Restoration Stage*, pp. 229–230.

29. Spence, *Anecdotes*, ed. Malone, p. 174.

30. Of Hart, in the rôle of Alexander, a courtier remarked: *"Hart* might Teach any King on Earth how to Comport himself" (*Rosc. Angl.*, p. 16).

31. Davies, *Dramatic Miscellanies* (1784), III, 161.

32. A story is told of the rivalry of Barry and Boutell in the two leading parts of Roxana and Statira and the near extinction of Boutell by the dagger of Barry. This episode might have taken place in some unrecorded performance after the union of 1682, or it may have been Marshall who was confused with Barry (*History of the Stage* [1741], 21).

33. An interesting line of research is revealed in the work of Lowenberg, *Ueber Otway's und Schiller's Don Carlos* (Lippstadt, 1886).

34. "Otway and Racine Compared," *British Magazine* (1760), I, 462. Cf. Lounsbury, *Shakespeare and Voltaire*, pp. 182–183, 193, for the irritation of Voltaire at this comparison.

35. Racine, *Oeuvres*, ed. Mesnard, II, 367.

36. *Don Carlos*, Preface.

37. A fairly heavy piece of Otway's wit is recounted in Walford's *Old and New London*, I, 102, the original source of which is in obscurity: how Otway calling several times without avail at Dryden's lodgings in Fetter Lane where he had been invited to breakfast finally out of patience scribbled over his door, "Here lives Dryden a poet and a wit," and how Dryden recognized the hand and looking across at Otway's lodgings added, "This was written by Otway, opposite." According to the story Otway, the next morning, saw the rhyme, "and being a man of rather petulant disposition told Dryden, that he was welcome to keep his wit and his breakfast to himself." Another anecdote that lends little more credit to Otway's reputation as a wit is told in *The Works of Mr. Thomas Brown* (1711), IV, 18. It need not be retold.

38. *Poet's Complaint*, pp. 4–6.

39. *Don Carlos*, Preface. Sir Formal Trifle was a character in Shadwell's *Virtuoso;* I'gad, the characteristic exclamation of Bayes in *The Rehearsal*. Otway in his Epilogue referred to an actress turning nun, a rather obvious cast at the recent action of Dryden's mistress, Mrs. Reeve.

40. *Don Carlos*, Preface.

41. *Ibid.* Booth the actor had it from Betterton that *"Don Carlos* was more applauded and drew better houses for many years than either *The Orphan* or *Venice Preserved"* (Letter to A. Hill, dated June 19, 1732, cited by Cunningham in his edition of Johnson's *Lives*, I, 213). Cf. *Rosc. Angl.*, p. 36: "all the Parts being admirably *Acted,* it lasted successively 10 Days; it got more Money than any preceding Modern Tragedy."

42. *The Works of Buckingham* (1704), p. 44.

Chapter VII

1. *Poems on Several Occasions. By the Earls of Roscommon and Dorset, &c* (London, 1714), pp. 62–63. The same volume (pp. 64–65) contains his poem *The Enjoyment.*

2. An elaborate argument was presented by Mr. J. C. Ghosh (*Notes and Queries*, 12th ser., XII, 103 ff.), questioning the authenticity of the legend that these letters were addressed to Barry or that the poet had ever had such a love affair. I answered in the same periodical, CXLIX, 165–167.

3. *Familiar Letters: Written by the Right Honourable John, late Earl of Roches-*

ter, and several other Persons of Honour and Quality. With Letters Written by the most Ingenious Mr. Thomas Otway (1697). In this work I have quoted from what seems an edition of 1705 (t.–p. missing). It differs from the first edition in being less heavily italicized.

4. R. Mosen, "Ueber Thomas Otway's Leben und Werke," *Englische Studien*, I, 429.

5. "The Playhouse," *Wks. of Th. Brown* (1720), III, 39. In the edition of 1708, III, 343, Barry is not mentioned in this connection. Cf. the following, from *The Players turn'd Academicks* (London, 1703), p. 3:

> And where's He or She breaths that dares but attest,
> That *B——* had ever Deceit in her Breast. . . .
> That she wickedly harbour'd a Lawless Intent,
> Or Traffick'd for *Debts* at a Hundred *per Cent*, . . .
> Who not to be Idle makes it all the same Case,
> If she's let out for *Woolen*, or *Linnen*, or *Lace*
> As Trunks full of each at her House do declare,
> She has *Dealt* more than *Once* for more than one *Ware*.

6. R. Gould, "The Playhouse. Writ in 1685," *Poems* (1689), p. 175. The poem continues:

> Thy *Orphan*, nay thy *Venice* too shall stand,
> And live long as the Sea defends our Land.

7. *Ibid.*, pp. 181–182.

8. "The Playhouse" (Advertisement), *Works of Robert Gould* (1709).

9. In the edition of 1709, I, 248, the word "sudden" is replaced by "cruel."

10. Gould (1689), p. 181.

11. "On the Death of John Dryden, Esq.," *Luctus Britannici: or the Tears of the British Muses; for the Death of John Dryden* (1700), p. 38.

12. "A Brief Supplement," *Apology*, II, 302.

13. *Ibid.*, II, 303.

14. Cf. Cunningham's note in *Memoirs of the Count Grammont*, ed. Vizetelly, II, 121.

15. "Brief Supplement," *Apology*, II, 302.

16. *Apology*, I, 159.

17. *History of the English Stage* (London, 1741), p. 14.

18. *Life of Mr. Thomas Betterton* (1710), p. 16.

19. "An Allusion to the Tenth Satyr of the First Book of Horace," *Critical Essays*, ed. Spingarn, II, 282.

20. *Familiar Letters* (1705?), I, 74–75.

21. *Familiar Letters of Love, Gallantry, and several Occasions* (London, 1718), pp. 31–32. The Epilogue to Mrs. Behn's *Abdelazer; or, The Moor's Revenge*, recited a few months after *Don Carlos'* production is imitative of Otway's indecent finale to that play, being spoken by a girl and probably the same little Mrs. Ariell who delivered Otway's Epilogue. It is possible that both are by Otway. The style and the thought are identical, and Mrs. Behn's was written by "a friend."

22. *Venice Preserved*, Act I, sc. i, p. 9.

23. Cf. Deschanel, *Racine* (Paris, 1884), I, 217 ff.; Lyonnet, *Les "Premières" de Jean Racine* (Paris, 1924), pp. 95–114.

24. "Racine's are the best crying plays" (Lockier in Spence's *Anecdotes*, p. 205).

25. "Un amant et une maîtresse qui se séparent, est-ce matière à tragédie?" (É. Deschanel, *Racine*, I, 214.)

26. Cf. D. Canfield, *Corneille and Racine in England*, p. 97, for a favorable judgment of Otway's skill as a translator, and A. de Grisy, *Étude sur Thomas Otway* (1868), pp. 109–110, for the inevitable French condemnation.

27. *Hist MSS. Comm., Bath*, II, 160.

28. *Friendship in Fashion*, Prologue.

29. *Ibid.*

30. Durfey, *Trick for Trick* (1678), Prologue.

31. *Athen. Oxon.*, IV, 169.

32. C. Dalton, *English Army Lists*, I, 208.

33. *Diary*, ed. H. B. Wheatly (1906), II, 335–336.

34. M. M. Verney, *Memoirs of the Verney Family* (1899), IV, 238.

35. Dalton, I, 208, 222. The regiment, in which Otway served, embarked July 2, and suffered much from sickness in camp near Brussels (p. 213). It was disbanded March, 1679 (*ibid.*, p. 210).

36. *The Souldiers Fortune* (1681), Act II, pp. 19–20.

37. *Ibid.*, Act V, p. 61.

38. *Ibid.*, Act IV, p. 40.

39. *Cal. of State Papers, Domestic, 1679–1780*, p. 38.

40. *Cal. of Treas. Books*, VI, 332, 814 ff., 823.

41. *The Souldiers Fortune*, Act I, p. 5.

Chapter VIII

1. *Rosc. Angl.*, p. 38. Cf. Gould (1689), p. 173.

2. Cf. D. H. Miles, *The Influence of Molière on Restoration Comedy*, p. 103.

3. *Friendship in Fashion*, Act III, sc. i, p. 27.

4. *Ibid.*, p. 26.

5. Malone, *Dryden*, I, i, 74–75.

6. *The Destruction of Jerusalem By Titus Vespasian, Part the First* (1677), the Epistle to the Reader.

7. *Poet's Complaint*, p. 6.

8. Nicoll, p. 311.

9. Langbaine, p. 398.

10. *Friendship in Fashion*, Prologue.

11. *Ibid.*, Act III, sc. i, pp. 25–26. Steele used this quotation with so much point to the Duke of Newcastle as to be deprived of his license (Lowe, *Betterton*, p. 121).

12. *Ibid.*, Act I, sc. i, p. 9.

13. "To Mr. Creech," *T. Lucretius Carus Done into English Verse* (Oxford, 1683).

14. Mrs. Behn, *The City Heiress* (1682). Prologue by Otway.

15. *The Souldiers Fortune* (1681), Epist. Ded.

16. *Rosc. Angl.*, p. 36.

17. *Apology*, I, 147–148. Cf. *Rosc. Angl.*, p. 41: "*Mr.* Leigh *was Eminent in the part of Sir* William, *&* Scapin. *Old* Fumble, *Sir* Jolly Jumble, Mercury *in Amphitrion, Sir* Formal, Spanish *Fryar*, Pandarus *in Troilus and Cressida*." The list needs no further commentary.

18. Besing has not observed this debt to Wycherley, of the duped husband go-between, in his pursuit of the debt to Molière. Wycherley borrowed directly from Molière and Otway generally from Wycherley with additions from Molière (Besing, *Molières Einfluss auf das englische Lustspiel bis 1700* [Borna-Leipzic, 1913], pp. 98 ff.).

19. *The Atheist* came largely from Scarron's novel, *The Invisible Mistress*, which had appeared in its most recent English reprint, 1682. Cf. Esdaile.

20. *The Atheist* (1684), Act I, p. 6. The form of the play juggles curiously between prose and verse, an evidence of its unsettled purpose.

21. *Theodosius*, Epist. Ded.

Chapter IX

1. *Hist. MSS. Comm. Bath*, II, 158.
2. *Collected Works of Rochester* (London, 1926), p. 254.
3. "To Mr. Lee on his Alexander," *The Rival Queens* (1677).
4. *The Works of Buckingham* (1704), p. 43.
5. *Ibid.*, p. 44.
6. *The Tory Poets* (1682), p. 5.
7. *A Character of the True Blue Protestant Poet* (1682).
8. *Titus and Berenice* (1677), Epilogue.
9. *A Supplement to the Narrative* (London, 1683).
10. Cf. B.M. Harl. MS. 7317, f. 175:
> But *Settle* that incorrigible Owl,
> That Composition of a knave and Fool.
11. *Poet's Complaint* (1680), p. 8.
12. *Lives of the Poets* (1753), II, 326.
13. *Pepys and the Restoration Stage*, p. 272; Nicoll, p. 16 n.
14. *Titus and Berenice* (1677), Epilogue.
15. "Caesar's Ghost," *A New Collection of Poems Relating to State Affairs* (1705), p. 232.
16. Mrs. Manley, *Secret Memoirs* (1720), I, 31 ff.
17. *Cal. of State Papers*, XXI, 351.
18. Cf. *Accounts and Papers*, LXII, i, 537; and the following from an official broadside: *A List of the Names of Knights, Citizens . . . Returned to serve in the Parliament of England, Begun the 6the Day of March, 1678/9.*
> Southampton—Borough of Newtown
> Sir John Holmes, *Knt.*
> John Churchill, *Esq.*
19. *The Character of a Town Gallant* (1675), p. 5.
20. A war in the pit.
21. *Aphra Behn*, ed. Summers, I, 107. In the notes there is no explanation of the lines beyond a list of pit-duels. After I had published an article, "Otway's Duels with Churchill and Settle" (*M.L.N.*, XLI, 73–80), Mr. Summers incorporated the findings into his *Otway* without any statement of source.
22. *Hist. MSS. Comm.* 7th Rept., Append., 473a.
23. *Ibid.*

Chapter X

1. *Poet's Complaint*, p. 21.
2. For the general account of these events, I have depended chiefly upon the following authorities: Trevelyan, *England under the Stuarts;* Pollock, *The Popish Plot;* Airy, *Charles II;* Haile, *Mary of Modena; D.N.B.* for Oates, Shaftesbury, etc.
3. There had been political attacks from the stage antedating those of the Popish Plot. Thus Marvell speaks of *The Politician: or, Sir Popular Wisdom* (1677) as being directed against "Shaftesbury and all his gang" (*Hist. MSS. Comm. Portland,* III, 357).
4. For a study of the influence of politics, cf. Nicoll. "Political Plays of the Restoration," *M.L.R.*, XVI, 224.
5. This has hitherto been written "correcter men"; however cf. *The Whiggs Lamentation* (1681), B.M.:

> Our Case to th' Carrecter-men, we must refer
> To *Shadwell*, and *Settle*, to *Curtis*, and *Carr*.

In *A Choice Collection of 180 Loyal Songs* (1685), p. 64, the word is spelled "Character."

6. *Theodosius* (1680), Prologue.

7. *The Medal Revers'd* (1682), p. 7.

8. *Whig and Tory, Or the Scribling Duellists* (1681). Yale.

9. Shadwell, *The Woman Captain* (1679), Prologue.

10. *The True News: or, Mercurius Anglicus* (Feb. 7, 1679/80).

11. Mrs. Behn, *The Feign'd Curtizans* (1679).

12. *Caius Marius*, Epilogue.

13. *Ibid.*, Act V, sc. i, p. 55.

14. *Caesar Borgia* (1680), Epist. Ded.

15. Act V, sc. ii, p. 69. Cf. *Paradise Lost*, Bk. III, 489–496.

16. For the Italian and French sources of *Caesar Borgia*, cf. Mehr, *Neue Beiträge zur Leekunde und Kritik, insbesondere zum "Cäsar Borgia" und zur "Sophonisba"* (Berlin, 1909).

17. "*taken before Sir* Joseph Jorden *Knight, and* Richard Lee *Doctor of Divinity, and Rector of* Hatfield, *and Chaplain in* Ordinary *to his Majesty.*"

18. His epitaph in Hatfield Church is given by S. E. Brydges in his *Censura Literaria* (1805), I, 176: "Depositum Richardi Lee, S.T.P. nuper Hatfieldi Episcopalis, alias Regialis, cum capella de Totteridge Rectoris, qui obiit A.D. 1684. aetat. suae 73. Hic requiescat spe laetae resurrectionis."

19. It was well advertised and went through several editions. Jacob remarks that it was "very famous at the time it was wrote" (*Hist. Account* [1720], p. 175).

20. *Poet's Complaint*, pp. 11–12.

21. *Tory Poets* (1682), pp. 6–8. This excessively rare poem I reviewed in *Notes and Queries*, January 1, 1927, CLII, 6–8. Summers made no use of it until his *Shadwell*.

22. Davies, *Misc.*, III, 110 ff.

23. *The Orphan*, Act II, sc. i, p. 15.

24. Act III, sc. i, pp. 25–26.

25. *The Patriot, or the Italian Conspiracy* (1703), Preface. Cf. Prologue by Dennis:

> The following Piece by fiery *Lee* was wrought,
> And judg'd his strongest and his noblest Draught.

26. MS notes to Langbaine. B.M.

27. Ed. Arber, I, 451.

28. Nicoll, p. 10 n.

29. Many of the titles in Rich. Lee's library show him to have been an avid purchaser of Whiggish pamphlets.

30. *Lucius Junius Brutus* (1681), Act III, sc. ii, p. 35.

31. "All the Parts in't being perfectly perform'd, with several Entertainments of Singing; Compos'd by the Famous Master Mr. *Henry Purcell,* (being the first he e'er Compos'd for the Stage) made it a living and Gainful Play to the Company: The Court; especially the Ladies, by their daily charming presence, gave it great Encouragement" (*Rosc. Angl.*, p. 38). The first quarto is almost unique among Restoration plays in having the music appended. Incidental music exists in MS in the B.M. for many of the plays mentioned in this work. It was an indispensable part of tragedy and comedy, and doubtless exercised an influence upon the whole tone of drama.

32. Act I, sc. i, p. 3.

33. Act II, sc. i, p. 27.
34. *Lucius Junius Brutus,* Epist. Ded.

Chapter XI

1. "Winter," pp. 646–648, *Complete Poetical Works,* ed. Robertson (1908), p. 209.
2. Cf. Malone, *Shakespeare* (1790), I, 281; Odell, *Shakespeare from Betterton to Irving* (1920), I, 51–52. *Romeo and Juliet* was considered by Pepys the worst play he had ever seen (H. McAfee, *Pepys and the Restoration Stage,* p. 74 n).
3. A few such references may be cited: Fielding, *Joseph Andrews,* Bk. III, chap. x; Pope, *The Epistle to Augustus;* Guthrie, *An Essay upon English Tragedy* (1757) p. 27; *Royal Magazine* (1763), IX, 39 ff.; *Memoirs of the Life of Robert Wilks, Esq.* (1732), p. 20.
4. *Thomas Otway,* ed. Hon. Roden Noel (Mermaid Series, n.d.), xliii.
5. *Lives of the English Poets,* ed. G. B. Hill (Oxford, 1905), I, 245.
6. *John Dryden,* ed. Malone, I, ii, 248.
7. *Lives* (Loeb Class. Lib.), IX, 563 ff.
8. Act I, sc. i, pp. 2–3.
9. And now for you who here come wrapt in Cloaks,
   Only for love of *Underhill* and Nurse *Noakes.*
10. *Caius Marius,* Act II, sc. i, p. 16. Cf. p. 33:
    Lavinia. Speak kindly, will my *Marius* come?
    Nurse. Will he? Will a Duck swim?
11. Act I, sc. i, p. 10.
12. *Ibid.*
13. Act I, sc. ii, p. 47.
14. *Alcibiades,* Act I, sc. i, p. 6.
15. "These 3 Plays [of which *The Orphan* was one], by their Excellent performances, took above all the Modern Plays that succeeded." (*Rosc. Angl.,* ed. Knight, p. 38.)
16. *Lives,* I, 245.
17. Lillo refers to Otway in his Prologue to *The London Merchant.*
18. *Friendship in Fashion* (1678), Act I, sc. i, p. 27.
19. *The Orphan,* Act II, sc. i, p. 31.
20. *Ibid.,* Act IV, p. 54.
21. *Thomas Otway* (Mermaid Series), xxxiv.
22. Cf. Gildon, *The Complete Art of Poetry* (1718), II, *passim; The Beauties of English Drama* (1777), *passim; Elegant Extracts* (1791), *passim.*
23. Act V, sc. i, p. 64.
24. *Ibid.,* p. 68.
25. *Ibid.,* p. 71.
26. (Gildon), *The Life of Mr. Thomas Betterton,* p. 40. Of Betterton, Cibber says that while "in Castalio he only excell'd others, in Othello he excell'd himself," and that "his voice was better adapted to give effect to rage and jealousy . . . than to sighs and tenderness" (*Apology,* I, 116). The legend that Bracegirdle acted in *The Orphan* at the age of six was destroyed by Fyvie, *Tragedy Queens* (1909), pp. 14–15.
27. Act V, sc. i, p. 69. The speech was severely handled by Saintsbury, but only after misquoting it. Cf. *Short History of English Lit.* (N. Y., 1910), p. 501.
28. *Essays of John Dryden,* ed. Ker, II, 145. Cf. Cibber, *Lives,* II, 332: "Dryden was often heard to say that Otway was a barren illiterate man, but 'I confess, says he, he has a power which I have not'; and when it was asked him, what

power that was? he answered, 'moving the passions.' This truth was, no doubt, extorted from Dryden, for he seems not to be very ready in acknowledging the merits of his contemporaries." Cf. Gildon, *Laws of Poetry*, I, 210.

29. 1676. Esdaile, p. 167.

30. *Oeuvres Complètes de Voltaire* (Paris, 1879), XXIV, 204 ff.

31. Act III, sc. iii. Efforts have been made to connect the play with R. Tailor's *The Hog hath Lost his Pearl* (1614). So far as I can detect there is only the most superficial resemblance between the two.

32. Voltaire, *op. cit.*, XXIV, 208. Voltaire was followed by De Grisy, *op. cit.*

33. *Collected Works*, ed. Waller and Glover, V, 355.

Chapter XII

1. Act V, sc. i, p. 59.

2. *Theodosius*, Epilogue.

3. Its principal source was La Calprenède's *Pharamond*, as translated by J. Phillips, 1677. For parallels consult Auer. The subject is the same as that of Massinger's *Emperor of the East*, but Lee apparently had no knowledge of the earlier play.

4. *Theodosius*, Epist. Ded.

5. *Lucius Junius Brutus*, Epist. Ded. Old Rome entered from Livy. Otherwise the source was Mlle de Scudéry's *Clélie*, recently reprinted, 1678, in an English translation. Cf. pp. 231, 284-285, 314-319. Shakespeare's influence is found in frequent verbal reminiscence from *Othello, Julius Caesar,* and *Macbeth*. Cf. Auer, *op. cit.*

6. *Lucius Junius Brutus*, Epist. Ded.

7. Act IV, sc. i, p. 57. Cf. Bacon, "Of Death": "*Pompa mortis magis terret, quam mors ipsa.* Groans and convulsions, and a discolored face, and friends weeping, and blacks, and obsequies, and the like, show death terrible."

8. *The Destruction of Jerusalem* (1677), the Epistle to the Reader.

9. "Discours du Poème Dramatique," *Oeuvres*, I, 24. Quoted from Pendlebury, *Dryden's Heroic Plays* (1923), p. 70.

10. *The Impartial Critick* (1693).

11. Cf. *Oeuvres Complètes* (Paris, 1877), II, 324.

12. *Miscellany Essays*, trans. T. Brown (1694), pp. 65 ff. Cf. Epist. Ded. of Mrs. Trotter, *The Unhappy Penitent* (1701).

13. *Clelia, An Excellent New Romance* (London, 1678), pp. 207, 215.

14. Dibden thought *Lucius Junius Brutus* one of Lee's finest productions (*A Complete History of the Stage*, IV, 185).

15. *Lucius Junius Brutus*, Epist. Ded.

16. John Dennis, *Original Letters* (1721), p. 63.

17. *Lucius Junius Brutus*, Act I, sc. i, pp. 11-12.

18. *Ibid.*, p. 12.

19. *Theodosius*, Act V, sc. iv, pp. 60-61.

20. *Lucius Junius Brutus*, Act I, sc. i, p. 4.

21. *Caesar Borgia*, Act V, sc. i, p. 60.

22. *Ibid.*, sc. ii, p. 62.

Chapter XIII

1. "To Mr. Dryden on his Poem of Paradise" (*The State of Innocence, and Fall of Man: An Opera* [1677]). Dryden alludes indulgently to Lee in his Preface.

2. Dryden made the following contributions to Lee: Prologue to *Sophonisba,* spoken at Oxford; Epilogue to *Mithridates;* Prologue to *Caesar Borgia;* the original Prologue and Epilogue to *The Princess of Cleve;* Epilogue to *Constantine the Great.* Beside these, a broadside Prologue and Epilogue was printed by J. Sturton for *Mithridates,* "the First Play Acted at the Theatre Royal this Year, 1681." According to MS notations by Luttrell, both were by Dryden. (Copy in the Huntington Library, with liberal corrections in MS.) In his MS *History of the Restoration Stage* (Harvard Library), p. 227, Collier states that he has the original MSS of these pieces which vary from the printed form in making an interval between the closing and opening of the theaters of two instead of four months.

3. Malone, *Dryden,* I, i, 74.

4. Dryden, *The Vindication: Or The Parallel* (1683), p. 42.

5. *Oedipus* (1679), Act II, sc. ii, p. 17.

6. For the relations of the various plays upon the subject of Oedipus, cf. W. Bentzien, *Studien zu Drydens "Oedipus"* (Rostock, 1910).

7. *Oedipus* (1679), Preface.

8. *Ibid.*

9. *The Complete Art of Poetry,* I, 237.

10. W.B. argues that by the introduction of the subplot of Creon and Adrastus, the collaborators spoiled their tragedy (*Letters of Wit, Politics, and Morality* [1701], p. 235).

11. *Oedipus,* Act V, p. 77.

12. "it took prodigiously being *Acted* 10 Days together" (*Rosc. Angl.,* p. 37).

13. A. Radcliffe, "News from Hell," *The Ramble* (1682), p. 4. The last line is a parody of a line in *Oedipus,* Act IV, p. 65.

14. Gould, *Poems* (1689), pp. 175–176.

15. Dennis, *The Impartial Critick* (1693), pp. 8, 12.

16. Quoted by Elwin, *Works of Alex. Pope* (1871), I, 55 n.

17. "The Stage," *A Collection of Original Poems* (1714), p. 27.

18. *The Spectator,* ed. G. G. Smith (London, 1897), I, 149–150.

19. *Heroick Love* (1698), Preface.

Chapter XIV

1. *Some Reflections upon the Pretended Parallel in the Play called The Duke of Guise* (London, 1683), p. 3.

2. *Ibid.,* p. 2.

3. *The Vindication: Or The Parallel* (1683), p. 41.

4. Nicoll, *Restoration Drama,* p. 311. Attended (December 1) by the King. Charles was an infrequent visitor of political plays.

5. *The Princess of Cleve* (1689), Epist. Ded.

6. *The Princess of Cleves* was published in translation, April, 1679. Lee was very active in following up the new translations with plays. His mistake in the title is due probably to the running title of the book, where it is spelled *Cleve.* The title-page has *Cleves.*

7. *The Princess of Cleve* (1689), Act I, sc. i, pp. 6–7.

8. *A Relation of the Barbarous and Bloody Massacre of about an Hundred thousand Protestants. Collected out of Mezeray, Thuanus, and other approved Authors* (London, 1678). Lee's *Massacre* was written perhaps the next year. It is difficult, in spite of a German thesis that strives to prove the case, to discover in Lee's tragedy any indebtedness to Marlowe's play of the same name. Cf. Griersbach,

Nathaniel Lee's Zeittragödien und ihre Vorläufer im Drama Englands (Rostock, 1907). Malicorn of *The Duke of Guise* clearly derives from Faustus.

9. *The Reasons of Mr. Joseph Hains Conversion* (1690), Pt. III, p. 28. Quoted by Griersbach. The play became almost a celebration piece for the return of Protestantism. Cf. Epilogue.

10. *The Massacre of Paris* (1690), Act II, sc. i, pp. 15–16.

11. *Ibid.*, Act I, sc. ii, p. 7.

12. Epist. Ded.

13. *The Prince (sic) of Cleve for Dorset Garden, being well-Acted, but succeeded not so well as the others* [Nero, Gloriana] (*Rosc. Angl.*, p. 38).

14. The signature of Lee was added in the fourth edition of Dryden's *Miscellany Poems* (1716), I, 15.

15. "To the Unknown Author of this Excellent Poem," *Absalom and Achitophel* (The Second Edition, 1681).

16. *To the Duke on his Return* (1682). Broadside.

17. The problem of the date of first production is solved by a MS notation on the Broadside Prologue, "30 Nov." and the date of acquisition, "4. Dec. 1682." Huntington Library.

18. *The Unbiass'd Satyr: Or Reflections On Manners* (1683). Guildhall.

19. *The Vindication: Or The Parallel*, p. 3.

20. *Hist. MSS. Comm., Buccleuch*, II, i, 108. Cf. *Hist. MSS. Comm., Rept. 15*, Append., Part VII, p. 108 (Newsletter of July 29, 1682): "A play by Mr. Dryden termed the *Duke of Guise*, wherein the Duke of Monmouth was vilified and great interest being made for the acting thereof, but coming to His Majesty's knowledge is forbid, for though his Majesty be displeased with the Duke yet he will not suffer others to abuse him." Cf. also *London Mercury*, August 28, 1682.

21. *Vindication*, pp. 2–3.

22. *Ibid.*, p. 4.

23. *The Duke of Guise* (1683), Act I, sc. i, p. 4.

24. Cf. *The Medal of John Bayes* (1682): "For the Association, which he next mentions, dropt out of the Cloudes, entred into, and subscribed by no body, and seen by no one of our Party that ever we could hear of. . . . "

25. It has been suggested that Lee composed *An Epode to his Worthy friend John Dryden, to advise him not to answer two malicious Pamphlets Against his Tragedy called "The Duke of Guise"* (*Ashley Catalogue*, II, 101). Such attribution can hardly be correct. Lee would not refer consistently to the play as if it were by Dryden alone. Nor does the *Epode* show any traces of his style.

Chapter XV

1. *The Souldiers Fortune*, Epilogue.

2. *Titus and Berenice*, Prologue.

3. "A performance of *The Orphan* was broken up by Nelly being called a name she never repudiated" (Doran, *Annals of the English Stage*, ed. Lowe [1888], I, 90).

4. *The Feign'd Courtizans, or, A Nights Intrigue* (1679), Epist. Ded.

5. *An Essay of Scandall.* B.M. Harl. 6913. Dated 1681 in Harl. 7319.

6. Henry Hart, *A Memorial of Nell Gwynne, the Actress and Thomas Otway, the Dramatist.* Nell's son, Charles Beauclerk, Earl of Burford, afterward Duke of St. Albans, was born May 8, 1670. The pension was granted June 11, 1679.

7. The young Duke of Richmond (*Life and Times of Anthony Wood*, II, 555). The position had been intended for Wycherley, with a stipend of £1,500 a year,

but was transferred to Duke upon the marriage of the former to the Countess of Drogheda. Cf. Spence's *Anecdotes,* ed. Malone, p. 120. Was it Duke that put Otway forward as tutor to young Burford?

8. Venn, *Alumni Cantab.* In answer to my inquiries, Mr. Venn was so obliging as to write that a search of the university records threw no light upon Otway's sojourn beyond the fact that he received the M.A. degree in 1680 as a member of St. John's, adding that "his name does not appear upon the admission book (as is usually the case with those incorporated from elsewhere)."

9. G. Jacob, *The Poetical Register* (1723), I, 193.

10. *Poems by the Earl of Roscomon. Together with Poems by Mr. Richard Duke* (1717), p. 515.

11. Duke composed an address to the queen upon this occasion, September 28, 1681, which may be found in his collected works. Cf. Luttrell, I, 130.

12. Roscomon, p. 517.

13. This poem first appeared in *Miscellany Poems* (1684), p. 221, as an "Epistle to *R.D.* from *T.O.*" The names were supplied in the version printed in Roscomon, p. 511. Summers apparently did not use this version, for he mistakes Beverly for Richard Bentley, the famous scholar.

14. *On the Universally Lamented Death of the Incomparable Dr. Short* (1685), Broadside.

15. J. Dennis, "Some Remarkable Passages of Mr. Wycherley's Life"; Pack, *A New Collection of Miscellanies* (London, 1725), p. 121. A William Wilson entered Trinity, Cambridge in 1671 with Richard Duke.

16. James Beverly, 1671 (cf. the name James in Duke's poem); Henry Finch, M.A., 1682. Edward Finch, M.A., 1679, composer, lawyer, and later chaplain to the queen is perhaps as likely a candidate as his brother Henry.

17. Roscomon, p. 517.

18. *Ibid.,* p. 509.

19. *Ibid.,* p. 508.

20. *Ibid.,* p. 514.

21. Dryden and Tonson, *Miscellany Poems* (1684), pp. 225–227.

22. In the *Sylvae: or, The Second Part of Poetical Miscellanies* (1685), pp. 155–161, appears a translation of "The Sixth Elegy of the First Book of Tibullus," which almost as certainly is by Otway. The poet had made other translations from Tibullus, printed in *The Works of Petronius Arbiter* (London, 1713). This unsigned translation of the *Miscellanies* is shot through with evidences of his style and thought. Cf. the following lines to those of his letter upon p. 87, and to lines in the *Letter to a Friend:*

> Oft I by Wine have try'd to lull my cares,
> But vexing grief turn'd all my wine to Tears.
> Each sprightly bottle did but still supply
> Another Fountain for my weeping Eye. . . .
> In vain, I sing, nor will my words command,
> This Gate ne're opens to an empty hand.

The poem continues in Otway's relaxed verse, complaining against the same rich rival with a vocabulary closely resembling that of the poem quoted on p. 182. It was a habit of Otway to select only those poems for translation that seemed most applicable to his own life. Naturally he did not append his name, with the facts of his love not yet public property.

23. The tone of complaint is pervasive throughout Otway's verse. Cf. *The Poet's Complaint* and his short lyric, *The Complaint.*

24. In *Friendship in Fashion* and *The Souldiers Fortune.*

25. One may compare this to the excerpt, given above, from the translation of

Tibullus, and to his general use of wine as a cure for love, narrated in his first letter.

26. Otway was fond of chains. Cf. "For when, as long her Chains I've worn," in *The Complaint;* and, "I cannot break soft Beauty's Chain," in his translation of the *First Elegy of Tibullus.*

27. Swains, remains, pains, complains,—one may observe everywhere in his verse the threadbare and mawkish rhymes. In *The Complaint* appears pain, swain; mind, unkind; prize, despise; dove, love, rove; charms, arms, etc., most of which are to be found in this *Letter.* Very nearly the whole list is in the *First Elegy of Tibullus* and in the Epistle of *Phaedra to Hippolytus,* with heavy stress upon the pains-complains complex.

28. Cf. Tom Brown's Epist. Ded. to the *Letters:* "The Passions in the raising of which, he had a Felicity peculiar to himself, are represented in such lively Colours, that they cannot fail of affecting the most insensible Hearts, with pleasing Agitations. I could wish we had more Pieces of the same Hand; for I profess an entire Veneration to his Memory. . . . "

29. *Familiar Letters* (1705?), I, 85.

30. *Congreve,* ed. Summers, I, 101. The letter mentions Custis.

31. *Familiar Letters,* I, 79–80.

32. The will of Eliz. Barry is in Somerset House, Leeds 239. She left a number of bequests, of which one of twenty pounds to Mrs. Bracegirdle is noteworthy and another to the same actress of two hundred pounds to save the "harmless from any debt of the Playhouse." To Gabriol Ballam, Gent. she gave her estate of mills at Newbury, the residue of her estate to John Custis, Gent., formerly Page to the Prince and to Abigal Shackhouse, spinster. The will was signed November 4, 1713.

33. B.M. Harl. MS. 6913, f. 345.

34. "The Complaint" (Mrs. Behn), *Miscellany, Being a Collection of Poems. By several Hands* (1685), p. 55. Mr. Summers states that he drew his text from Dryden's second *Miscellany* (date not given), and he printed the first quoted line *Rivals* for *Rival's,* as in late reprints. The sense is changed completely.

35. *Familiar Letters,* I, 79.

36. Cf. *Dramatic Works of Etherege,* ed. H. F. B. Brett-Smith (Boston, 1927), p. xxx.

37. B.M. Harl. 6913, f. 345. The interesting part of the satire, *On Three Late Marriages,* is the unnoted fact that Mrs. Barry, "at thirty-eight, a very hopeful Whore," seems either to have projected or accomplished marriage. It is all quite obscure as to the man, but we are supplied with the epithet "slattern Betty Barry" and the rate of her pay, fifty shillings a week.

38. *Familiar Letters,* I, 78–79.

39. Oldys' MS notes to Langbaine.

40. *The Tory Poets* (1682), p. 6.

41. *Familiar Letters,* I, 79.

Chapter XVI

1. Prior, *Dialogues of the Dead,* ed. Waller, p. 56.

2. *Venice Preserved,* Epist. Ded.

3. Nicoll, p. 311. It is noteworthy that between April 5, 1678, and this February 11, 1682, Charles is recorded as having visited, at the Duke's Theatre, three plays by miscellaneous poets, two by Aphra Behn, two by Dryden, and five by Otway, and, if we add the next succeeding visit, six by Otway.

4. The fact that the play was dedicated to Portsmouth is of significance. She was second only to James as a political issue.

5. *The Dramatic Censor* (1770), I, 313. Bellamira and Ascanio in Lee's *Caesar Borgia* may have suggested the general treatment.

6. The date is printed on the broadside. For Dryden's Prologue cf. *John Dryden*, ed. Noyes, p. 132.

7. Malone supplies the date (*Dryden*, I, i, 121). It has not been observed, so far as I can discover, that Dryden's famous Prologue "To the Duchess," beginning "When factious Rage to cruel Exile drove," was written to accompany this production of *Venice Preserved*. It is so noted by Luttrell upon the broadside in the Huntington Library.

8. *Rosc. Angl.*, pp. 37–38. Her three great rôles were Monimia, Belvidera, and Isabella. "She forc'd Tears from the Eyes of her Auditory, especially those who have any Sense of Pity for the Distress't" (*Apology*, I, 160).

9. Davies, *Miscellanies* (Dublin, 1784), III, 140–141. This is said to have been first written by a contemporary (B.M. MS History of the Stage [11826.r], XIII, 388).

10. *A Satyr, 1682*, B.M. Harl. 7319, f. 225; Harl. 6947, f. 233.

11. For the history of this infamous attack upon Dryden, cf. Malone, I, i, 129.

12. Settle, *A Narrative* (1683).

13. *Venice Preserved,* Prologue. Cf. *The Recovery* (1682?):
   Here first were rais'd, the wondr'ing World to scare,
   The Armies *Harris* mustered in the Air.

14. A song on Nicky Nacky had appeared some months earlier in Mrs. Behn's play, *The Roundheads*, staged *ca*. December, 1681.

15. Davies, *Dramatic Miscellanies* (1784), III, 128.

16. Prologue.

17. Taine, *History of English Literature*, trans. Van Laun (N. Y., 1875), II, 242.

18. H. C. Robinson, *Diary*, ed. Sadler (London, 1869), I, 187–188.

19. *Venice Preserved* (1682), Act II, p. 20.

20. *The Idler*, No. 60. Cf. *The Spectator*, No. 39; *Misc. Aurea*, p. 24.

21. Prologue.

22. The task has been performed admirably by A. Johnson, *Étude sur la Litt. comparée de la France et de l'Angleterre à la fin du XVIIe siècle* (Paris, 1901), and by McClumpha, *Thomas Otway*, pp. 304 ff.

23. G. H. Nettleton, *English Drama of the Restoration and Eighteenth Century* (1921), p. 102. Pierre's speech upon Honesty, Act I, sc. i, may be compared to Falstaff's upon Honor.

24. *Venice Preserved*, Act II, sc. ii, p. 31.

25. Act I, sc. i, p. 15.

26. *Venice Preserved*, Act I, p. 11.

27. *Ibid.*

28. *History of Music* (1789), III, 589 n.

29. "Vision of the Election of the Poet Laureat," *The Censor*, No. 41 (1717). In "The Apotheosis of Milton," *Gentleman's Magazine* (1738), IX, 20, Lee is discovered sitting between Otway and Dryden.

30. *Lucius Junius Brutus*, Act V, sc. i, p. 65.

31. *Venice Preserved*, Act V, pp. 70–71.

32. *Lucius Junius Brutus*, Act III, sc. iii, p. 39.

33. *Collected Works*, XI, 402.

34. *Venice Preserved*, Act V, p. 68.

Chapter XVII

1. "A Supplement to the late Heroick Poem," B.M. Harl. 6913, f. 230. Shadwell, a Whig ruined by Tory ascendancy, had no play produced between *The Lancashire Witches,* September, 1681, and *The Squire of Alsatia,* May, 1688.

2. *Loyal Protestant,* February 18, 1681/2, and May 20, 1682. The play is dated by Malone in his MS note to *Biog. Dram.*

3. *The City-Heiress: or, Sir Timothy Treat-all* (1682), Prologue.

4. This probably is a reference to the failure of her adaptation of Randolph's *Jealous Lovers* under the title of *Like Father Like Son.* It was produced just before this time, but was never printed. The Prologue and Epilogue were issued in broadside. Cf. Thorn-Drury, *A Little Ark* (1921), p. 45 n.

5. The comparison is to Mrs. Behn's play of the preceding December, *The Roundheads or, The Good Old Cause.*

6. *The Tory Poets,* p. 8.

7. *The City-Heiress,* Prologue. This exists, also, in separate broadside.

8. *The Atheist* (1684), Prologue.

9. Cf. Powell, *The Treacherous Brothers* (1690), Preface: "The time was, upon the uniting of the two Theatres, that the reviving of the old stock of Plays, so ingrost the study of the House, that the Poets lay dormant; and a new Play cou'd hardly get admittance, amongst the more precious pieces of Antiquity." For a list of revivals cf. *Rosc. Angl.,* pp. 39–40.

10. "A Satire on the Modern Translators," *Dialogues of the Dead and Other Works in Prose and Verse,* ed. Waller, p. 47. This poem is here attributed to Prior, but was disowned by him, according to a MS note by Pope in his copy of *State Poems* (1705). B.M.

11. *T. Lucretius Carus* (Oxford, 1683).

12. "A Description of Mr. Dryden's Funeral," *Poems on Affairs of State* (1703), II, 231.

13. MS in possession of Mr. W. R. Baker, Esq., of Bayfordbury, Herts., who kindly permitted me to have it photographed.

14. *The Atheist,* Epilogue.

15. *Ibid.,* Prologue.

16. Epist. Ded. For the character of Elande, cf. *Savile Correspondence* (Cam. Soc. Pub.), *passim.*

17. Epist. Ded.

18. *Les Soupirs de la Grand Britaigne: or, the Groans of Great Britain* (London, 1713), p. 67.

19. Oldys' MS notes to Langbaine. He writes to the Earl of Oxford, February 23, 1730/1 of "the intelligence I gained about a twelve-month past of some considerable remains . . . of that late famous tragic poet Nat Lee" (*Hist. MSS. Comm., Portland,* VI, 37).

20. Dennis, *Letters upon Several Occasions* (1696), p. 56. He adds: *"Otway* and He are safe by Death from all attacks."

21. Oldys' MS notes to Langbaine.

22. Wycherley, *Miscellany Poems* (1704), pp. 301–302.

23. Oldys' MS notes to Langbaine.

24. A MS note on the broadside (Prologue and Epilogue) fixes the date of production as November 12, 1683. Cf. Malone's MS notes to *Biog. Dram.* Bod.

25. *Constantine the Great* (1684), Prologue. The broadside has no indication of authorship.

26. *Life and Times of Anthony Wood,* III, 112.

27. *Poetae Britannici* (n.d.), p. 18. Reprinted under title, "Of Poetry" in Samuel Cobb's *Poems on Several Occasions* (Third Edition, 1710), p. 20.

28. Wycherley, *op. cit.*, p. 303.

29. *The Works of Mr. Tho. Brown* (1707), II, ii, 78.

30. Oldys' MS notes to Langbaine.

31. T. Cibber, *The Lives of the Poets* (London, 1753), II, 230.

32. Oldys' MS notes to Langbaine.

33. Wycherley, *op. cit.*, p. 300.

34. *A Search after Wit; Or, a Visitation of the Authors* (London, 1691). The stanza on Settle is quoted out of its original position.

35. Wycherley, *op. cit.*, p. 301.

36. *A General View of the Stage. By Mr. Wilkes* (1762), p. 298.

37. "Satyr against the Poets," B.M. MS. 162. B. 8 (7317). The passage is annotated in another contemporary hand: "Nathan[1]: Lee A Poet y^t is crak brain'd & very often put in Bedlam, hath written very fine Plays." Cf. p. 155.

38. *Observator,* p. 5. February, 1685. Noted by Schumacher, *Thomas Otway* (Bern, 1924), pp. 168–169. He draws no conclusions.

39. *Athen. Oxon.,* IV, 170.

40. (Mrs. Behn), *Lycidus: or the Lover in Fashion* (1688), pp. 81–82. Summers incorrectly states that he prints from Mrs. Behn's *Miscellany* of 1685. The poem does not appear in that volume.

41. *Windsor Castle, in A Monument to our Late Sovereign K.Charles II* (1685), pp. 14–15.

42. "Remarks upon Mr. Pope's Translation of Homer," *Critical Essays of the Eighteenth Century,* ed. Durham, p. 242.

43. Settle had recanted his Whiggish doctrines in *A Narrative* (1683). Cf. F. C. Brown, *Elkanah Settle,* p. 24.

44. Gould, "To Julian, Secretary of the Muses," *Poems* (1689), p. 279. A different version is to be found in his *Poems* (1709). He revised his authentic poems in this second edition, and there seems little doubt but that this was of his composition. It has been variously attributed. The names have been filled in from *The Works of Buckingham* (1704), pp. 20–23.

45. *Athen. Oxon.,* IV, 170. Cf. *The Tatler,* May 9, 1710, where it is stated that he "died at a sponging-house on Tower-Hill, known by the sign of the Bull."

46. *Lives,* ed. Hill, I, 247.

47. *The Lives of the Poets* (1753), II, 333–334.

48. Ed. Singer (1820), p. 44. Malone, in his edition of Spence, spells the name *Blakiston.*

49. Burney Collection. B.M.

50. I, 304.

51. The outline of the Blakiston affair I announced in *T.L.S.,* January 14, 1926.

52. Burney Collection. The same advertisement appeared in other papers.

53. In 1719 W. Mears and R. King brought forth *Heroick Friendship,* purporting to be the lost tragedy. It contained a feeble imitation of Otwavian devices and characters, but for "the last play of Otway" it was amazingly optimistic. The verse cannot be his by any stretch of the imagination, and the source was one never tapped before by the poet. It was all the baldest hoax, and would not be deserving of notice, if it did not bear witness to the magic of Otway's name.

54. "The Bee," No. VIII, *The Works of Goldsmith,* ed. Cunningham (1854), III, 128.

55. *T.L.S.,* August 9, 1923; June 26, 1930. *The General View* first appeared in Dublin during 1759 and was dedicated to Viscount Wellesley, the father of Wellington.

56. The fact that two of Otway's poems—*The Complaint* and *A Pastoral*—appeared posthumously in Mrs. Behn's *Miscellanies* of 1685 and 1688 lends plausibility to this final visit. The latter poem is unfinished and supposedly was written by Otway upon his deathbed.

57. *A General View of the Stage* (The Second Edition, 1762), pp. 245–246.

58. This mistake seems to have arisen from T. Cibber's incorrect dating of *Venice Preserved* (*Lives*, II, 336).

59. *Works*, ed. Cunningham, III, 127.

60. *Athen. Oxon.*, IV, 170. There is no commemoration in S. Clement Danes, though one was placed in the church at Trotton during the nineteenth century. For its text, cf. Fleet, *Glimpses of our Sussex Ancestors* (2d ser.), p. 241.

61. *The Lives and Characters of the English Dramatic Poets* (1699), p. 107. This is Gildon's continuation of Langbaine. Cf. Jacob's characterization (*Poet. Reg.*, I, 194). The song has been identified more or less satisfactorily as that discovered by Edw. Rimbault and printed in *Notes and Queries*, 1st ser., V, 337.

62. *D.N.B.* (Article on Nath. Lee by Sir Sidney Lee). I have been unable to authenticate this fact.

63. *Rosc. Angl.*, p. 38. Its late printing may be accounted for by its early lack of success.

64. "November 15, 1681, being the Quean of Brittain's birth-day, it was keeped by our Court at Halyruid house with great solemnitie, such as bonfyres, shooting of canons, and the acting of a comedy called *Mithridates, King of Pontus,* before ther Royall Hyneses, &c., wheiren Lady Ann, the Duke's daughter, and the ladies of honour ware the onlie actors" (Dibden, *The Annals of The Edinburgh Stage* [Edinburgh, 1888], p. 28). Marjorie Bowen, *The Third Mary Stuart*, p. 13, tells that the Princess Ann, in familiar correspondence, was addressed by the title *Semandra*.

65. *London,* Printed for *Abel Roper* at the *Bell* in Fleetstreet. 16(89), date clipped. The only known copy of this poem is in the Guildhall Library, London. Another unnoticed poem—of no great interest, however—is to be found in the *Oxford and Cambridge Miscellany Poems* (1709), p. 318: "A Song upon Fancy By Nath. Lee," while unimportant lyrics are to be found in the *Poems on Affairs of State*.

66. Oldys' MS notes to Langbaine.

67. *A General View of the Stage*, p. 297.

68. Register, S. Clement Danes. Cf. *D.N.B.* (Nath. Lee).

69. *A General View of the Stage*, p. 297.

70. *Memoirs Relating to the late Famous Mr. Tho. Brown* (London, 1704), p. 17. The last couplet is here quoted out of its normal place, which is following the third quoted line.

71. *Collected Works*, XII, 35.

Index

	DATE DUE		